I0812414

IMAGES
of America

ATWATER

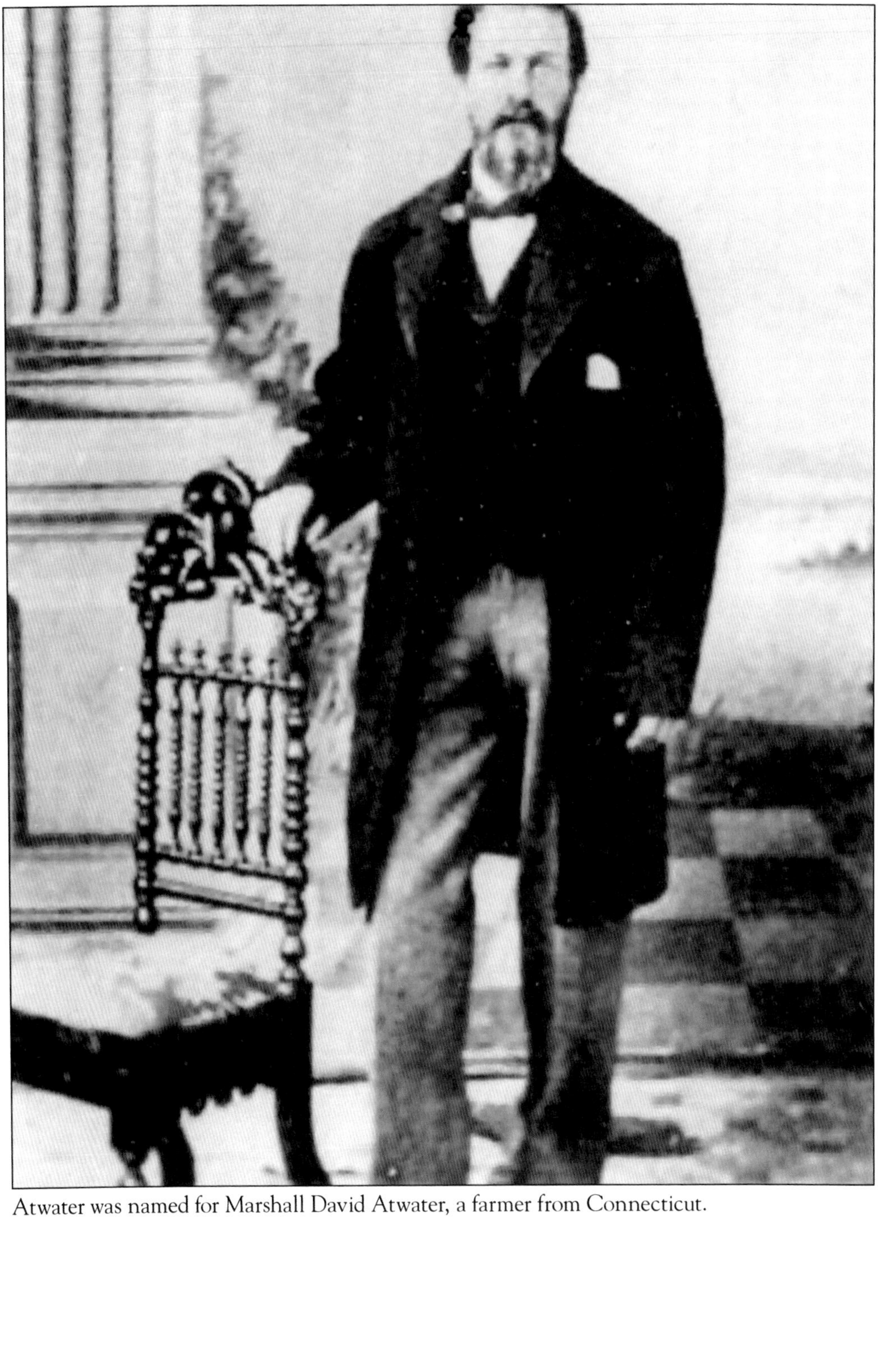

Atwater was named for Marshall David Atwater, a farmer from Connecticut.

IMAGES
of America

ATWATER

Atwater Historical Society

ARCADIA
PUBLISHING

ISBN 978-0-7385-2891-5

Published by Arcadia Publishing
Charleston, South Carolina

Printed in the United States of America

Library of Congress Catalog Card Number: 2005923147

For all general information contact Arcadia Publishing at:
Telephone 843-853-2070
Fax 843-853-0044
E-mail sales@arcadiapublishing.com
For customer service and orders:
Toll-Free 1-888-313-2665

Visit us on the Internet at www.arcadiapublishing.com

We wish to dedicate this book to the memory of Mary E. Stanfield, who gave us most of our research in her 1958 work Brief History of Atwater.

Contents

ACKNOWLEDGMENTS

The Atwater Historical Society would like to thank the following for their contributions: Phil Anderson; James and Lillian Apolinaro; Scott Atherton of Turlock Memorial Park; the Atwater Pentecost Association; the Avellar-Maciel families; Jay Baldwin; Manuel Barrios; Jack Bleiman, who wrote "A Brief History of Atwater" articles for the *Atwater Signal*; Ida Bleiman; Audrey Bonifay; Castle Air Museum Curator Dale Griffin; Tom Corvelo; Atwater historian Paul Crookham; Debbie Machado Court; Gayle and Stan Court; Anthony Dixon; Janie Henderson Estep; Carmel Ferreira; Phyllis Avellar Glass; Erica Groth Goss; Joyce Reynolds Gregory; the E. A. Heller family; the C. E. "Pete" Hinds family; Jean Mello Ivers; Ivan Klingelhofer; Richard Koster; Don Lencioni; Judy Alvernaz Lyons; Edith MacDonald; Vern and Norma Mattos; Isabelle Neves; the Owen-Peck family; Nada Lubisich Pazin; Greg Olzack; the Louis Passadori family; Tom Prothro, the Atwater Police Department; Helen Kangis Rice; Joe and Laura Saca; Fred Silveira; F. M. Sherrill; Greg Simay, of Burbank, in memory of his father Julius L. Simay stationed at Merced Army Flying Field in 1943; Vera Chase Smith; Ron Souza; Don and Marilyn Thornhill, "History of Merced County by Robert Outcalt," 1925; the Winton Historical Society, specifically Rosalie Heppner and Lorraine Richards; and Roger and Chichi Wood.

INTRODUCTION

Atwater is located in Merced County in the large valley known as the San Joaquin. The area's rolling plains and large rivers made it possible to turn the land into an agricultural paradise. Originally occupied by Yokut Indians and then by the Spanish, the face of the area saw dramatic change after the February 1848 Treaty of Guadalupe-Hidalgo, which ended the Mexican-American War, and California became a part of the United States.

The discovery of gold in 1849 brought a flood of people into California who were looking for quick riches; however, it also brought men of great moral character and vision. One such man was John W. Mitchell, who arrived in San Francisco following his brother Asal on February 22, 1851. After working in the city long enough to buy equipment, John and his brother went into business cutting hay and cordwood around Stockton. They sold these items to teamsters working the mines and soon had their own wagon and tent. They rented out one-half of the tent for $50 a month. An entrepreneur of the first order, John saved money to buy land from the federal government at a rate of $1.25 in greenbacks (paper money), or 75¢ in gold, per acre. He had 500,000 acres in his name even before the official U.S. survey was completed.

Reared on a farm in the Woodbury area of Litchfield County, Connecticut, Mitchell had always been lured by the call of the land. He convinced other people from his home state, including the families of his three nieces, to come west and try their hand at dry-land farming. He provided those who rented from him with seed to get started, farm equipment, and even houses. Buying and selling thousands of acres in the San Joaquin Valley, Mitchell influenced the delevopment of the land in the Atwater vicinity. He died on November 26, 1893, at the age of 65. Though he had a wife, Jane, she died before him, and they had no children. Three nieces inherited the bulk of his estate: Mrs. Henry Geer (Mary), Mrs. Stephen Crane (Emma), and Mrs. George Bloss (Ella). All three women were children of Mitchell's sister, Mrs. Stone.

Marshall David Atwater came to California from Bethany, Connecticut, as early as 1855. He spent several years working in the Mokelumne Hills area before arriving in 1868, after John Mitchell prompted him to make the move. As one of the first settlers, he farmed wheat on acreage that he rented from Mitchell. Marshall also purchased 6,000 acres of his own, north of what would become Atwater at the "Winn Ranch." He became one of the largest grain growers in the area. In 1872, when the Central Pacific Railroad pushed through the valley to Merced, Atwater and Mitchell induced the railroad to add a spur at the warehouse where Atwater stored his grain. This became known as "Atwater Switch" and made it easier for Atwater to ship large amounts of grain. About this time, he also purchased a ranch of some 4,480 acre northwest of nearby Merced. By 1876, Atwater, his wife, Laura, and their daughter Eliza moved to their new home on this ranch. He became a diversified farmer, growing different grains, citrus fruit, and livestock, and he also invented a huge grain harvester that was pulled by 24 mules. He operated this farm for over 30 years and passed away at the age of 80 in February 1905.

George Bloss Sr., who settled in Atwater in 1884, administered the Mitchell estate and his wife was one of the nieces that inherited land from Mitchell. In 1887, Bloss and Henry F. Geer subdivided 480 acres into 20-acre parcels and called the area Atwater Colony. In 1888, the Merced Land and Fruit Company laid out the town and sold lots at auction. George S. Bloss and his wife, Ella Stone Bloss, approved this plan, and the town was given the name of the colony. Atwater was not going to be a fast developer, for at the turn of the century only 100 people lived in the area, and its weekly newspaper didn't start until 1911. Atwater was, however, lucky to have George Bloss as a town benefactor. He had been president of Fin de Siecle Investment Company, which was created by the families of all three nieces to handle the Mitchell holdings. When the company was liquidated, it was divided into thirds—one for the Bloss Land and Cattle Company, one to the Crane Brothers Company, and one to the Geer-Dallas Investment Company. Bloss's third was used to benefit the town with a library, built in memory of his grandson, and a hospital in memory of his wife Ella. George Bloss Jr. and his wife, Christine, later continued these philanthropic endeavors.

This book pictures the progress of one town in the valley from its inception as a grain warehouse to a thriving community. Despite its slow start, the town did indeed develop. Situated in the population belt of the valley, over half of the county's population is now centered in the Merced-Atwater area. The Santa Fe Railroad was laid north of town and, along with Highway 99 passing through town, brought excellent transportation opportunities. The Atwater Canal brought irrigation to the area, while the advent of the Merced Army Flying Field (later Castle Air Force Base) brought people and increased commerce. From the days of the colony, Atwater is now a fully developed community.

One

THE FOUNDERS

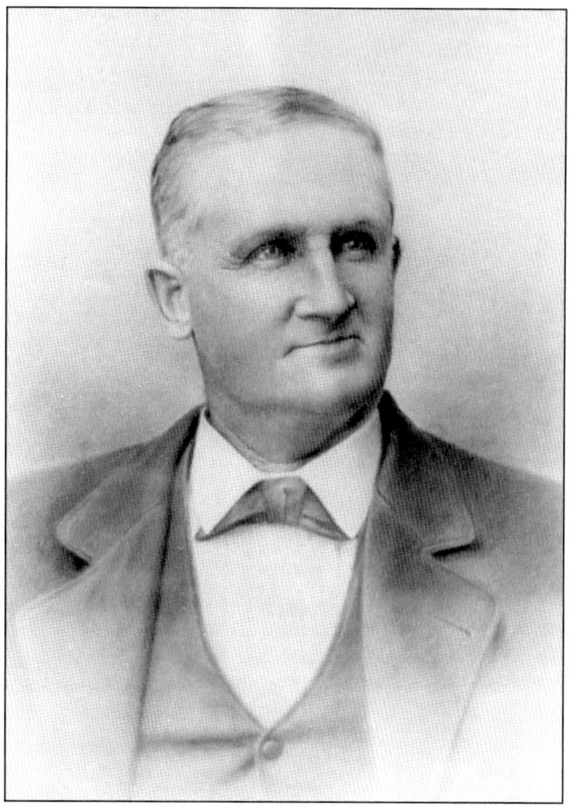

John Mitchell was known for his honesty, and it was said that he never went to law against anybody; his friends do not remember any suit ever being brought against him. Though his business was immense, for many years he never employed a bookkeeper, and he had no assistant. The accounts he kept were few, and he retained his affairs in memory. Prior to his death, he met with each individual that owed him money, and settled with them for whatever they could afford at the time. This way, he had all of his affairs in order when he passed away. His body was kept in a vault at the Masonic Cemetery in San Francisco until 1902, when a family mausoleum was erected in the cemetery in Turlock, California—the town he had founded and lived in. While he belonged to no religious denomination, shortly before his death, he said to a friend: "I love God; I love Christ; I love your Bible." It would seem he lived by these tenets.

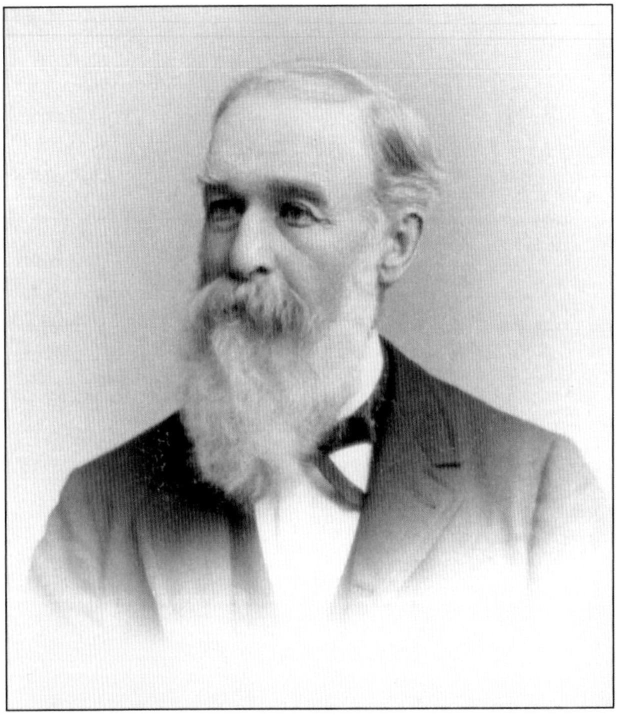

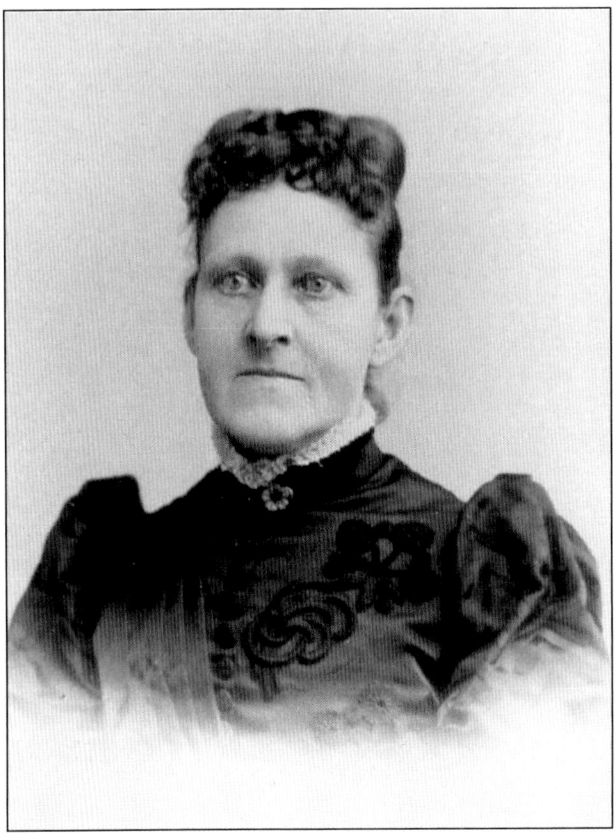

Marshall David Atwater's first wife, Eliza R. Allen, died in April 1852, only two years after their marriage and before he left Connecticut for California. In 1870, Atwater married Laura Allen of Woodbury, Connecticut, who was Eliza's sister. Laura had come west on the newly completed railroad, and they established their permanent home on a large ranch northwest of Merced in 1876. It was there that they raised their only child, Eliza, who was born August 18, 1872, in Stockton, California, which was the closest hospital. In 1925, Mrs. Atwater died at her daughter's home in Merced at the age of 88.

Eliza Atwater married Fredrick Henderson in 1899. Fredrick was a prominent attorney in Merced and also served as the first city attorney for the town of Atwater. In 1911, the Henderson's built a spacious home in Merced and the family, including Mrs. Atwater, moved there. The Henderson's had one child, Allen Atwater, who also became an attorney and practiced private law until he was appointed deputy district attorney in 1935. In 1938, he was elected to this office and served for four years. After his term expired, he took over full duties on the old home ranch (Atwater-Henderson Ranch) until it was sold in 1956. Eliza Henderson passed away at her home in Merced in 1954.

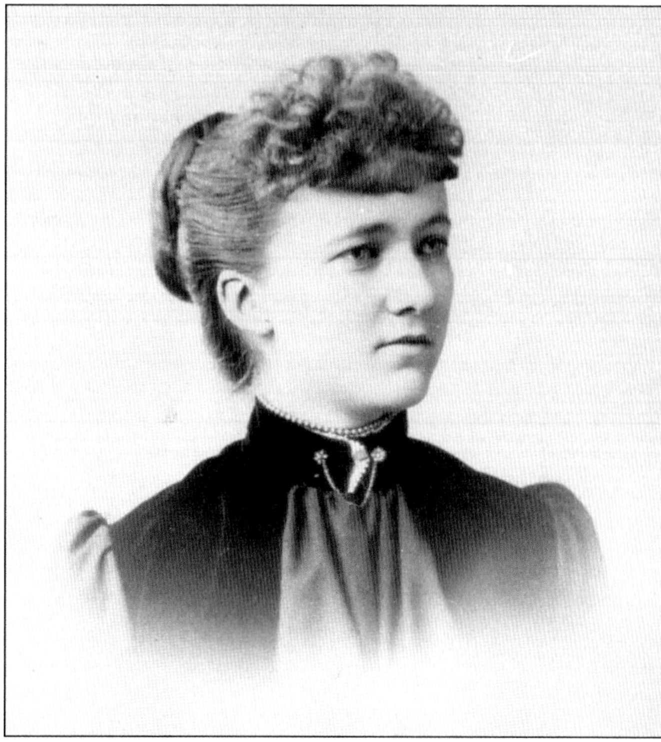

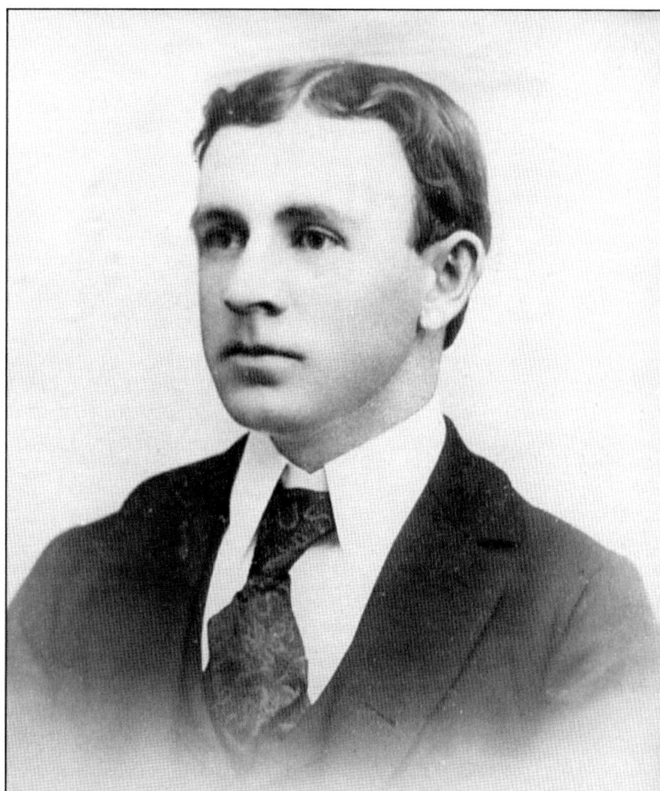

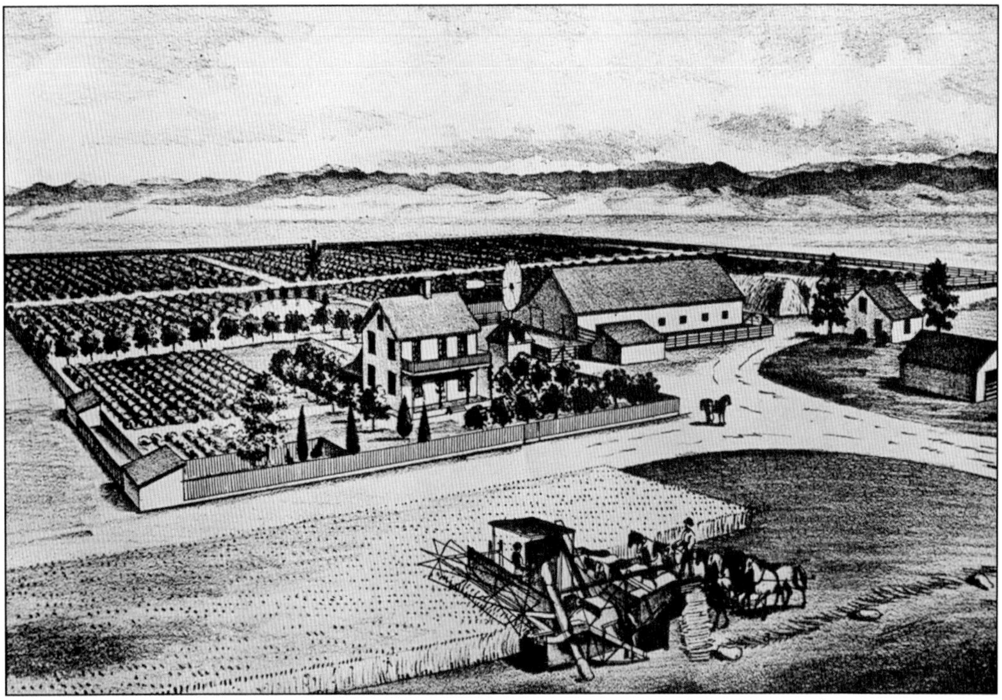

The Atwater ranch was one of the most progressive operations of its time, with a vineyard and a 10-acre orange grove—the first in the San Joaquin Valley. Atwater bordered the navel and Valencia orange groves, with olive trees to protect it from frost and wind. He always found a ready market for his fruit, and the olives were sold to a private concern that made pickled olives and oil from them. The major crops however, were still wheat, barley, and maize, and these were still part of the dry-land farming process.

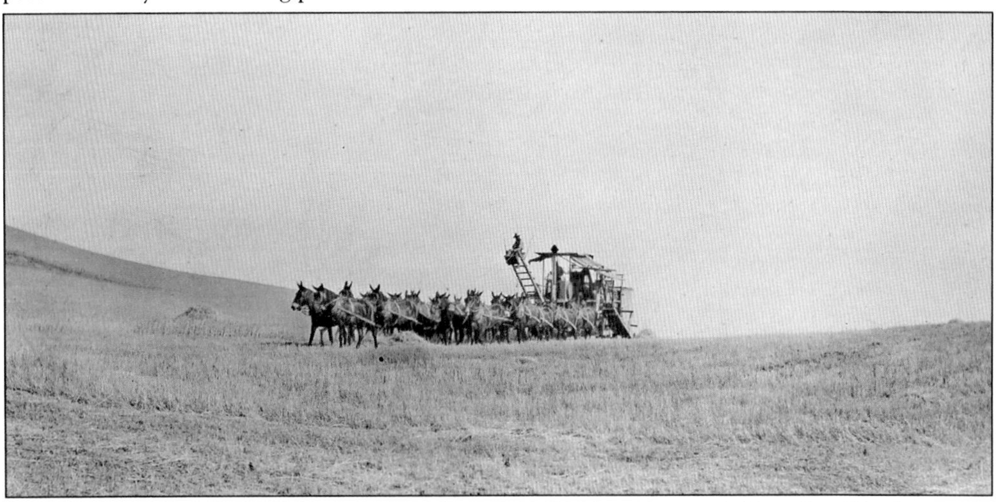

This image shows a typical harvester of the era, pulled by a team of 20 mules. The harvester Atwater invented was named the "Little Patent" and consisted of a 24-foot header, thresher, and straw wagon, and was operated by 5 men and 24 mules. In full operation, as reported in the September 1879 *San Joaquin Valley Argus*, it could do the cutting, threshing, sacking, and housing of the straw from 50 acres of land per day. It was also stated that the harvester, as an economical laborsaving machine, would prove advantageous to the entire farming interests in the state.

George Samuel Bloss came with his wife, son, and daughter from Woodbury, Connecticut, in 1884. They moved into a small dwelling that stood on the corner of what is now Third and Atwater Boulevard, where the Bloss Building stands today. He soon became engaged in farming, and in 1892 he erected a fine two-story home on his property south of the railroad. His wife Ella Bloss died in 1893, shortly after moving into this home. Mr. Bloss then married Edna Thompson Hull, another lady from the same area in Connecticut where he and his first wife were reared. The new Mrs. Bloss was instrumental in planting trees on the streets of Atwater and, along with a hired hand, hauled water in barrels from their house to irrigate the trees. Many of the older tree-lined streets that are enjoyed by today's residents are due to her concern and attention.

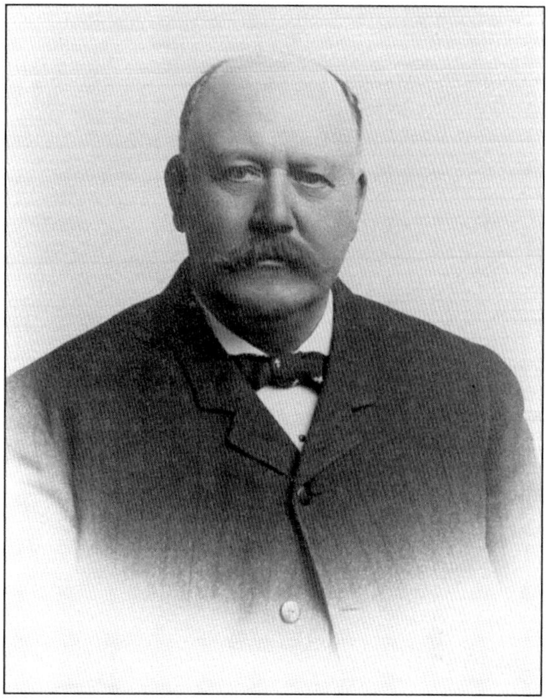

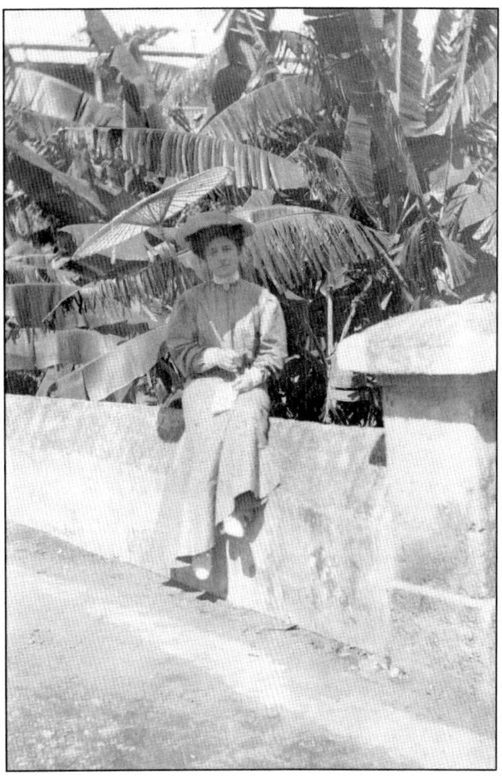

This picture of Edna Bloss was taken at Fort Santiago, in Manila, on November 28, 1907. The only sibling of George Jr., she accompanied him and other family members on an around-the-world tour. She married a Mr. Thorne and lived her adult life in San Francisco. They did not have children.

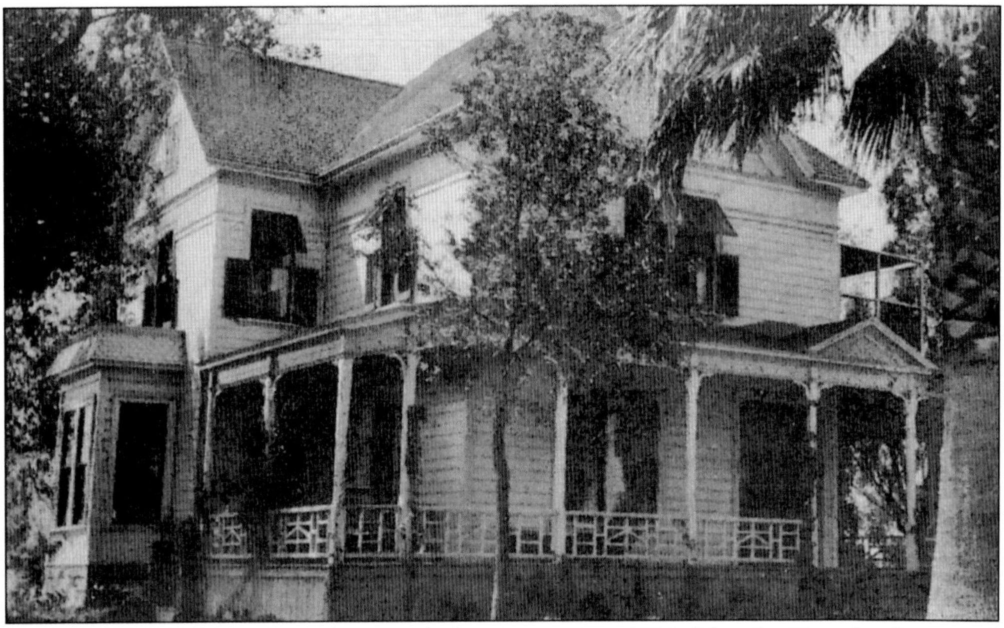

This house was built in 1892 and was ready for occupancy in 1893. After the Bloss Sr. clan passed away, it was rented to Dr. Cotton, then sold to Dr. Jackson, and then sold to others over the years. Unfortunately, this house is no longer standing, but it was the first structure built on the original layout of the town of Atwater.

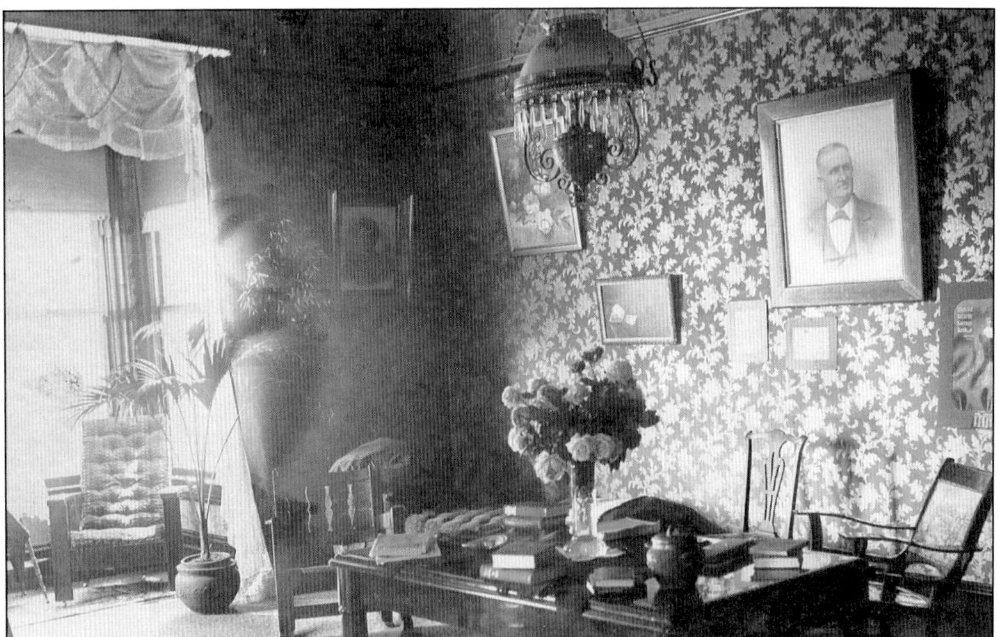

This photograph shows the parlor in the George Bloss Sr. home. The large picture of John W. Mitchell that is seen hanging on the wall is now on display on the first landing of the Bloss Home Museum in Atwater.

Born in Bethlehem, Connecticut, George Stone Bloss, at age 10, came to Atwater with his father, mother, and sister in 1884. He attended school in his hometown and continued his education at the Mitchell School in Atwater, Merced Academy for high school, and Santa Clara College for two years. In 1911, George married Christine Thompson of Bethlehem, Connecticut. Christine was the niece of Edna Thompson Bloss, the second wife of George's father. In 1914, the couple completed the construction of their own home at First and Cedar Streets. This was the same year their only child, George Thompson Bloss, was born. As a young man, George Jr. became interested in raising cattle. Successful in this work, he was able to enlarge his holdings in the Bloss Land and Cattle Company and was always considered an authority on raising stock. George Jr. became the first mayor when Atwater incorporated in 1922, and later he served as a councilman and a director of the Merced Irrigation District. He belonged to the Masons, was a Shriner, and was a member of most of the area service clubs. When George died April 13, 1963, at the age of 89, he willed the Bloss home to the City of Atwater, with the provision that Christine remain in residence until her death. George was always known as George Bloss Jr., though his middle name was different than his father's. Perhaps this was because their middle names both started with the letter S. Today we bow to common practice and refer to them as senior and junior.

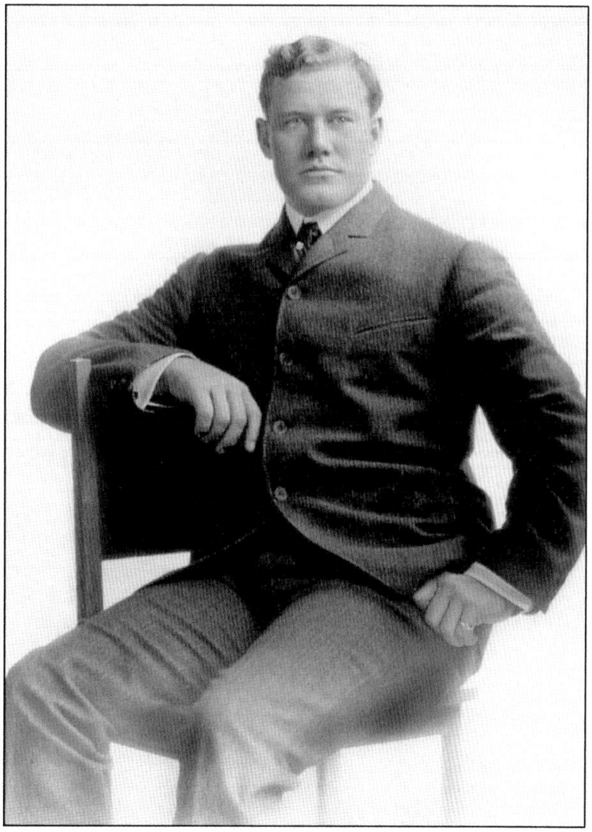

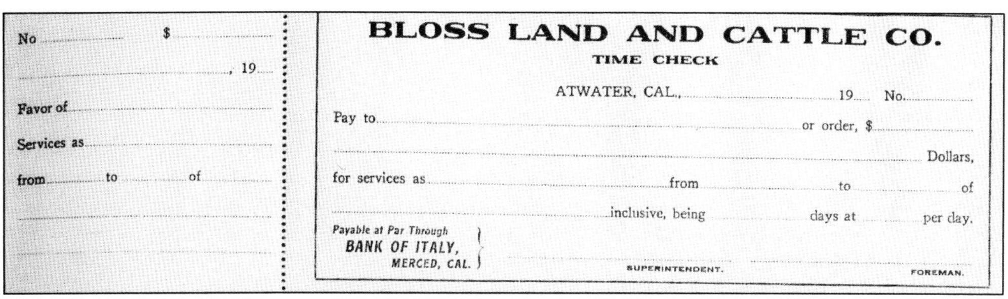

No .... $ ....

........, 19....

Favor of ....

Services as ....

from .... to .... of ....

BLOSS LAND AND CATTLE CO.

TIME CHECK

ATWATER, CAL., ... 19.... No. ....

Pay to .... or order, $ ....

.... Dollars,

for services as .... from .... to .... of

.... inclusive, being .... days at .... per day.

Payable at Par Through
BANK OF ITALY,
MERCED, CAL.

SUPERINTENDENT. FOREMAN.

This blank check for the account of Bloss Land and Cattle Company could be drawn on the Bank of Italy. Mr. Bloss was on the board of directors for the bank.

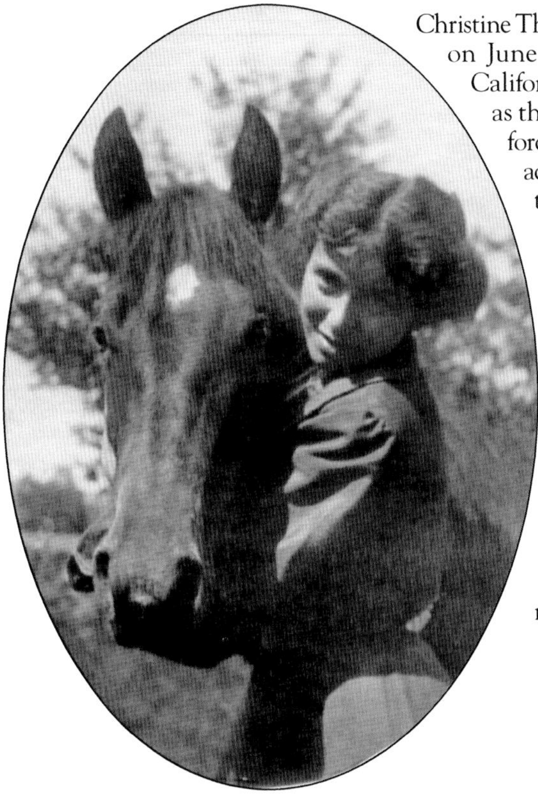

Christine Thompson was born in Bethlehem, Connecticut, on June 23, 1890, and passed away in Atwater, California, on December 18, 1971. During her years as the wife of George Bloss Jr., she was a quiet but forceful member of the Atwater community. She achieved many philanthropic endeavors, one of the most important being the establishment of a trust that awards scholarships to graduating high school seniors in the Merced County area. The Bloss Memorial Scholarship Trust gives thousands of dollars a year to young people who are continuing their education and it is based solely on academic achievement. Before she died, she also endowed a library in her hometown of Bethlehem. Christine was known for her involvement with children's groups. Many former Girl Scouts recall going to the Bloss house one Thursday every month to bake cookies with Mrs. Bloss. The community remembers her with fondness.

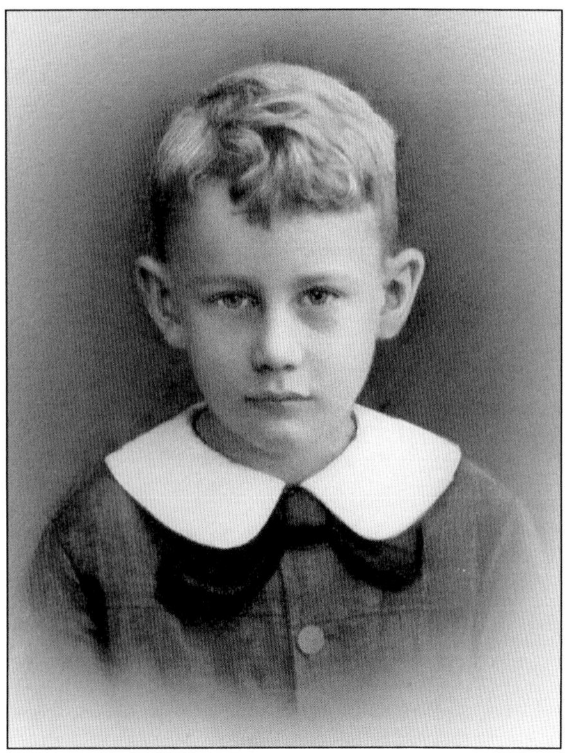

George Thompson Bloss (called Thompson) was born June 22, 1914. He was the beloved only child of George and Christine. He had a typically active childhood, but his life was cut short by the menace of measles. The story is that the Blosses took him to San Francisco to seek further medical help with this disease and he died there from complications on April 18, 1922, just about two months short of his seventh birthday.

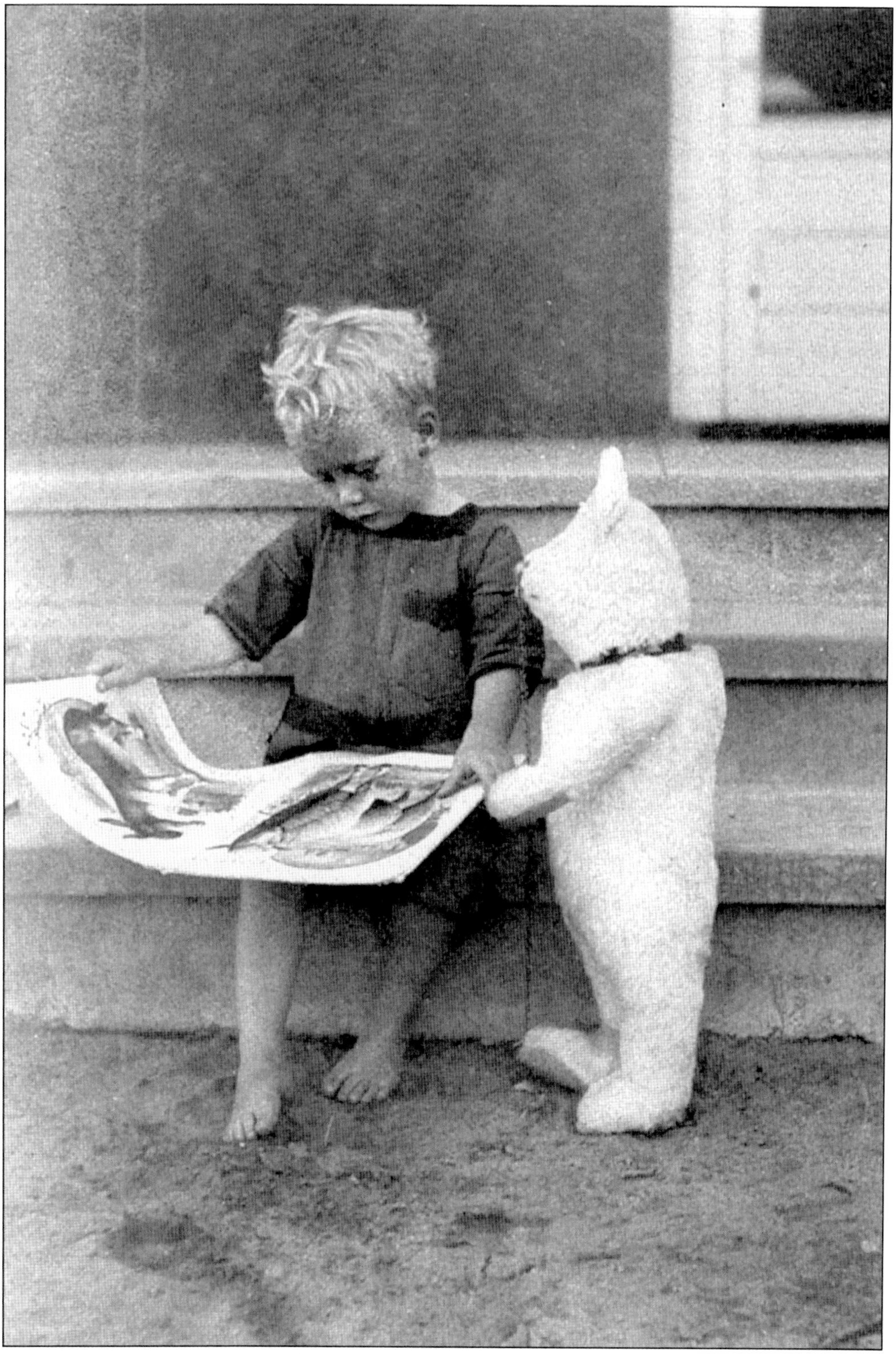

Sitting on the back steps of the Bloss home, Thompson reads to his bear.

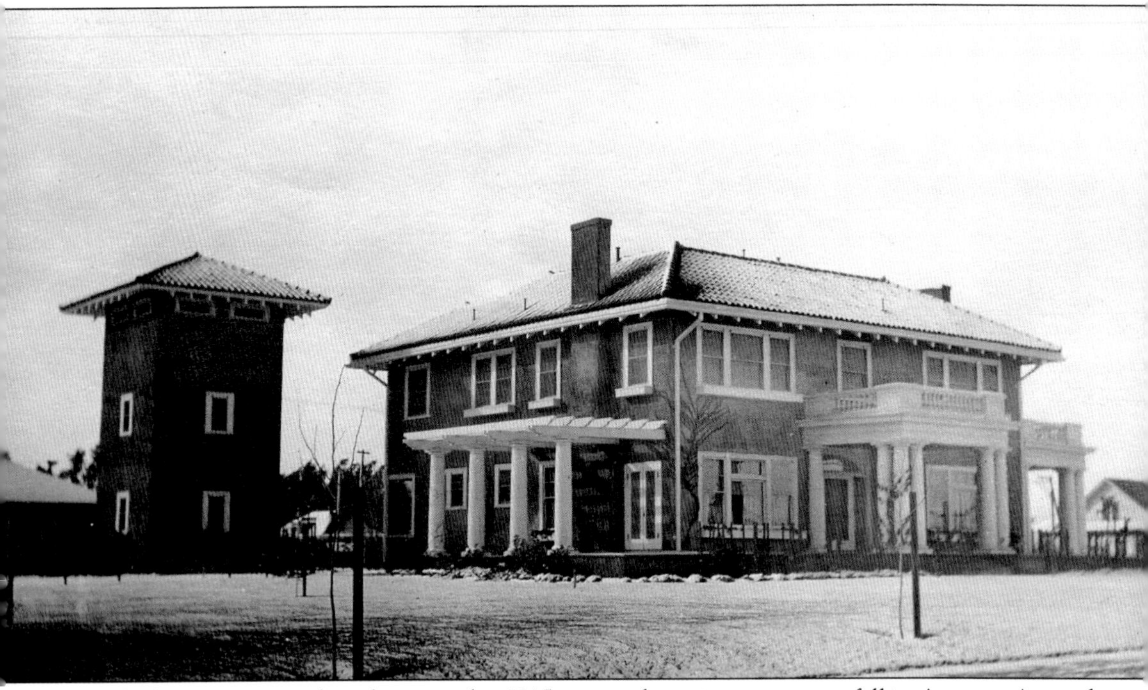

The home was new when shown in this 1915 picture depicting a rare snowfall in Atwater. Around 1932, a tower was added to the east side (where the French doors are located) to accommodate an elevator from the dining room to the bedroom above. Square footage of the home is 4,080 and was built at the cost of $11,954. The tower toward the rear is the tank house, which was common to most homes of the era. A well is underneath the building and water was pumped to a tank housed on the top floor. The water was then gravity-fed into the house. Unusual for the time, there are four full bathrooms on the second floor of the home and a powder room on the first floor. Mr. Bloss's bathroom also has a separate shower that sports seven showerheads. The architect-engineer for the house was William E. Bedesen, who drew the plans for many structures in the area and passed away in 1986 at the age of 102. The home is now a museum located at 1020 Cedar Avenue.

Two

EARLY ATWATER

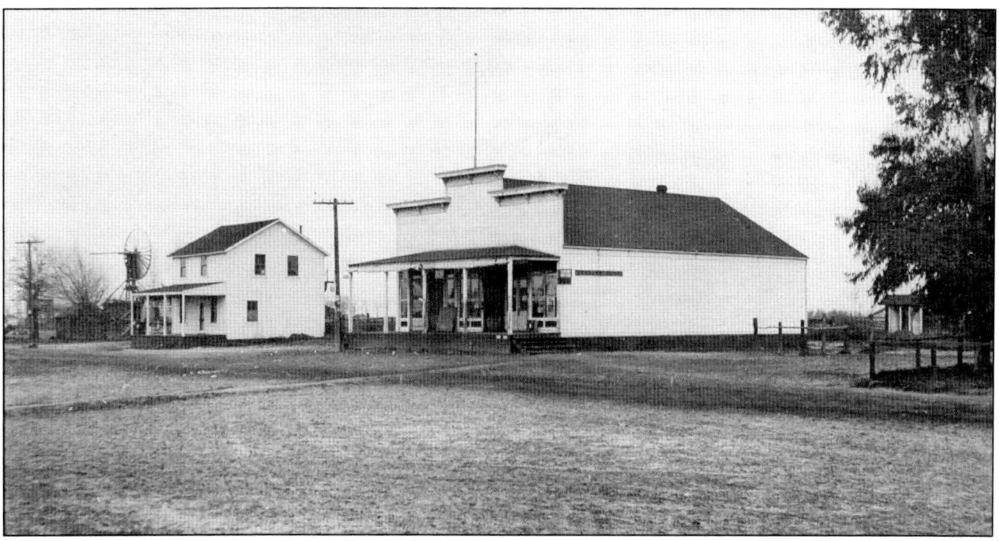

Here is Front Street around 1902. The two-story building on the left is believed to be the old store that was moved to its location from across the road when the depot building was moved in from Vallejo, California. Tom Harrell rented this two-story building and opened a pool hall. Mrs. Harrell also started a notion store in part of the building, and later the branch of the Merced County Library also occupied part of her business. Mrs. Harrell was the assistant librarian. The second floor served as their residence. The old buildings that housed the express and freight offices were dismantled. At this time there were about 100 people living in Atwater. The J. B. Osborn building is on the right.

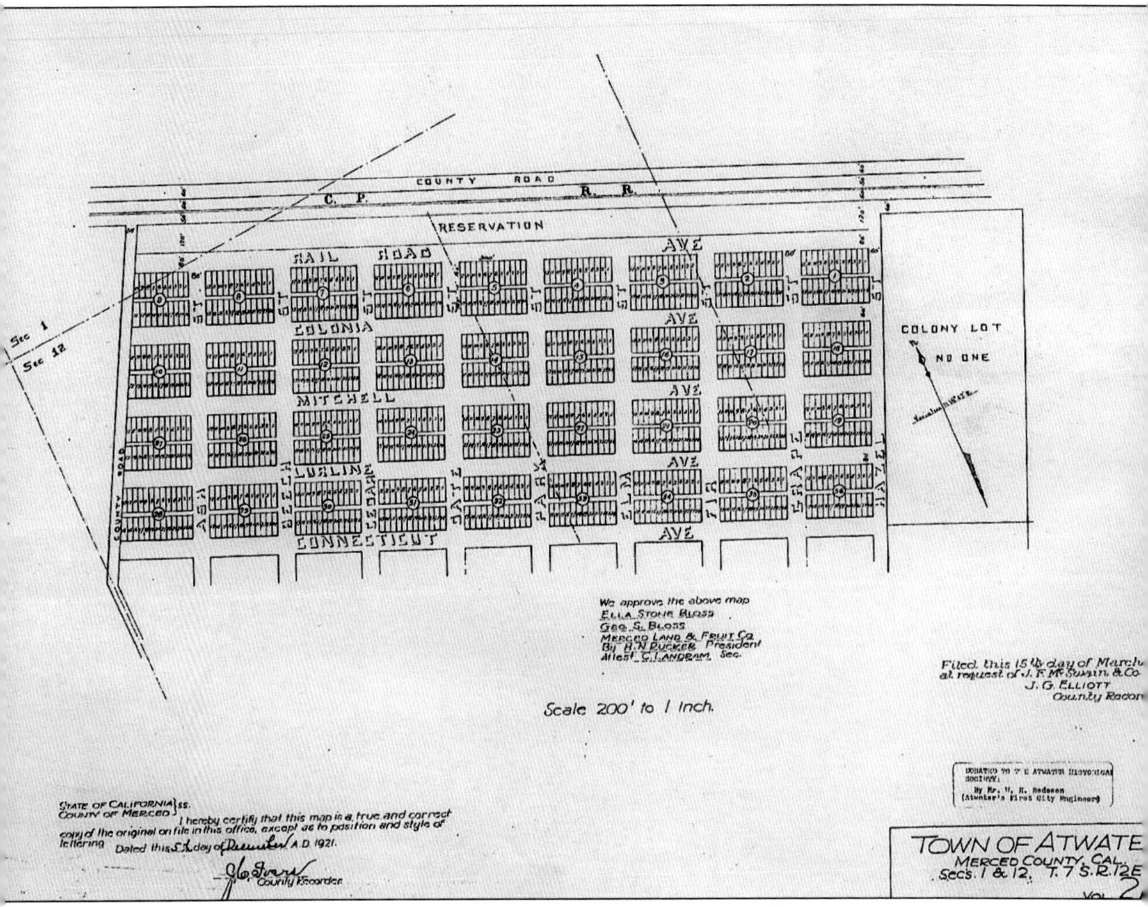

This March 1888 map shows the original plan for the town of Atwater. It was surveyed and proposed by the Merced Land and Fruit Company and approved by George Samuel Bloss and Ella Stone Bloss, who owned the property. The only buildings that were constructed on this land were the Bloss Sr. home and, eventually, other commercial buildings. The State Highway 99 Freeway occupies a strip of this land.

Clark Ralston came to California for the first time in 1849 by way of Cape Horn. He worked in the gold mines for five years and then returned east to live. He married Eliza Butler in Piqua, Ohio, in 1847. Clark entered the Civil War and became a major in the 66th Illinois Volunteer Infantry. After the war, the Ralstons and their family of six children came overland to California. They made their home in Pope Valley, Napa County, and San Francisco for several years; here two more children joined the family. In the late 1880s, the family came to Merced County and lived in Merced, Landrum Colony, and about 1890 they moved to the Giannini property in Atwater. Mrs. Ralston helped organize the Atwater Women's Improvement Club (later called Atwater Women's Club). This organization helped to refurbish Mitchell Hall for use by the community. They were also given the project of naming the streets in Atwater in 1908. When their youngest son Frank died in 1905, the senior Ralstons took their three grandchildren, Clark, Sadie, and Bert, to rear. Frank's wife, Gussie Bedesen Ralston, predeceased him in 1896. In 1912, Major Ralston died at the age of 93. Mrs. Ralston moved to one of her daughter's home in Oakland and lived there until her death in 1913. Ralston Park in Atwater is named for this family.

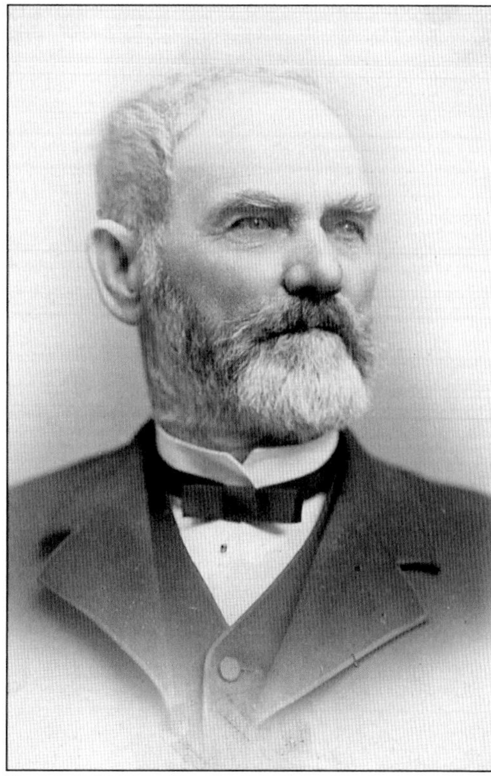

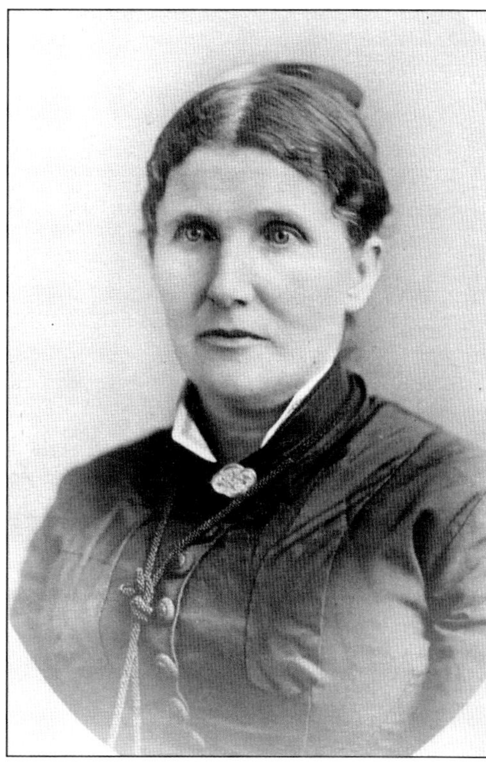

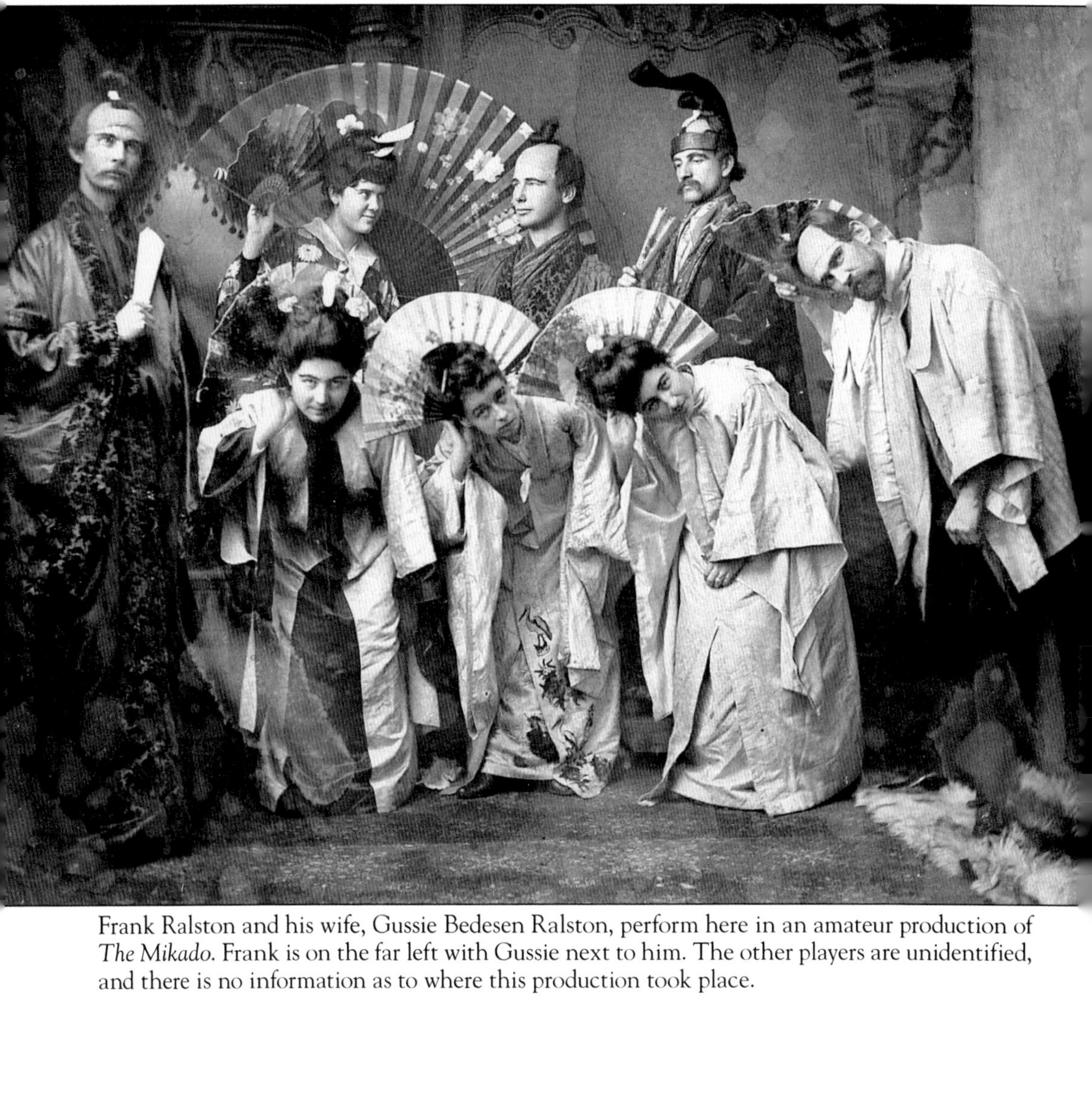

Frank Ralston and his wife, Gussie Bedesen Ralston, perform here in an amateur production of *The Mikado*. Frank is on the far left with Gussie next to him. The other players are unidentified, and there is no information as to where this production took place.

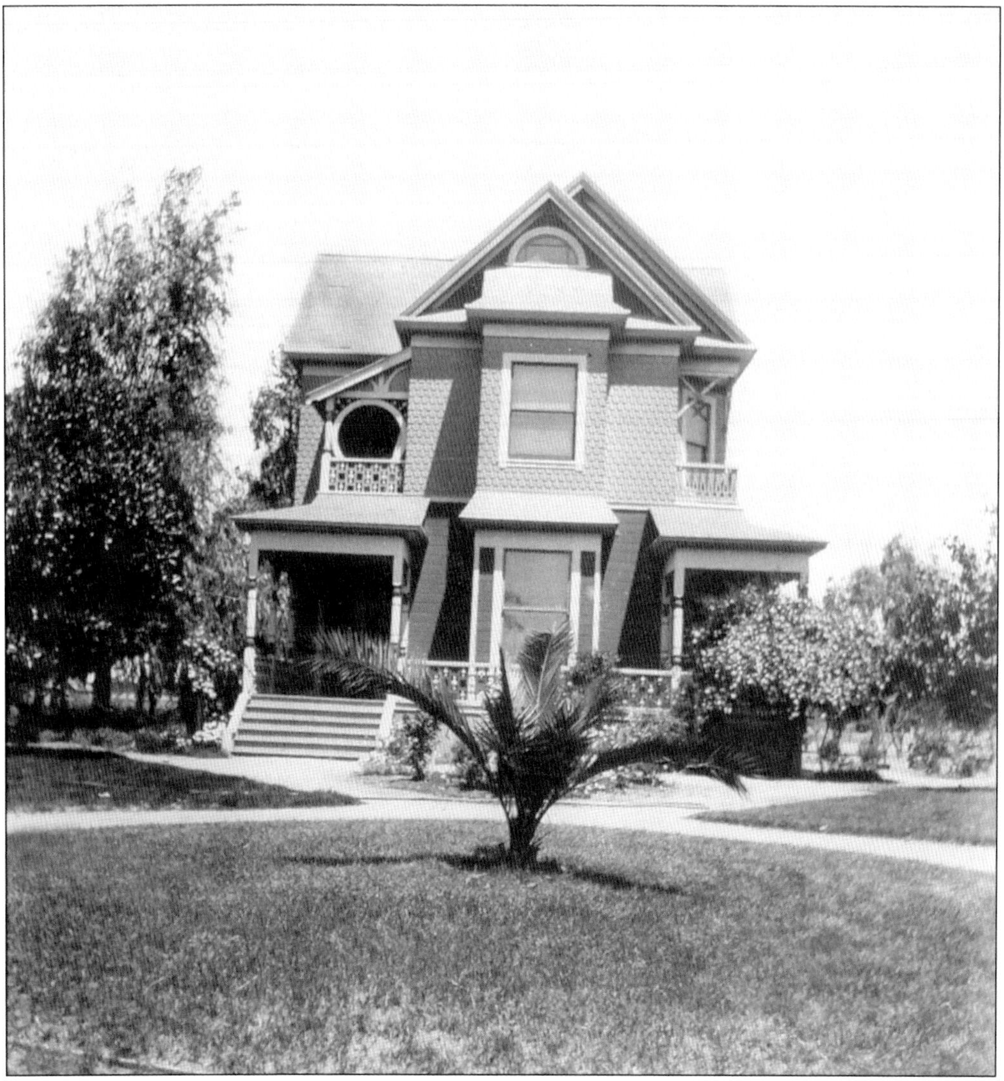

Built by David Ripley Miller around 1893, this farm home faced what is now Atwater Boulevard. Mr. Miller purchased the land from C. C. Mitchell, who was a brother of John Mitchell, and it was planted with peach trees. In 1945, the Cabazut family purchased the home and moved it one block back from its original location to Broadway Avenue. Though the house was turned into apartments, it has been used as a single-family dwelling for the past several years. After the home fell into disrepair, the owners sold the land to a church group, who in turn gave the house away for a small stipend for their building fund. The house was moved to Jones Road in Winton to be restored. Until its relocation in 2004, it had been the oldest house in Atwater and the only remaining Victorian.

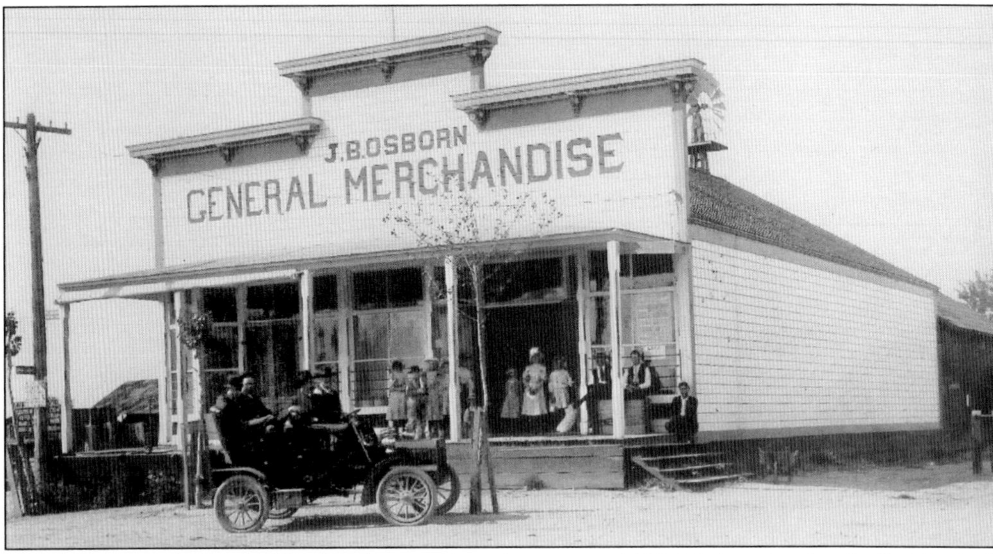

John Benton Osborn and his family moved to Atwater in 1892. He bought the C. C. Mitchell home and property, and the John Giddings store. He took charge of the post office, the depot, and the express and freight offices that stood by the store. In 1901, he bought two lots in the Fin de Siecle Addition of Atwater, where he erected the large general merchandise store pictured above. This building was occupied in 1902. Mr. Osborn died suddenly on January 19, 1912. In July of the same year, Osborn and Son was burned to the ground in a fire that swept out almost the entire block on Front Street (now Atwater Boulevard).

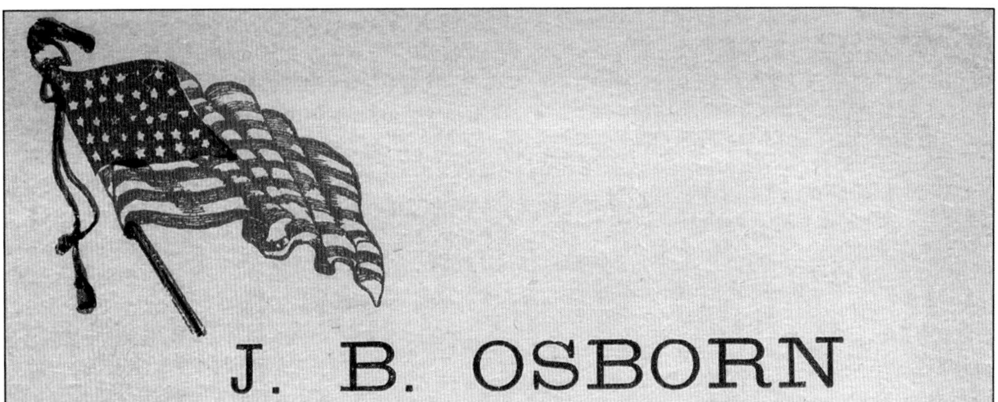

J. B. Osborn ran for supervisor of Merced County District No. Three on November 8, 1898. The card he passed out during the campaign shows that he was the "Regular Republican Nominee." He lost the election, but in time his son Charles became one of the first city councilmen when Atwater was incorporated in 1922.

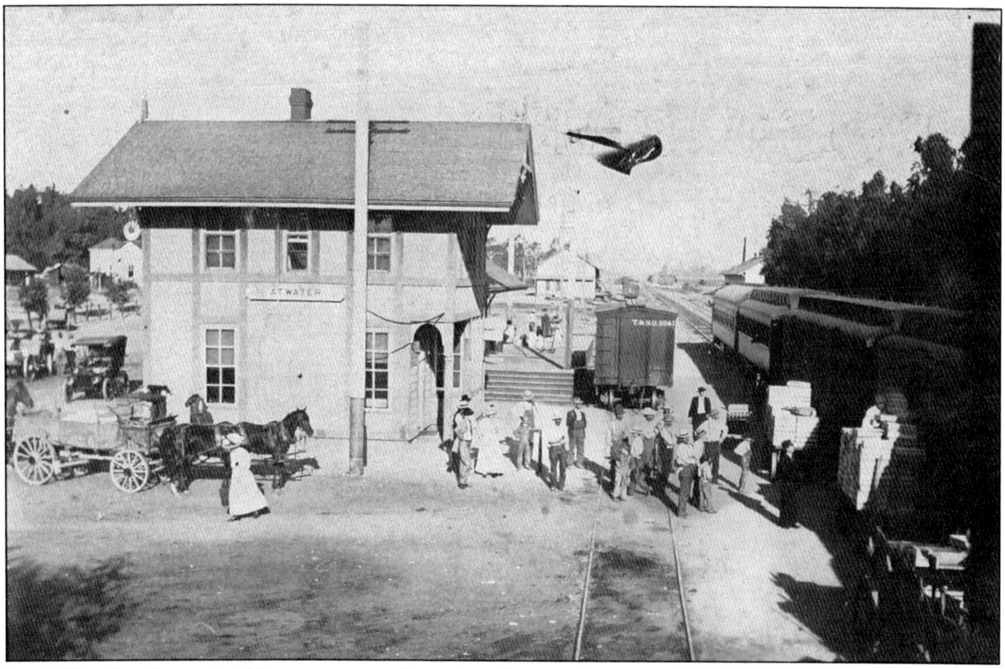

In 1902, the depot building was purchased and moved in sections by train from Vallejo. The old building, which housed the express and freight offices, was dismantled. The original store building was moved across the road near the Osborn store. The depot served the area from 1902 until 1959. From 1959 to 1962 it was subleased from the railroad by Mr. and Mrs. Ralph Smart and used as a railway express office and Greyhound Bus Depot. In 1962, the railroad decided not to lease it again and the building was demolished. A footnote for this building is that during the year of 1912, an average of 30 to 40 carloads of fresh fruit and vegetables were shipped each day during the harvest season to the east by fast freight.

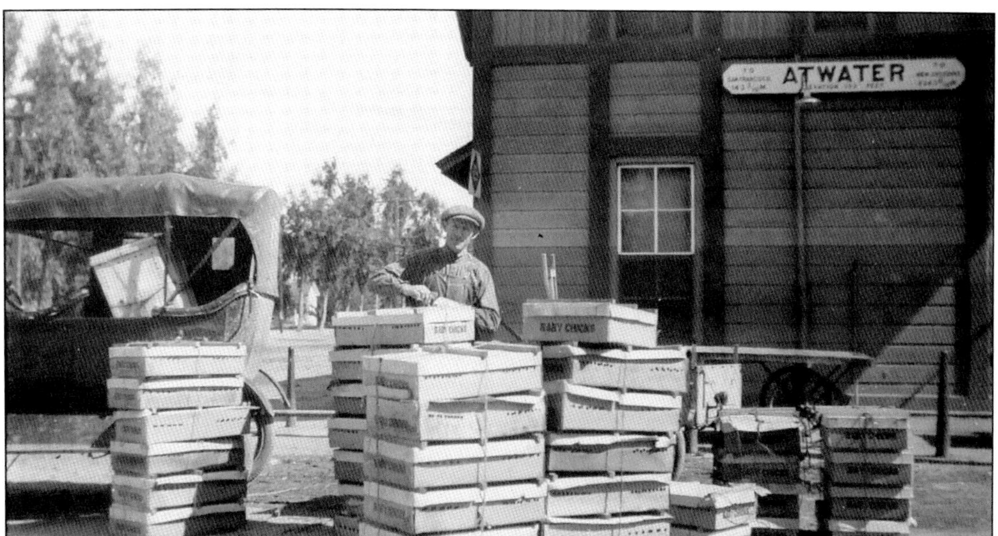

The railroad agent is shown loading boxes of baby chicks for shipment. The agent is believed to be Mr. John Lamberty.

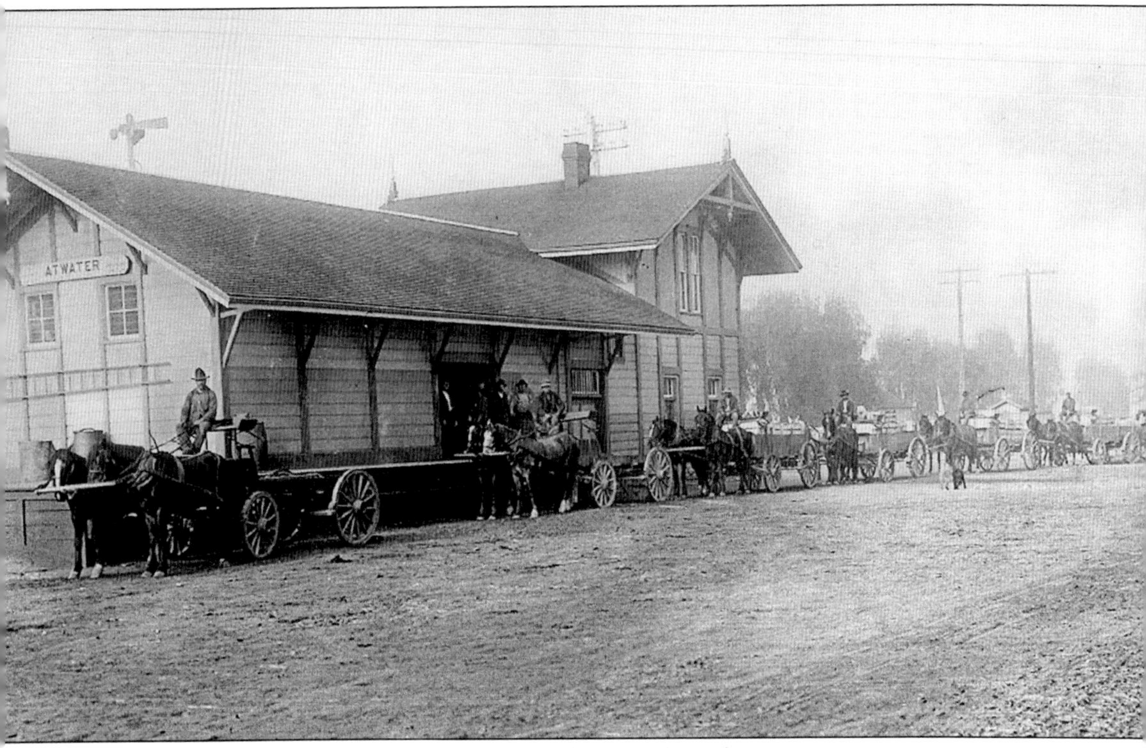

Farmers line up to unload their products for shipment by rail.

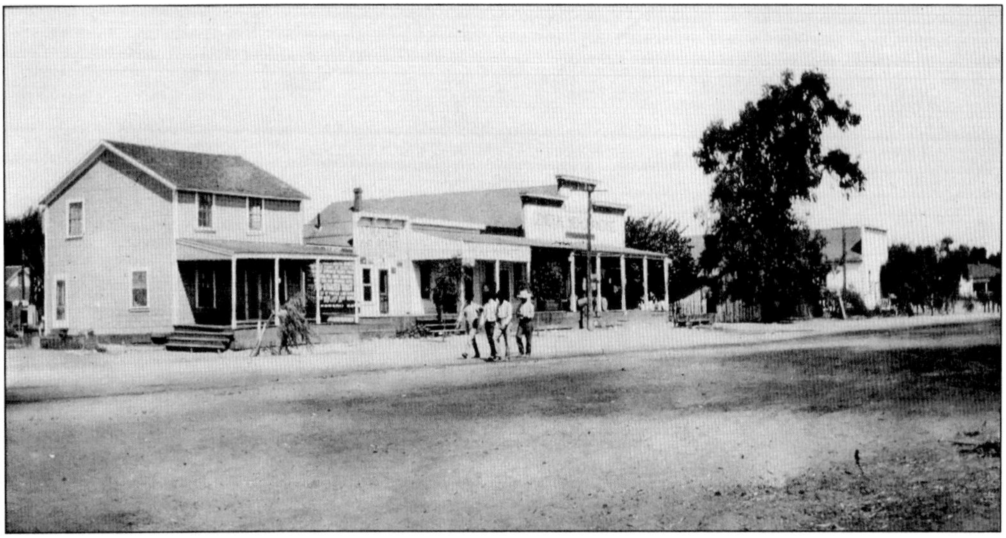

Front Street (now Atwater Boulevard) is pictured across from the railroad station prior to 1909. Located here were the J. B. Osborn General Merchandise Store, Hinds Meat Market, J. T. Harrell residence, Merced Building and Loan Association, Atwater Branch of Merced Security and Savings Bank, Owen and Bowles Furniture Store, Owen Brothers Real Estate and Produce Office, A. J. Dunlap's residence and barbershop, an ice cream and candy store, a library, and a post office. This was all in a one-block area between Third and Fourth Streets. A fire started in the meat market, and the whole block, with the exception of the small grocery store on the corner of Fourth Street operated by the Williams, burned to the ground in 1912.

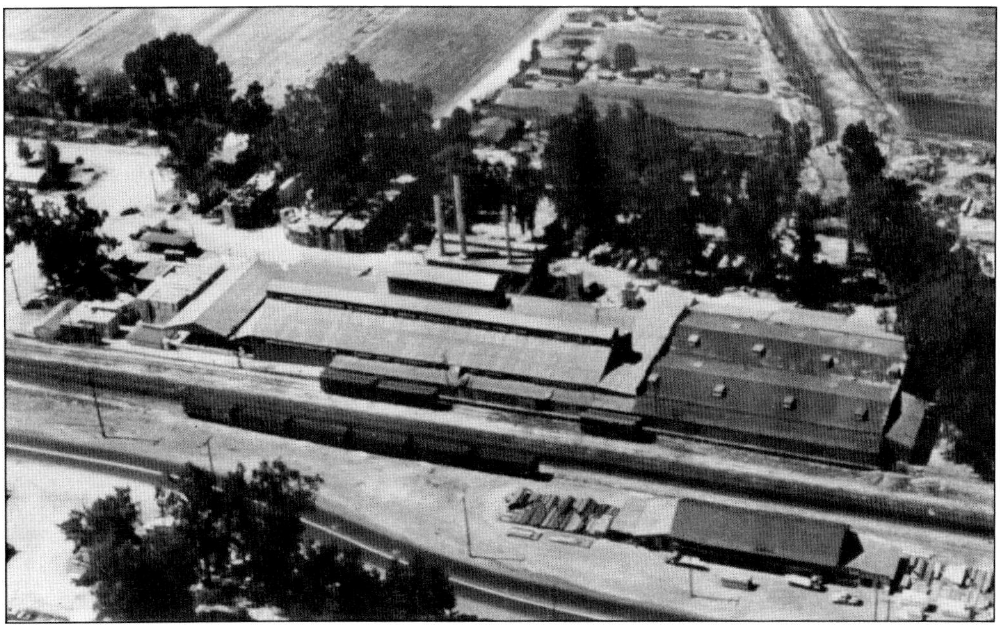

The Atwater Cannery was built in 1905 when Atwater fruit growers formed a co-op company to operate their own cannery. It was built on the original town site that had been set aside for the town of Atwater in 1888. Some of the shareholders were George Bloss Sr., George Bloss Jr., L. F. Herrod, the Owens Brothers, and J. B. Osborn, who became the manager. The cannery operated under the name of Del Monte until 1939.

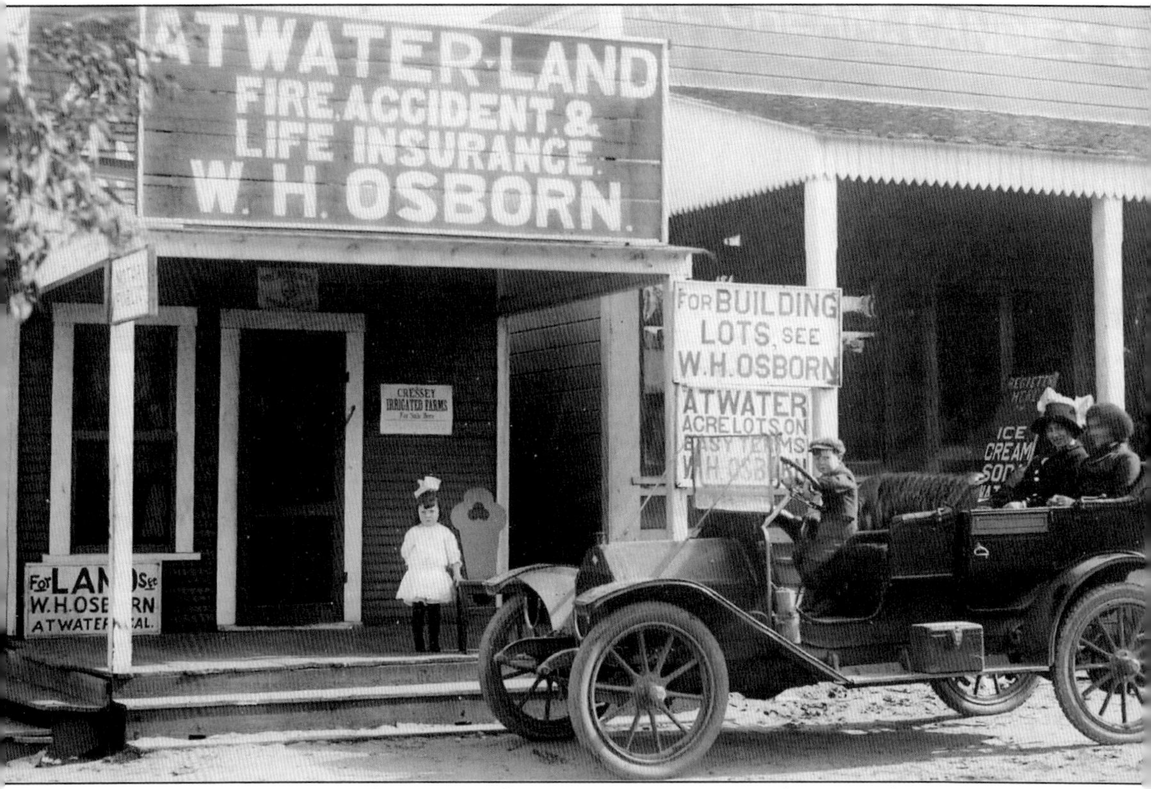

William H. Osborn, son of Henry, was born in San Francisco. He became a farmer when he was 21, and in 1877 he rented two and a half sections in Turlock from John Mitchell, his step-uncle. He married Lucinda Bonnett in 1878. In 1896, the couple moved to Atwater, where he farmed 50 acres of peaches. In 1907, Mr. Osborn became a realtor and was the agent for the Jordan/Atwater Colony No. 2. He also had an insurance agency in his office. William was appointed justice of the peace for the Atwater Township in 1913 and was elected to this office in 1914. He held this position until his death in 1943. During his lifetime, he saw the tiny hamlet grow into a thriving town with an estimated population of 1,300. Osborn took an active part in the growth of Atwater; he was always ready to lend a hand in the affairs of the town. A member of the United Methodist Church, he helped organize the first Sunday school.

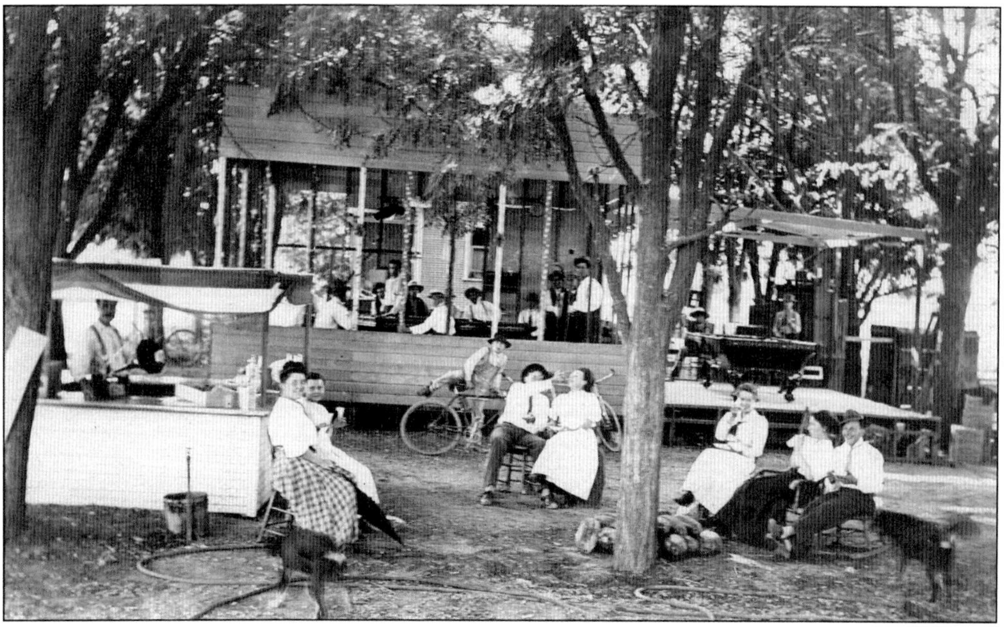

Pictured above is Harry Logue's open-air ice cream parlor and poolroom. Logue, pictured below, was born in St. Louis, Missouri, on October 22, 1856. His family moved by covered wagon to Colorado in 1860. Harry received his education in Colorado schools and became interested in mining, the business in which his father was engaged. He followed this line of work in Colorado, New Mexico, and Arizona. While in Arizona he served as a U.S. Marshall and also married Mrs. Virginia Clark, widow of Robert E. Clark. He adopted Virginia's son Robert, and then five more children were born of this union. The Logues first came to California in 1894, and in 1907 they made their home in Atwater. Harry opened a blacksmith shop and later opened the first open-air ice cream shop and poolroom. This business was located on Front Street (Atwater Boulevard) and Fourth. He also formed the stock company that built the Atwater Hotel in 1908. Seeing opportunity in real estate and insurance, he helped lay out and settle Parr Colony in the Fruitland area. After that, he became resident agent for the Cooperative Land and Trust Company of San Francisco. This business took an option to sell and help colonize the Winton area. Logue helped form the Winton Cemetery District and was involved in the Winton Water Works. A man of many vocations and avocations, Mr. Logue obtained a patent for an automatic headlight for automobiles and, as an accomplished carpenter, helped do the finish work on the alter in the temple room of the Mormon Temple that was being built in Salt Lake City, Utah. Mr. Logue passed away on September 28, 1932, at the age of 77.

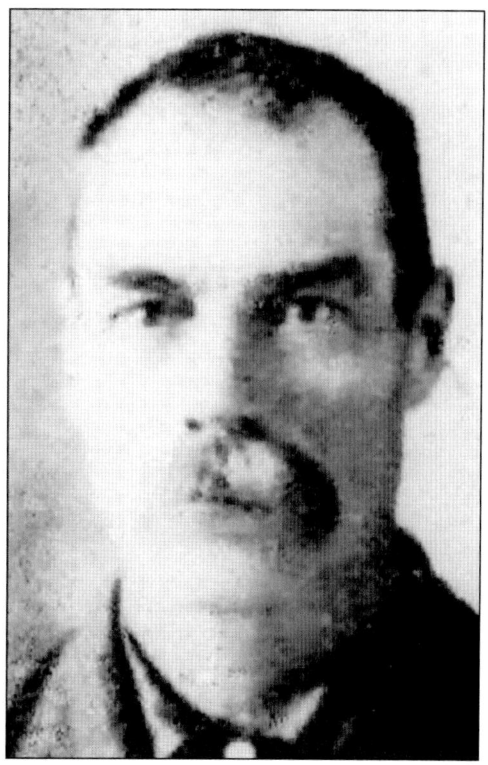

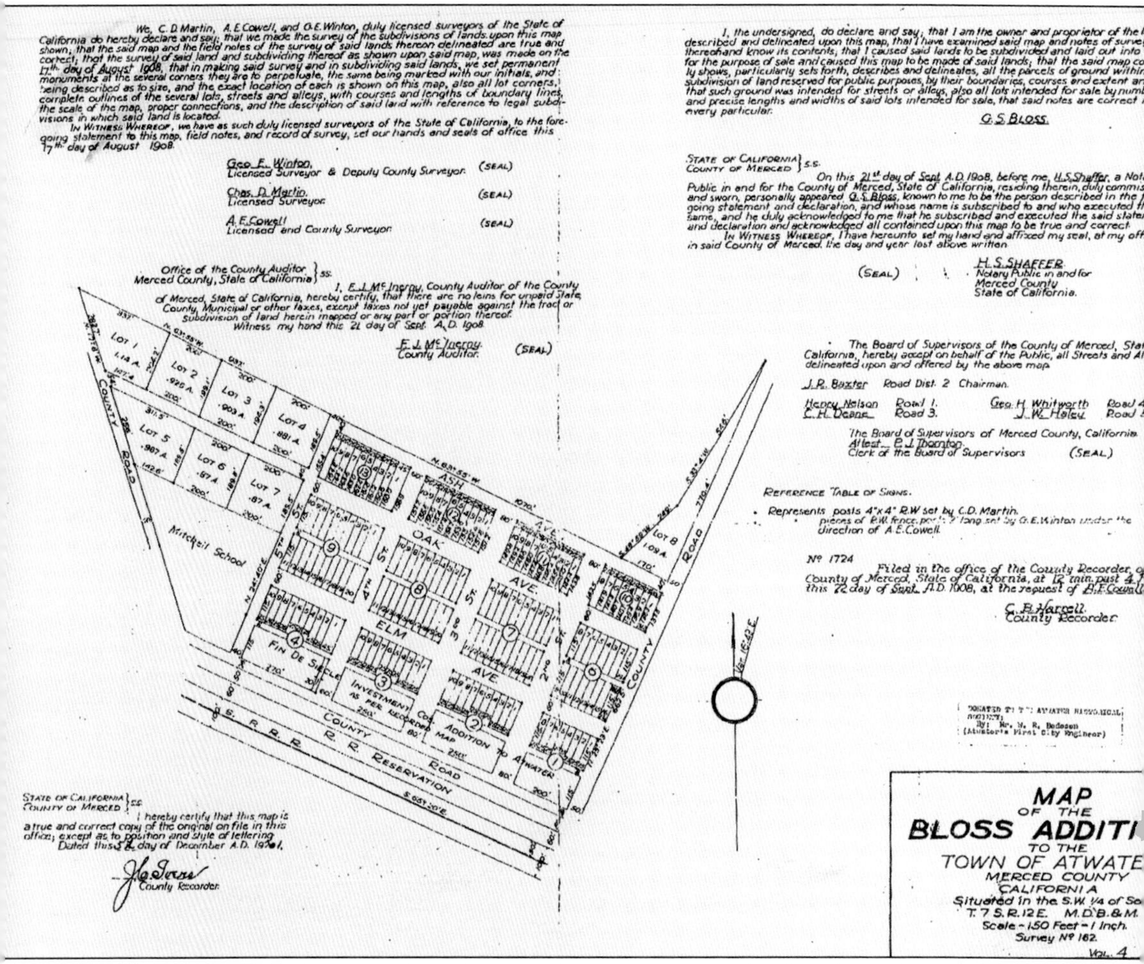

Showing the 1899 Fin de Siecle addition to Atwater, this map for the Bloss addition depicts how Atwater first developed. The Fin de Siecle addition was the beginning of the business district for the new town. Note that the names of the tree streets are no longer the same. Elm is now Broadway, Oak is Cedar, and Ash is Drakeley. These names were changed sometime prior to 1927.

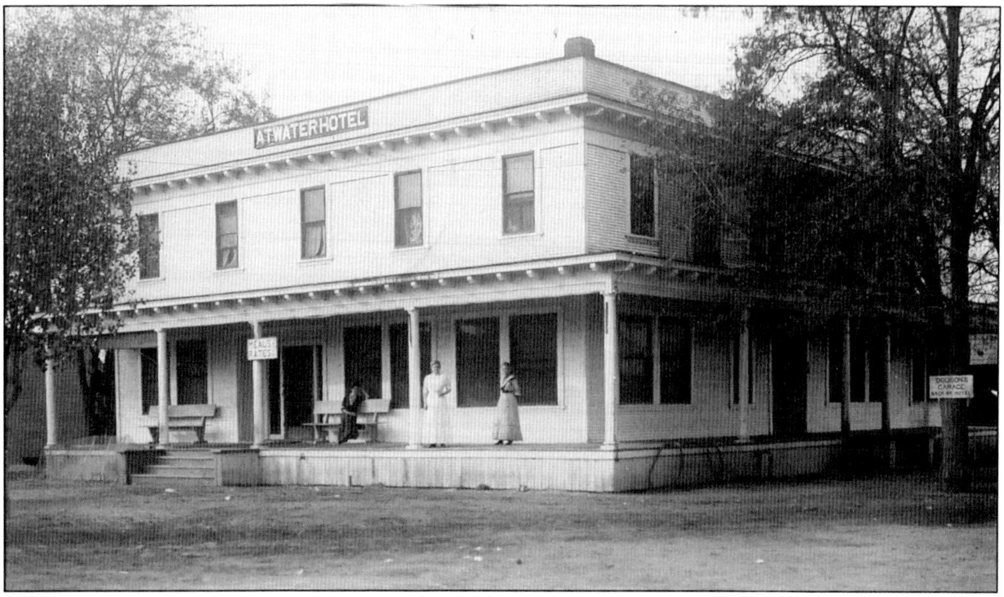

The Atwater Hotel was a cooperative project and built in 1908. Harry Logue promoted the idea, and shares were sold at $500 each. George Bloss Sr. donated the lot, and the building was erected at a cost of $5,000. Some of the shareholders were George Bloss Sr., George Bloss Jr., the Owen brothers, Charlie Shaffer, and G. H. Drakeley. The hotel had a family living room, a lobby, a dining room, a kitchen, and 14 bedrooms. A later addition was an annex of eight rooms. There was a need for the hotel at this time, for with the cannery and grape packing sheds in full operation during the harvest, employees needed accommodations. The sign on the tree is for Dodson's Garage in the rear. The hotel occupied the corner of Atwater Boulevard (Front Street) and Fourth Street from 1908 until 1955.

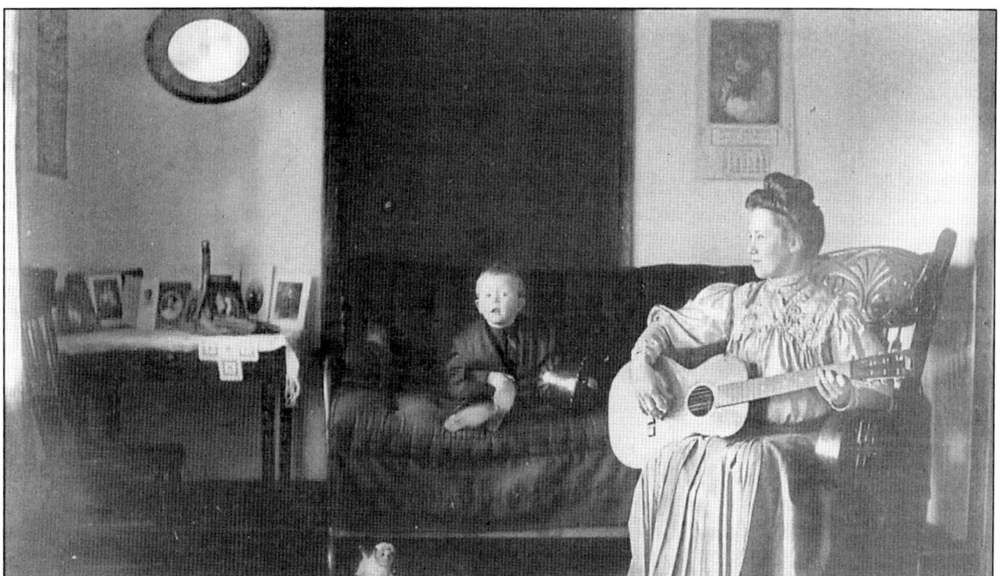

Pictured are the wife and son of the first manager of the Atwater Hotel, Mr. Will Gerard. The historical society also has a picture of the building with the sign reading Gerard Hotel, so it is assumed that the hotel was called by the manager's name until he left in 1909.

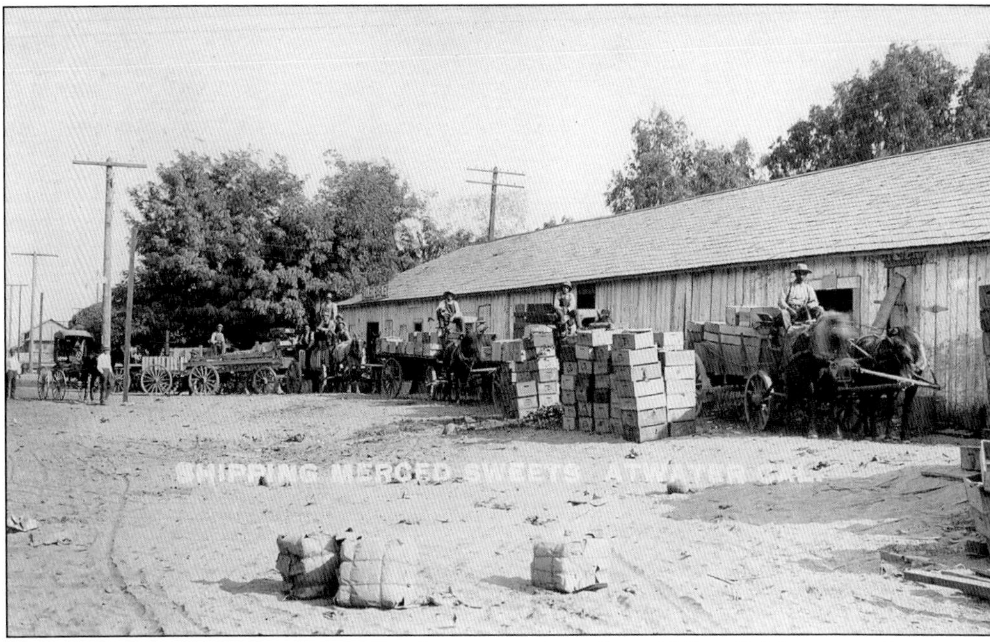

J. C. Boynton and Z. T. Smith, both teachers, came from Grass Valley, California, to the vicinity of Atwater in 1878. They were the first people to plant sweet potatoes in Merced County in the early 1880s. Mr. Boynton bought seed from New Jersey, while Mr. Smith bought his from North Carolina. Sweet potatoes did well in the sandy soil of the Atwater area and soon became one of the leading crops. Pictured are farmers bringing their harvest to be shipped to market. Some of the growers that bought and sold sweet potatoes were Frank Dutra, John Souza, J. J. Pimentel, and J. M. Trindade—known as the "big four."

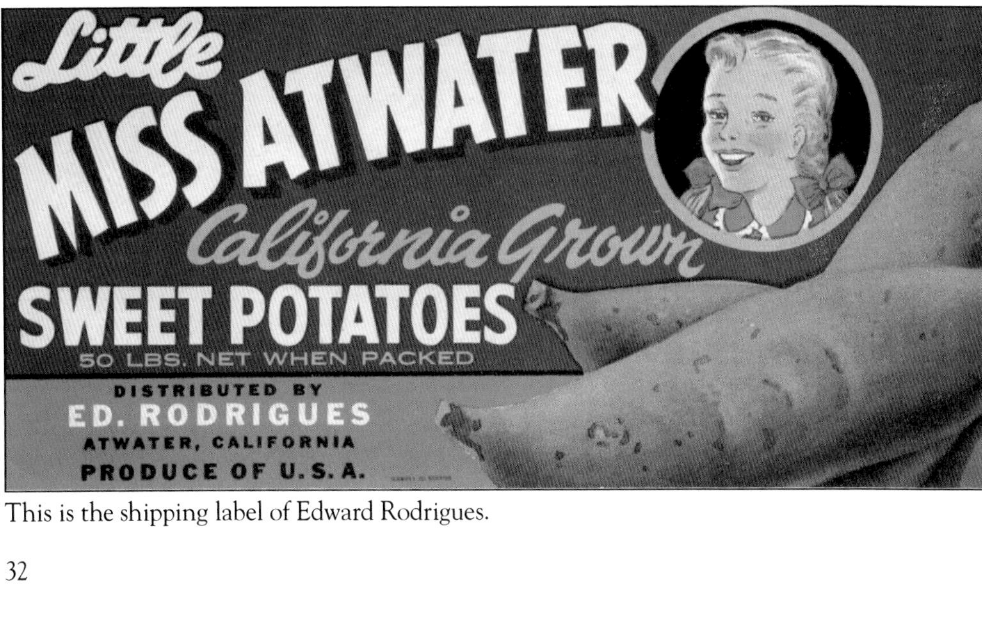

This is the shipping label of Edward Rodrigues.

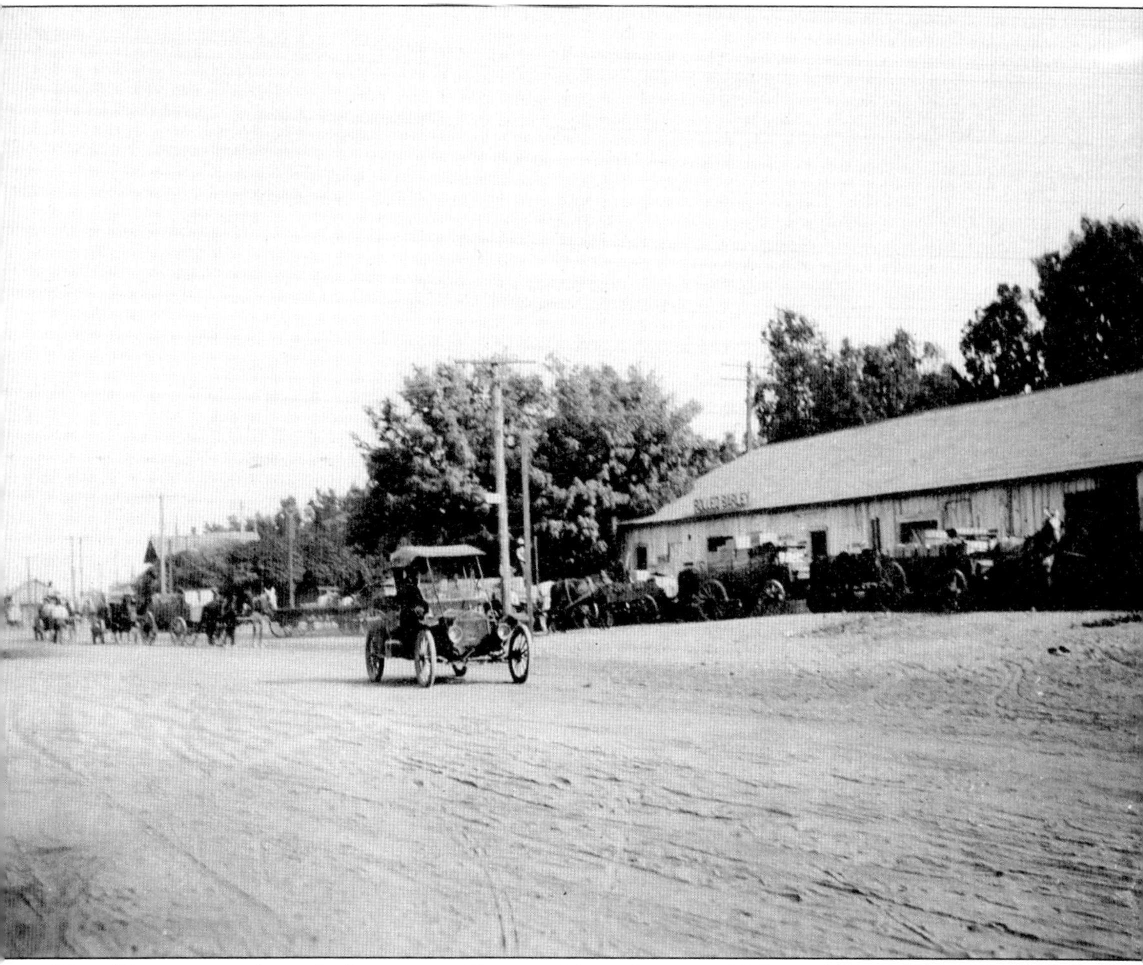

The old station packing shed is pictured here on Front Street in 1910.

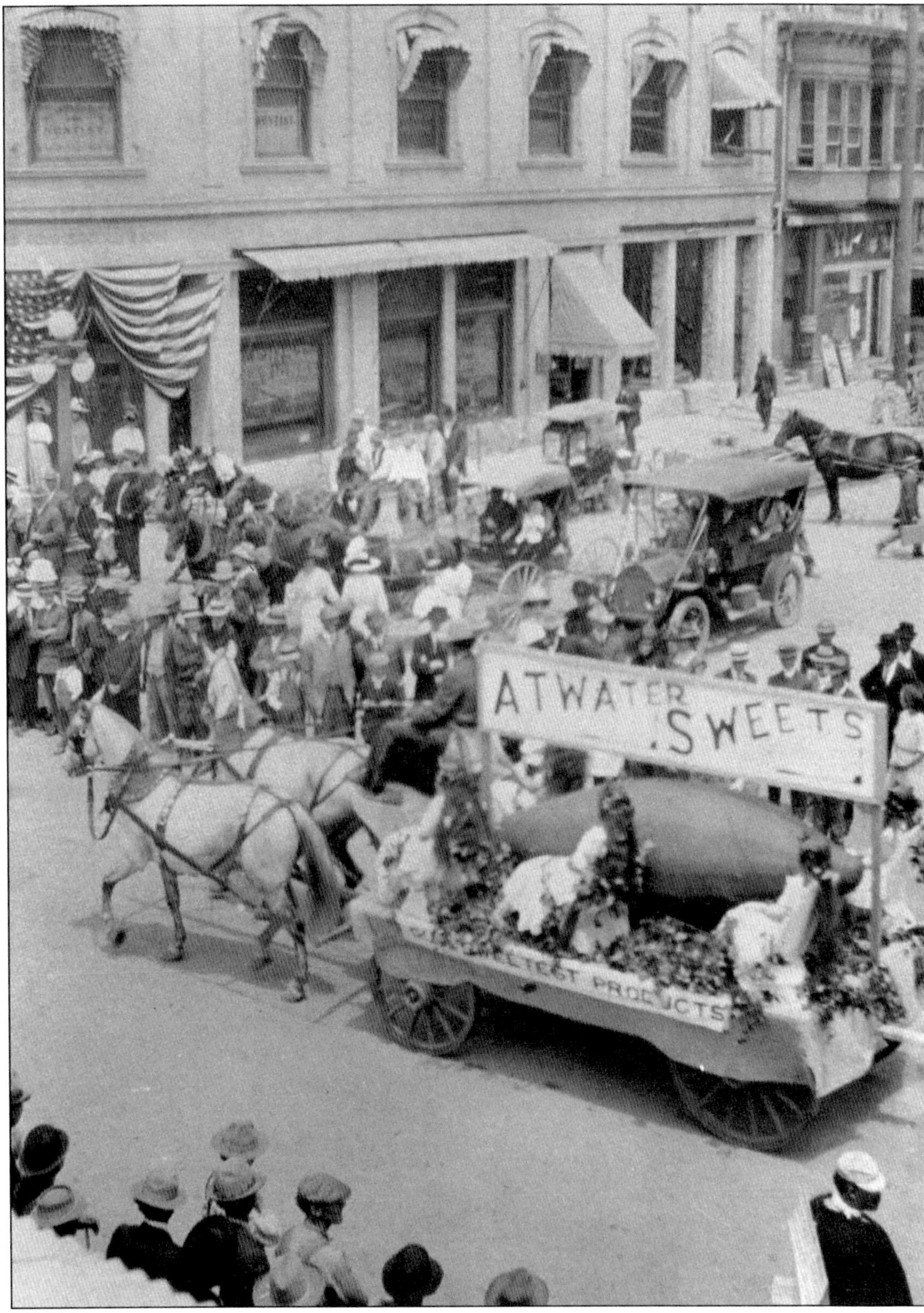

The Atwater Sweets float for the 1914 Merced County Fair was built in C. E. Hinds's yard in Atwater for the Atwater Chamber of Commerce. The paper mache and burlap sweet potato was made by Emery "Pete" Hinds and his wife Anna. Pictured on the float are Catherine Hinds Cunningham, Ruth Oswald Hurd, Edna Green Ralston, Aileen Hinds Colburn, and Cleo and Cliffe Owen. The driver is Walt Oswald.

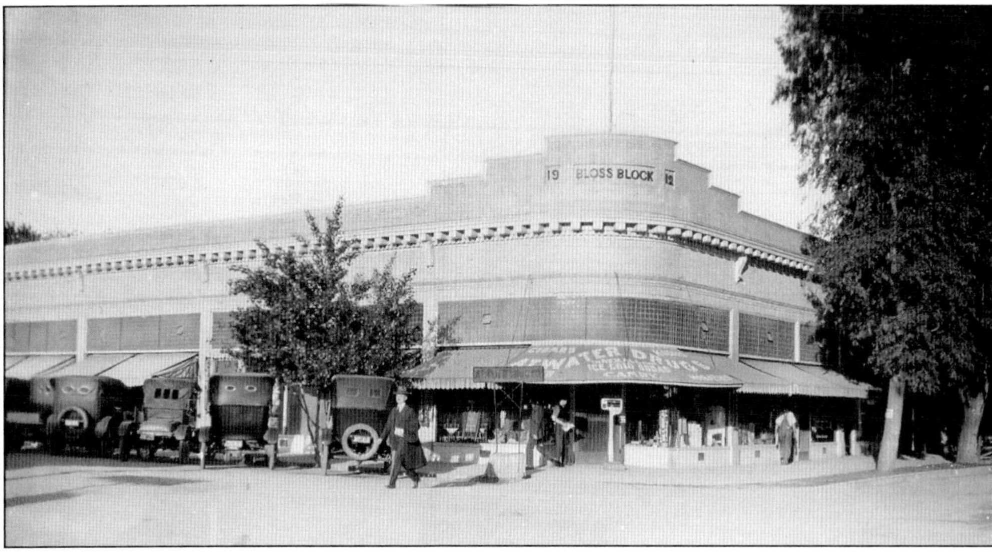

Built in 1912 on the corner of Front Street and Third, the Bloss Block was built after the fire that leveled the business section; it occupies that corner to this day. The building cost $21,000 and contained seven well-planned rooms. Dr. Kinney, the first doctor to open a practice in Atwater in 1910, also opened a drugstore in the Bloss Building. In 1917, this business was sold to Elias Allen "Pop" Heller, a pharmacist from Madera, California. Mr. Heller operated the drugstore at this location until 1951, when he, along with his son Jim, opened one of the most modern Rexall drugstores in the state. Charles Osborn moved his store and the post office into the largest rooms and Jack Dunlap opened a barbershop in the building. A pool room, a shoe repair shop, and Manuel Ray's Dry Goods Store opened in the other rooms. Today this building is occupied by many small businesses and the old drugstore in now Eric Lee's insurance office.

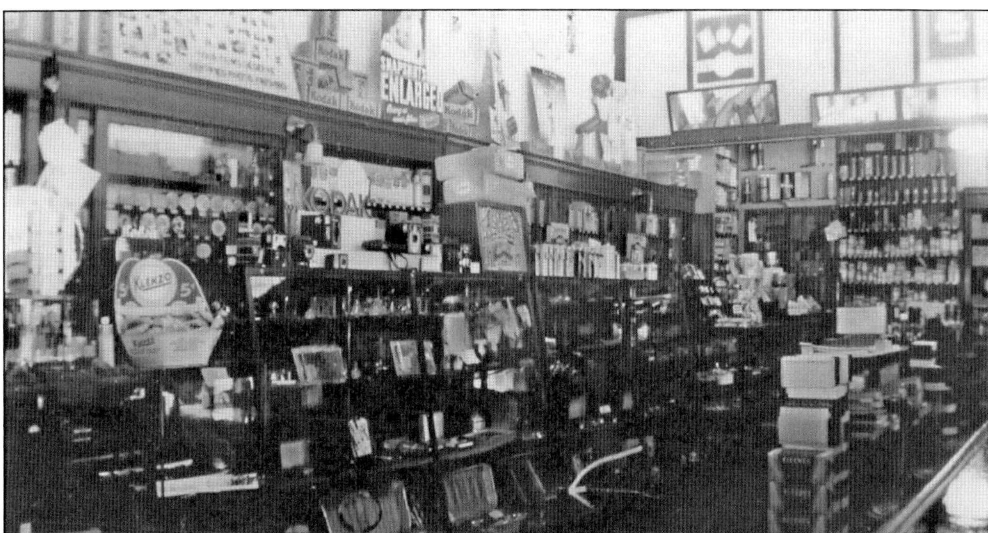

This is an interior photograph of the Atwater drugstore, taken after E. Allen Heller bought the store from Dr. Kinney. Kodak film was sold here along with many other items for personal use. Mr. Heller was quite taken with photography, and many of the images used in this book were available due to his avid interest.

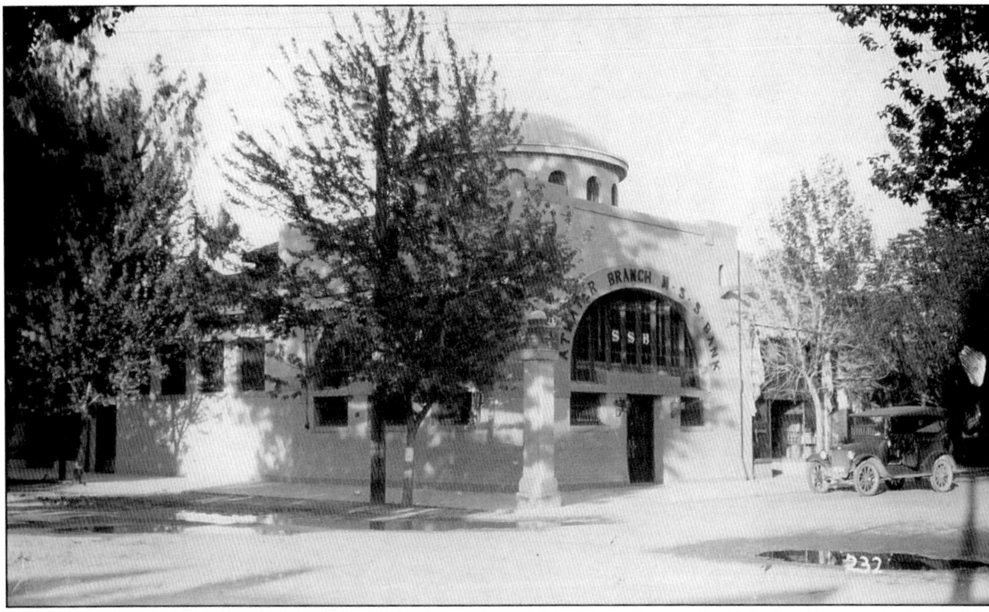

Pictured here is the Merced Security Savings Bank, Atwater branch. This building is located on the North East corner of Broadway and Third Street.

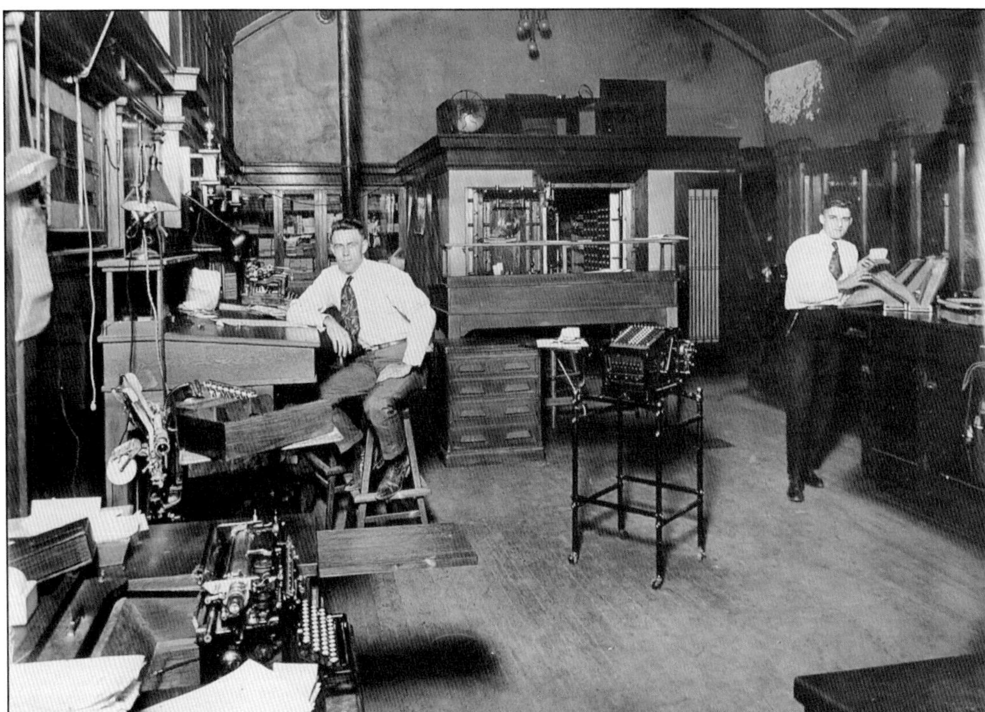

Arch Rector and Anthony Thomas posed for this photograph in the bank office and vault area on June 7, 1921.

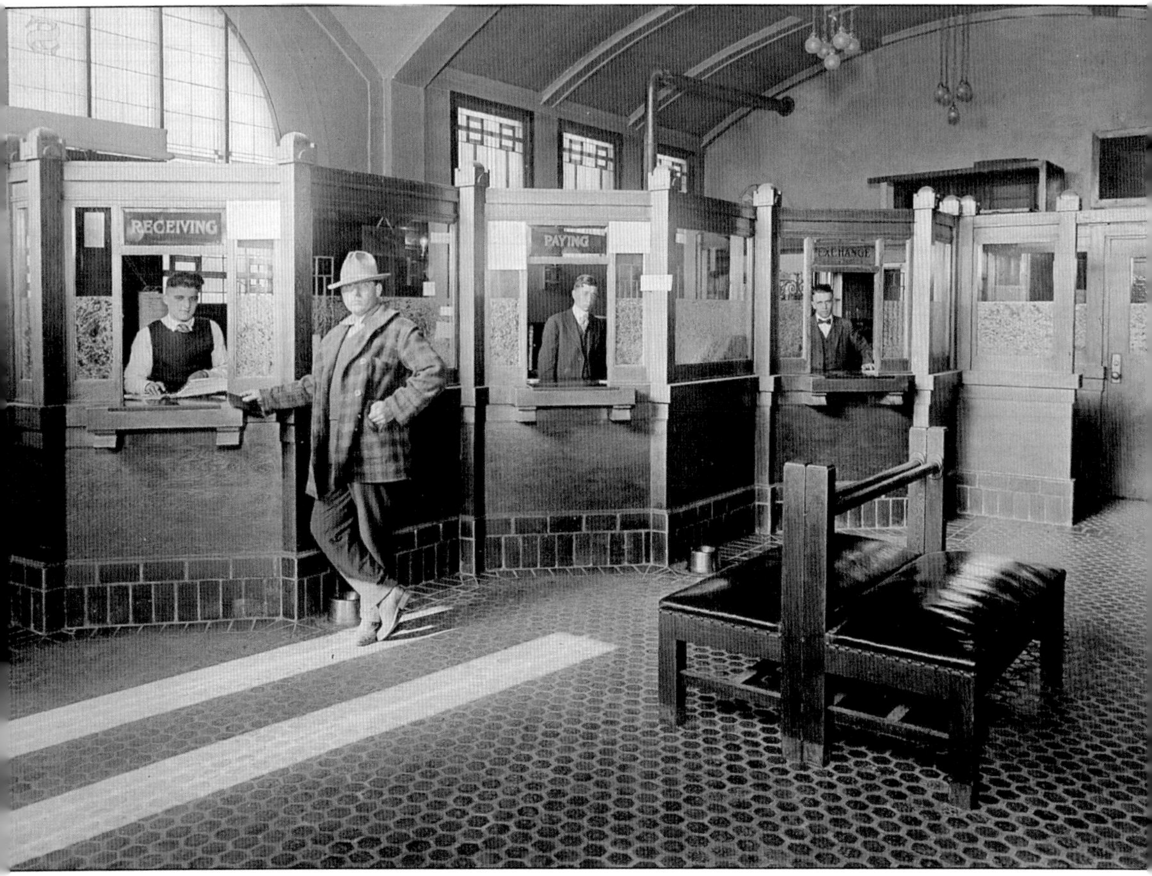

This image shows what banking looked like in Atwater in December 1920. Anthony Thomas is in the first teller window, Clark Ralston in the second, and Arch Rector is in the third. The customer is Joe Alvernaz Sr., a sweet-potato grower in the Livingston area. The bank was rushed to completion in 1912, due to the downtown fire. In 1927, the Bank of Italy purchased the Merced Security Savings Bank, and in 1930 the name was changed to Bank of America. The building remained the same, with just the name change, until the Bank of America built a new building on the corner of Fourth Street and Broadway in 1950. The building was sold to Louis Passadori, the dome was removed, and it has gone though many transformations but remains in the same location. Residents remember that Atwater Stationery occupied the corner store for many years.

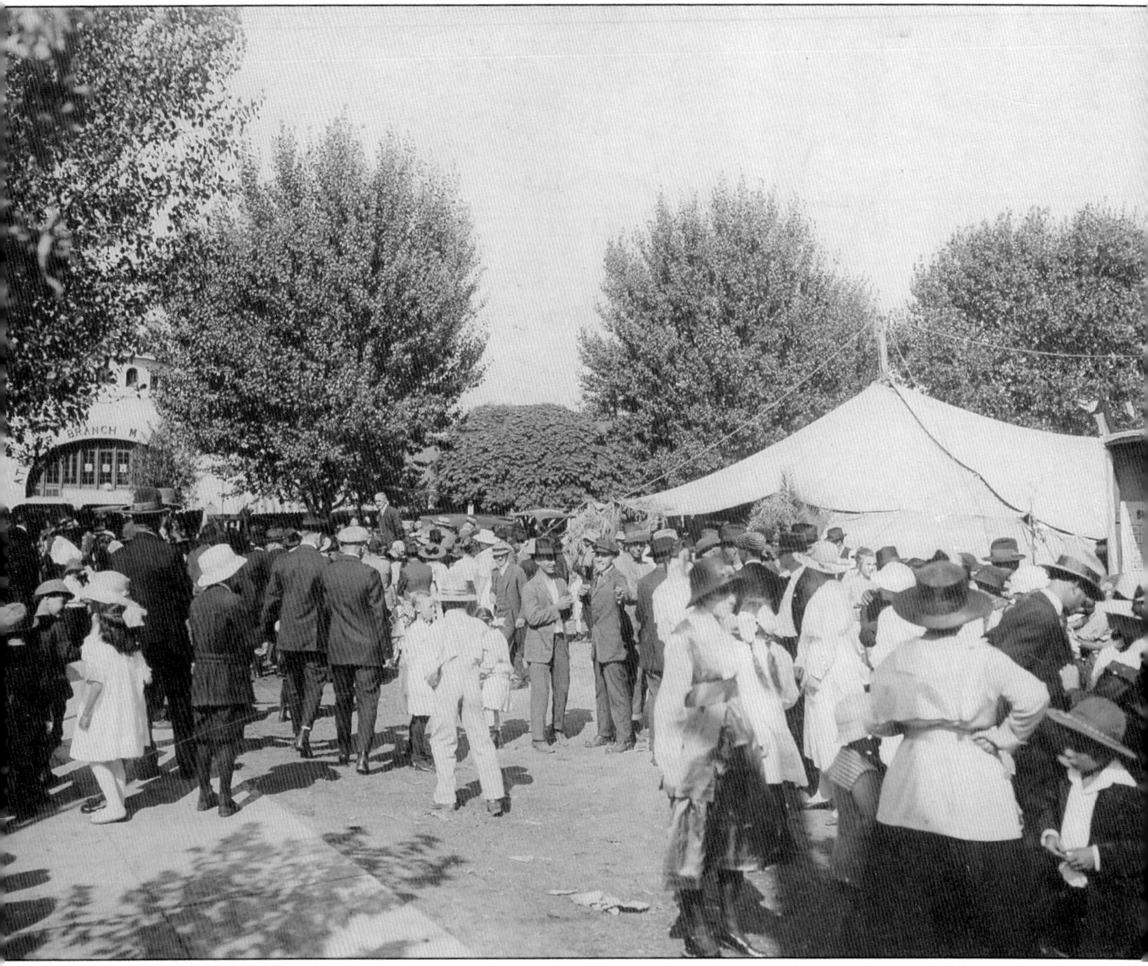

The Agricultural Fair was held on the South East corner of Third Street and Broadway in 1918. This site was later to become Dr. Jackson's office building. The ladies of the Women's Improvement Club of Fruitland had a booth at this fair. They recorded a profit of $46.85 and, after deducting expenses, were able to give $39.85 to the Atwater branch of the Red Cross.

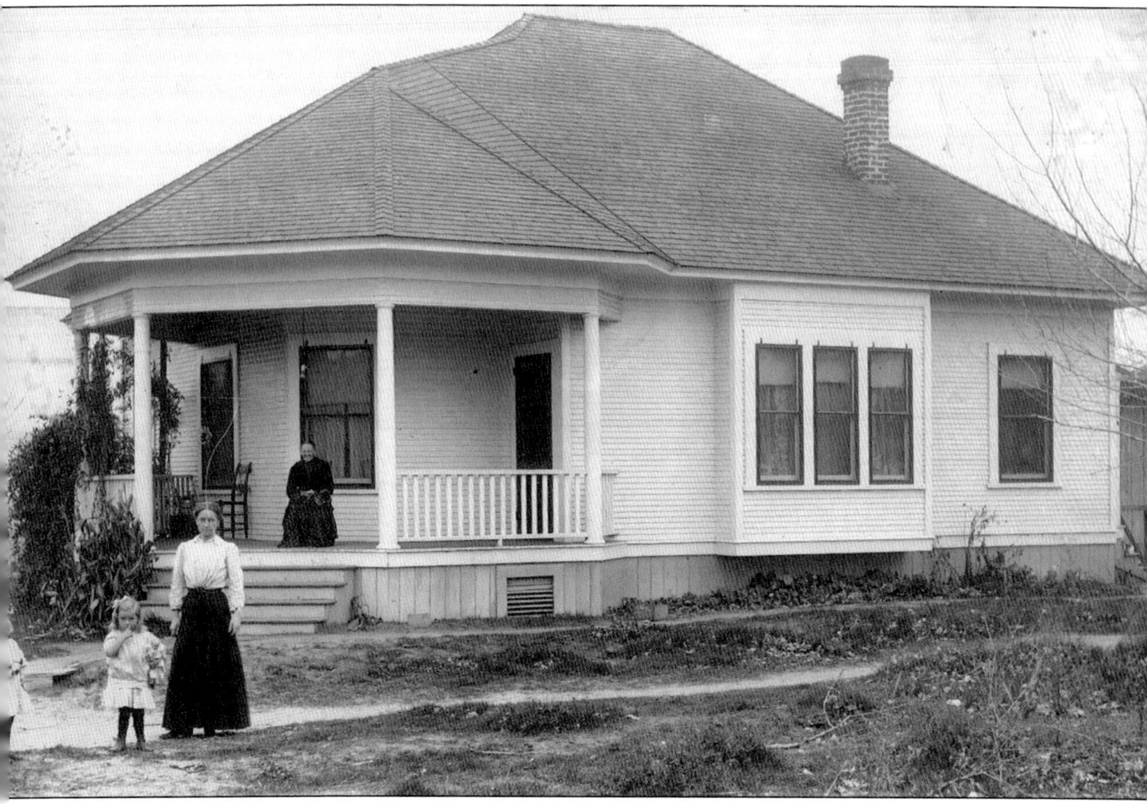

This home sat on the northwest corner of Broadway and Third Street. Pictured on the porch is Mrs. Caroline E. Smith; in the foreground is Mrs. Harry Foster (Belle Smith) with her daughters Elberta and Evelyn. In 1946, Louis Passadori constructed a new building on this site, and Salter's Pacific Food Market moved into the building. This house was moved to the corner of Sierra Vista and Olive Avenue. In October 1988, the house was moved once again, to a site in Modesto, California.

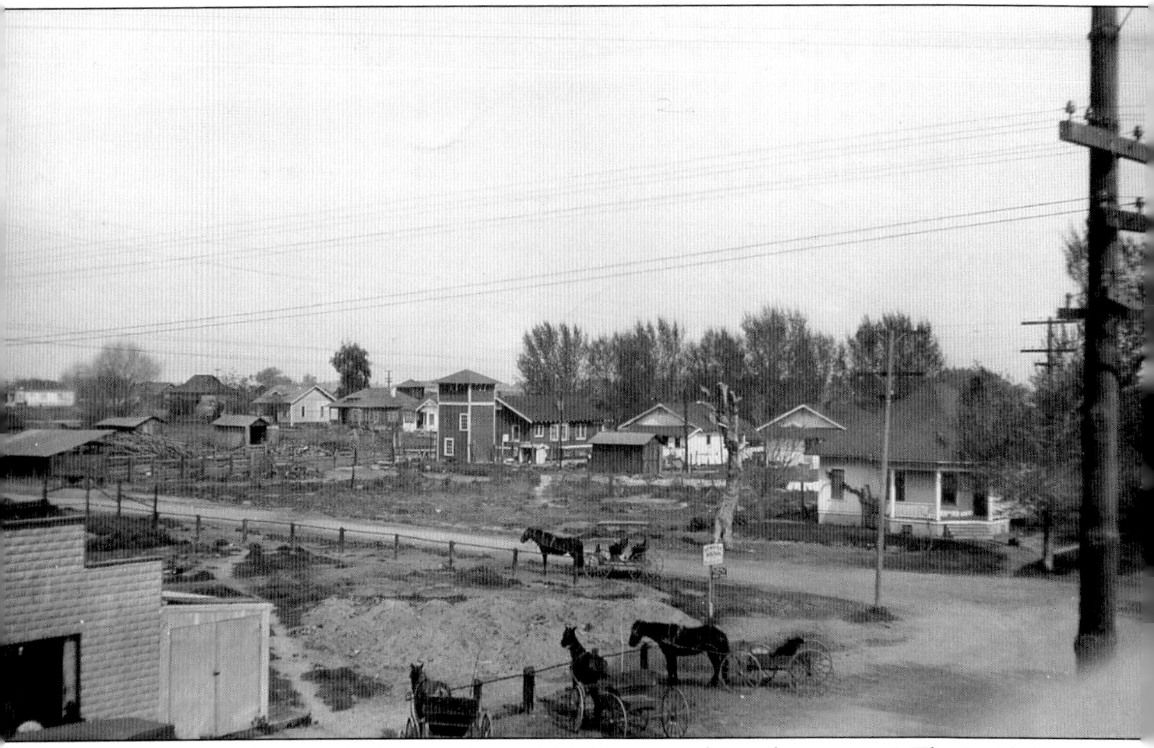

Shown in this image is the intersection of Third Street and Broadway, c. 1916. The Smith house is on the corner opposite to where the horses are tied. Waltamath's machine shop is in the lower left-hand corner. The other homes in the picture are on what is now Cedar Avenue. The modern downtown area of Atwater would develop on Broadway between Second Street and Winton Way.

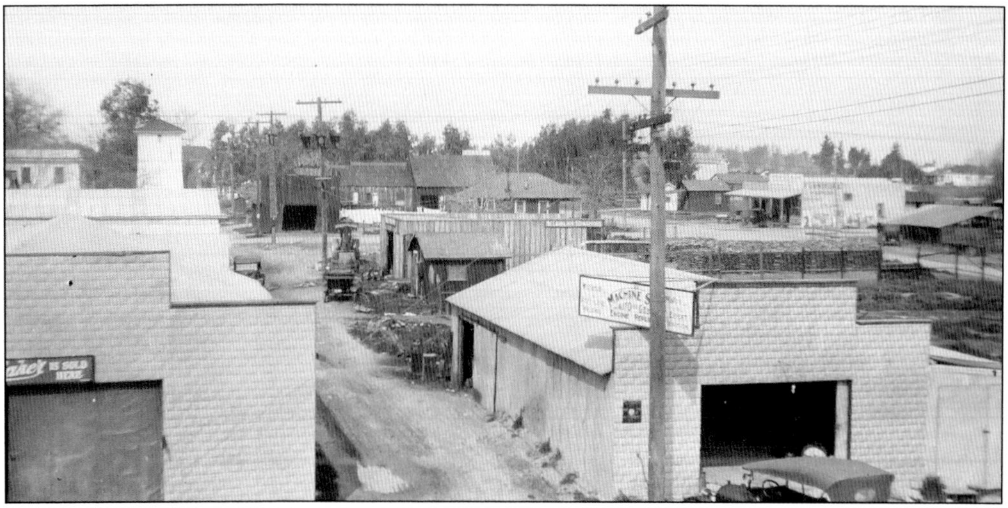

Depicted is Waltamath's Machine Shop on Third Street, between Broadway and Front Street (Atwater Boulevard). In 1935, this building was demolished to make way for Passadori's store, which occupies the entire corner. Across the alley is a building advertising that "The Studebaker is Sold Here." Other structures seen in this photograph are Neves Merchandise (upper right), Atwater Hotel (upper left), and part of the corral for the livery stable (center).

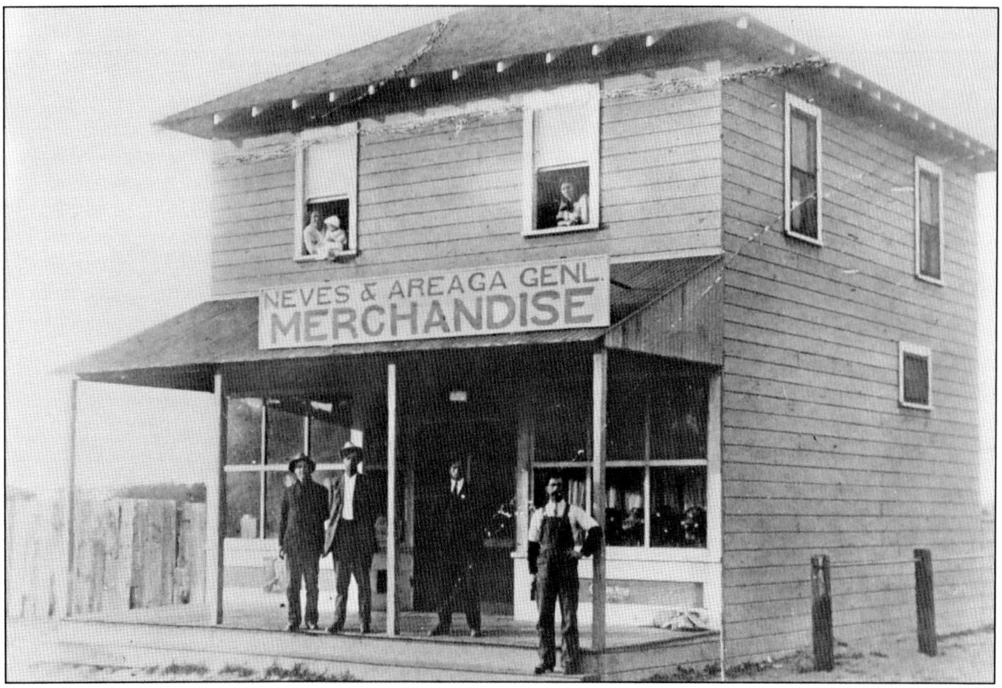

Alfred Neves came to Atwater from the Azores Islands in 1903. His first job was as a farmhand on the Bloss Ranch. Then, with his wife, Maria Leal Neves, he raised stock and cultivated sweet potatoes near Atwater until 1912. That year, he opened a small store on the corner of Fourth Street and Broadway. He entered this business with Manuel Ariaga, and the Neves family lived upstairs in the store. The baby being held by his grandmother on the ledge of the second-floor window is Harry Leal Neves. Harry later served as a mayor of Atwater. No information was available for Manuel Ariaga, though the spelling of Areaga versus Ariaga is noted in another photograph.

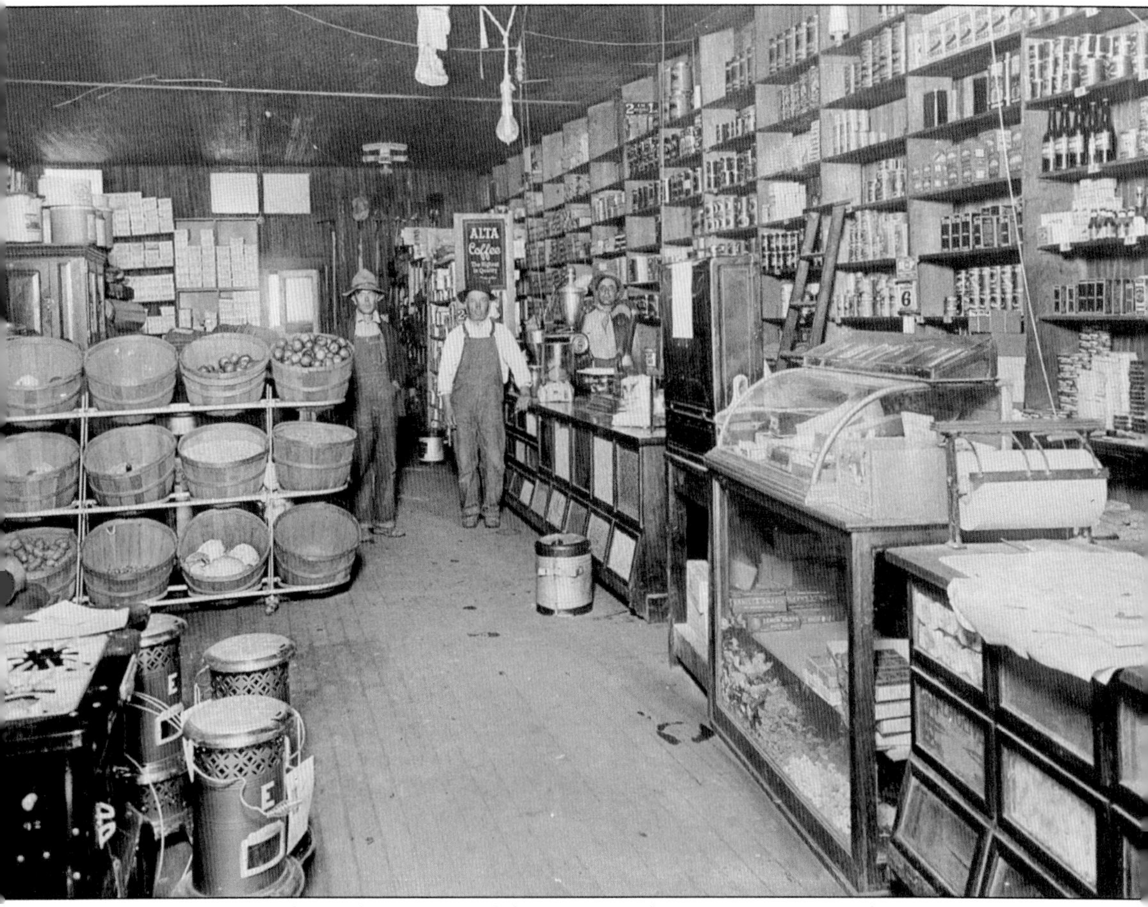

This photograph shows the interior of the Neves and Areaga store around 1913. The variety of goods that were sold is apparent. Note the kerosene heaters in the foreground.

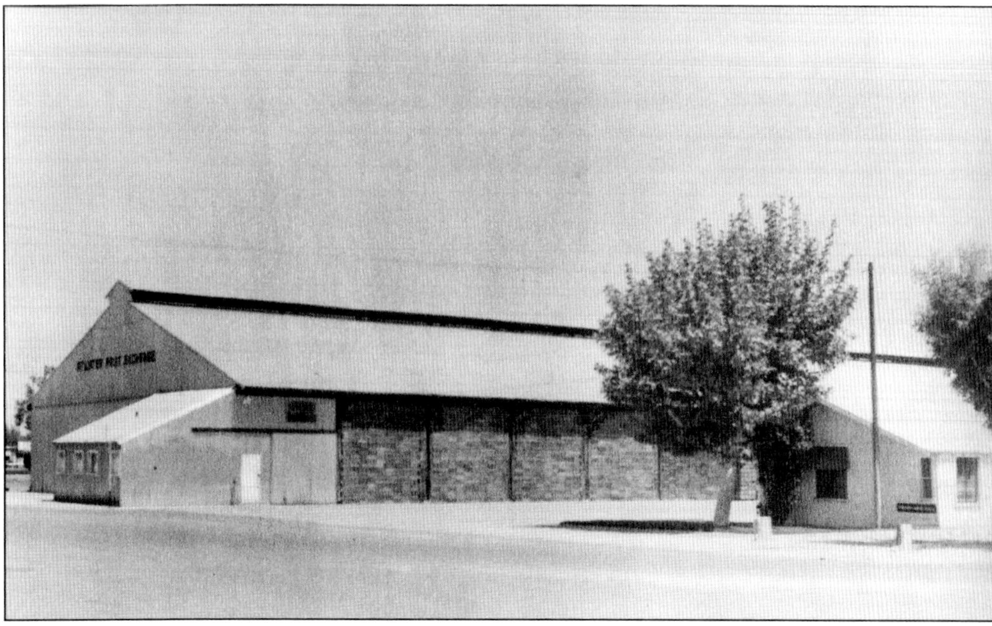

A new cooperative, the Atwater Fruit Exchange, was formed in 1918 with 32 members who were interested in improving the sales of their fruit. Shown is the large shed for packing and shipping peaches and grapes. The first manager was W. H. Spann. Elmer Wood was the next manager, a position he held for eight years. Many of the members of this exchange resigned their membership with the California Fruit Exchange to support this cooperative.

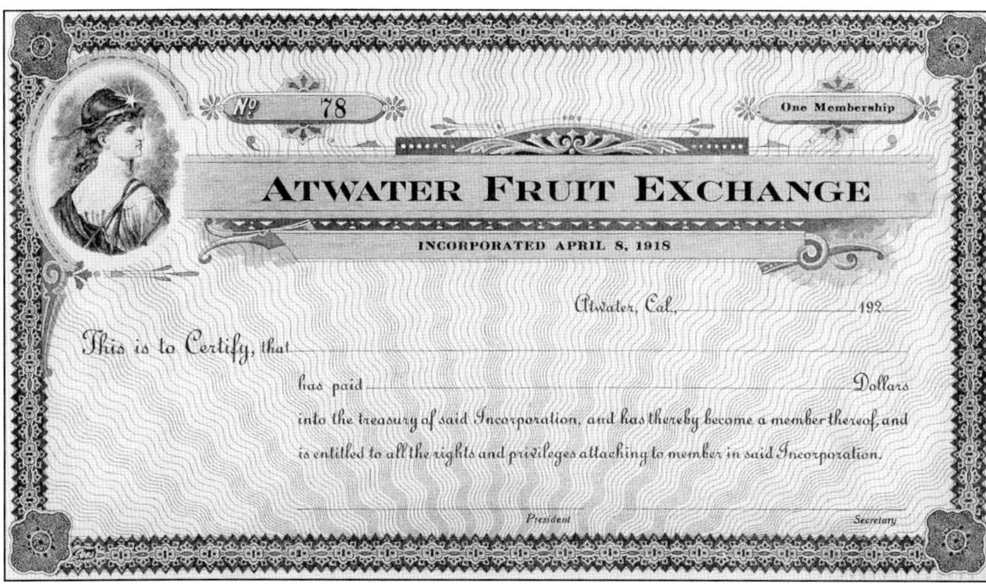

No 78

One Membership

ATWATER FRUIT EXCHANGE

INCORPORATED APRIL 8, 1918

Atwater, Cal., 192

This is to Certify, that

has paid Dollars

into the treasury of said Incorporation, and has thereby become a member thereof, and is entitled to all the rights and privileges attaching to member in said Incorporation.

President

Secretary

This certificate apparently was issued each year as a receipt of dues. It shows that the exchange was incorporated on April 8, 1918.

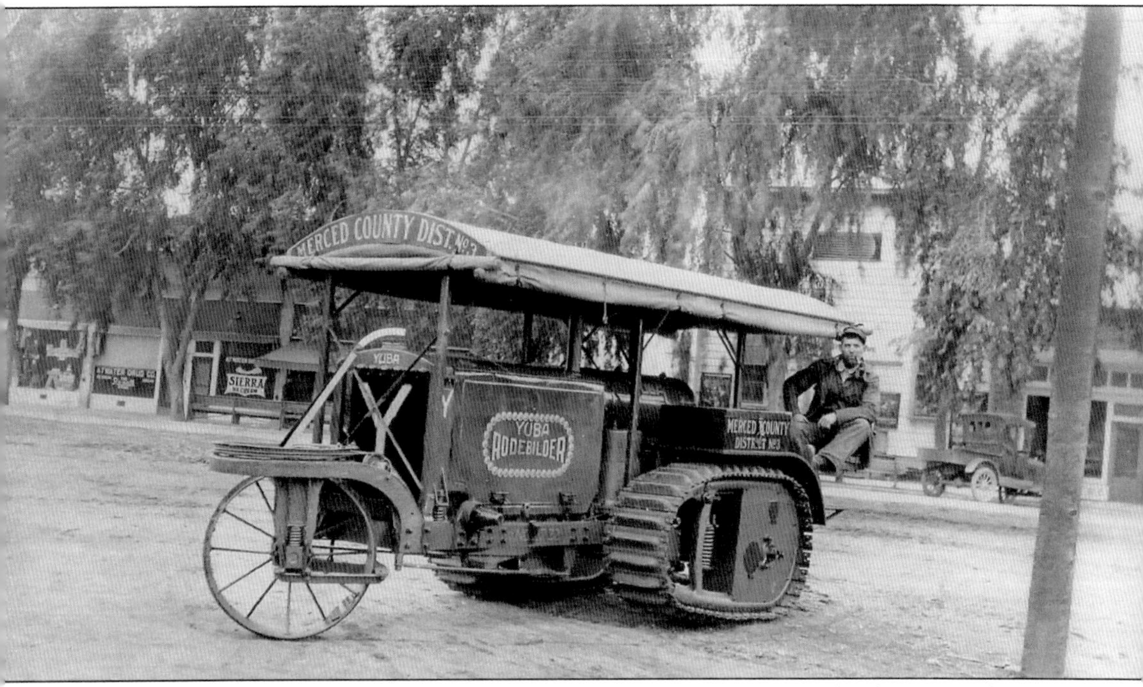

This Yuba Rodebilder was used in Merced County District No. 3. The driver is John Henry Wisdom. The two-story building in the background is the old Mitchell Hall on Front Street (Atwater Boulevard), which was used by the community for so many activities until it burned in 1923. There are posters for silent movies in the windows. This image is one of only two that the historical society has of this building.

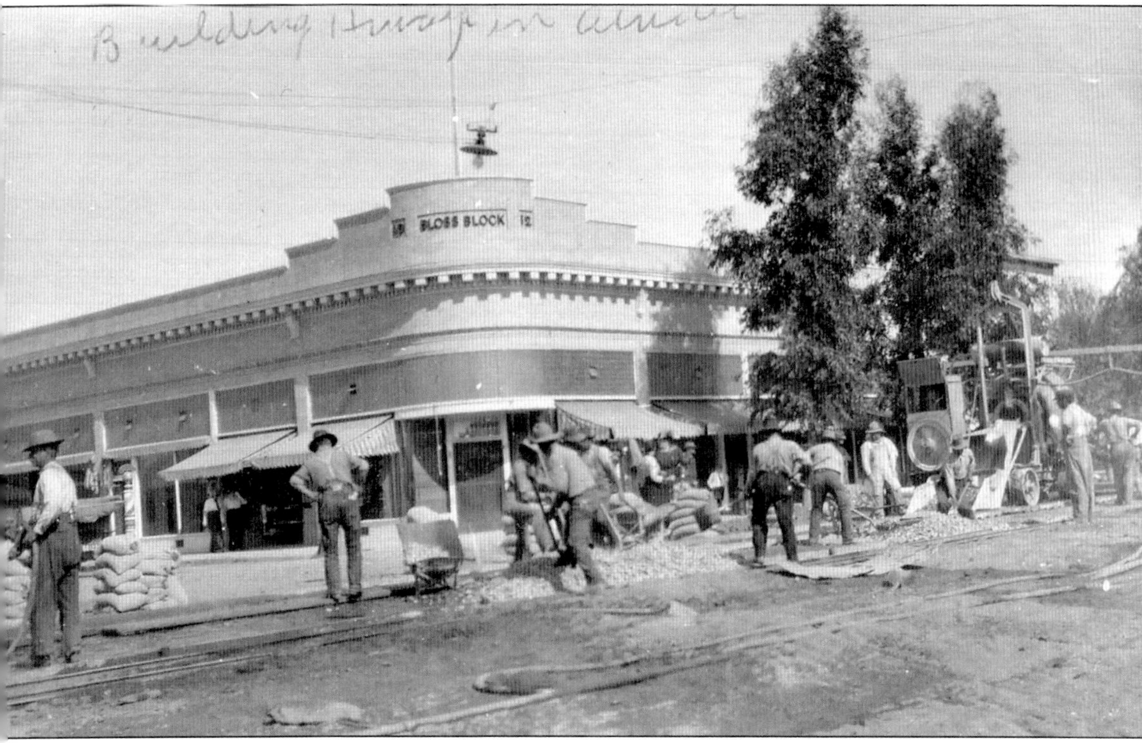

With the Bloss Block Building and the old Mitchell Hall in the background, workers are shown paving Front Street (Atwater Boulevard) with concrete between 1918–1920. During this period, only one lane was paved, as there were still more horses and wagons using the streets than automobiles.

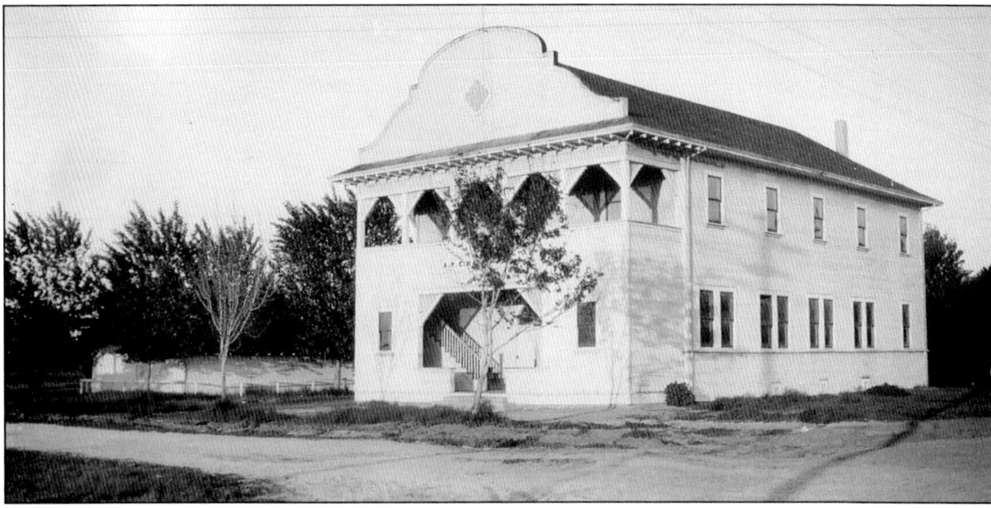

In 1911, the Atwater Pentecost Club was founded at a potluck gathering in what was known as Osborn Grove. Promoted by prominent businessmen and farmers in the area, the "Festa of the Holy Spirit" was a celebration to help raise money to build St. Anthony's Catholic Church. Early records show that 4,000 to 5,000 people attended these festas. In 1916, the club purchased property at 1420 Third Street for a $10 gold coin. In 1917, the hall pictured was built and the club was incorporated. The community used the APC hall for many other functions. In 1972, it was demolished and replaced by a more modern building.

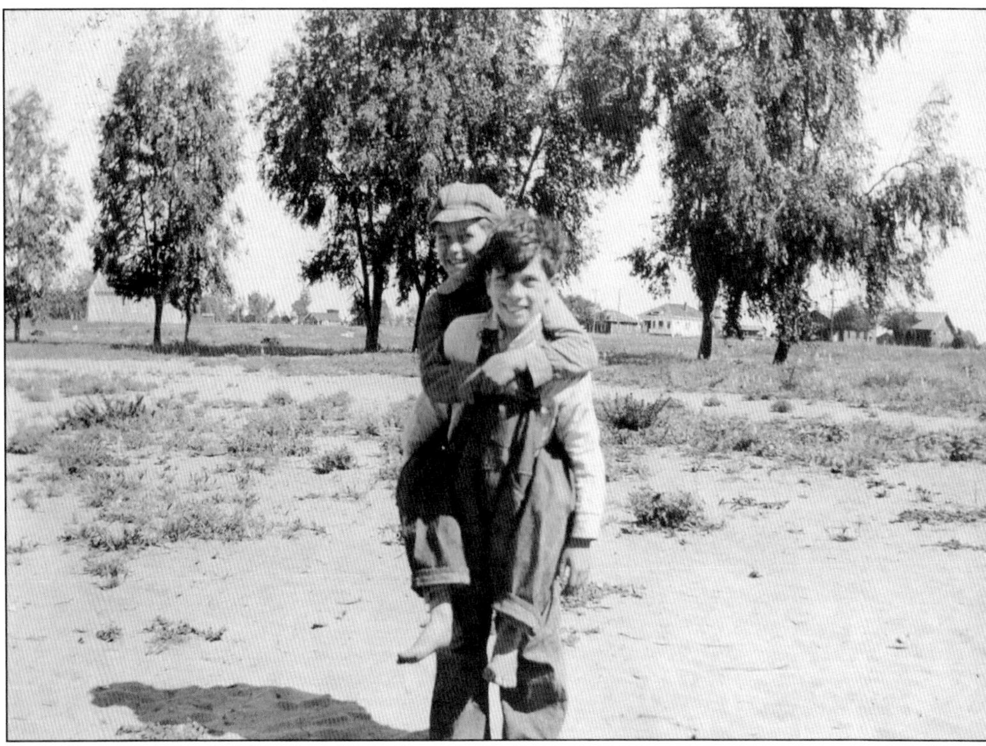

This photograph of Willie Vincent and Lee Wisdom was taken in 1918 or 1919. It is most likely that the site was the playground at Mitchell School. Lee is the son of John Henry Wisdom, who operated the Yuba Rodebilder for District No. Three of the County of Merced.

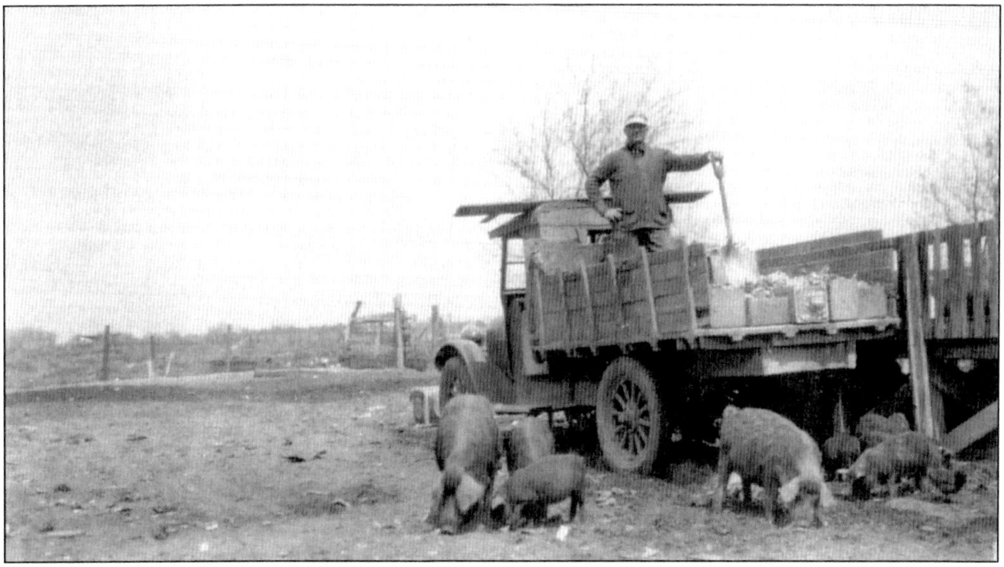

An Atwater-area farmer tends his hogs. The tailgate for the truck is stowed on top of the cab.

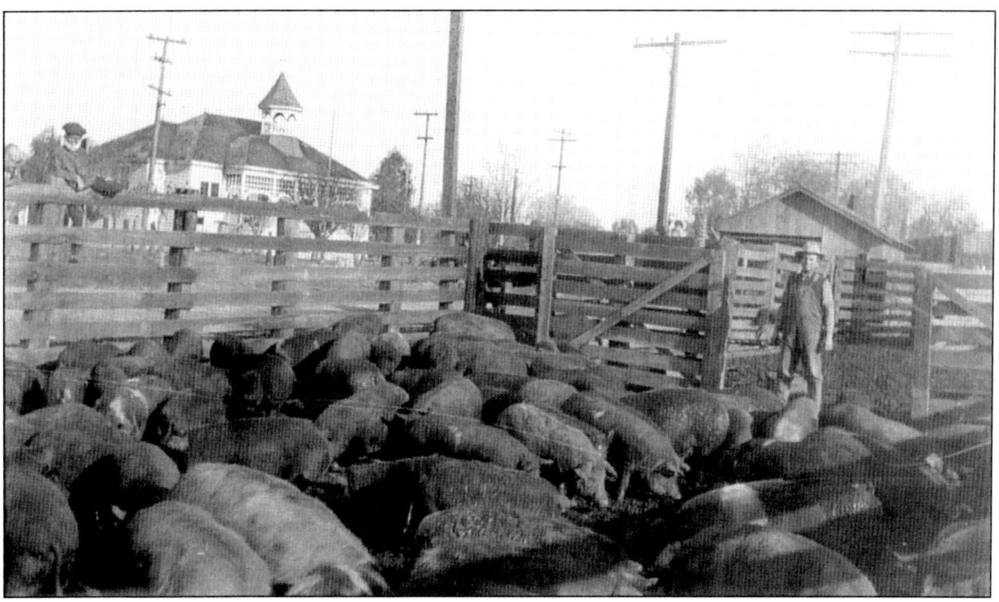

To the west of the Atwater Train Depot were the holding pens used for hogs that were going to be shipped by rail. Lee Thompson is the man in the photograph, and the children on the fence are James and Rosalie Heller. The small shed on the right housed a scale for weighing the hogs. The children are pictured with masks that were worn to protect against the severe influenza epidemic of 1918. Mitchell School is in the background.

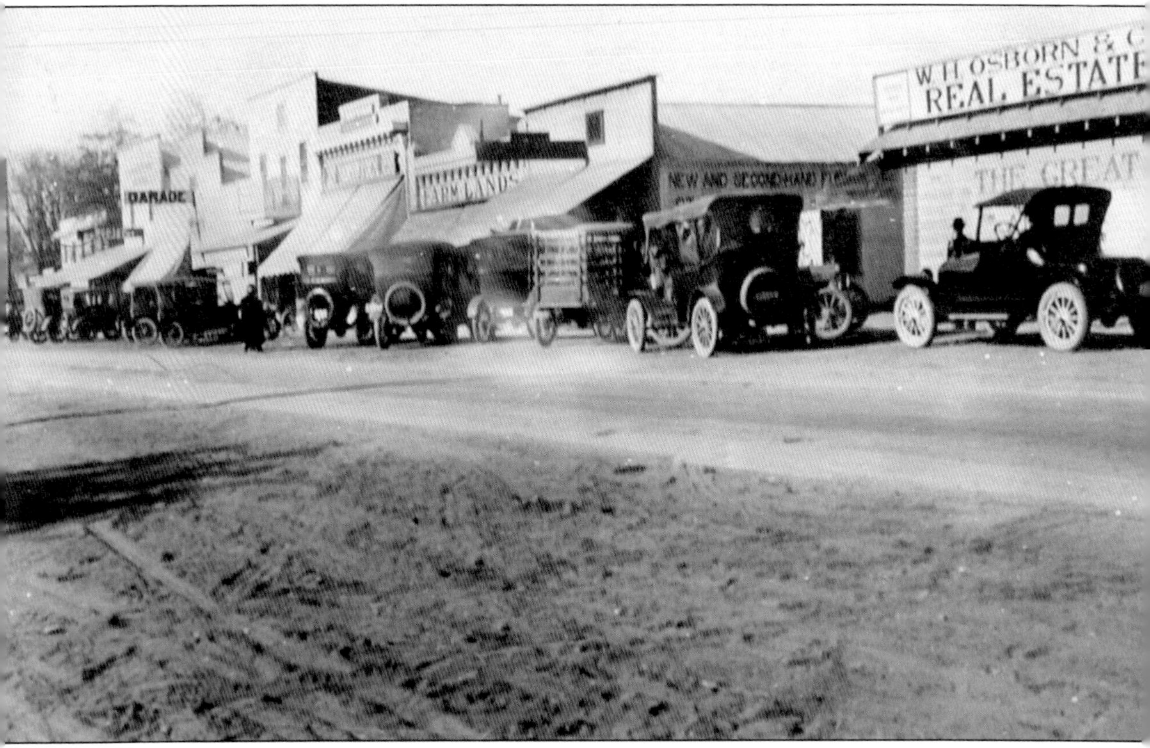

In 1916, John Fernandes built a two-story building on Front Street (Atwater Boulevard) between the Owen brothers' brick building and the Pregno grocery store. Joe Rodrigues opened a grocery store in this building and, a year or so later, sold the store to Thomson, Diehl, and Sargent. Also pictured is William Osborn's real estate office.

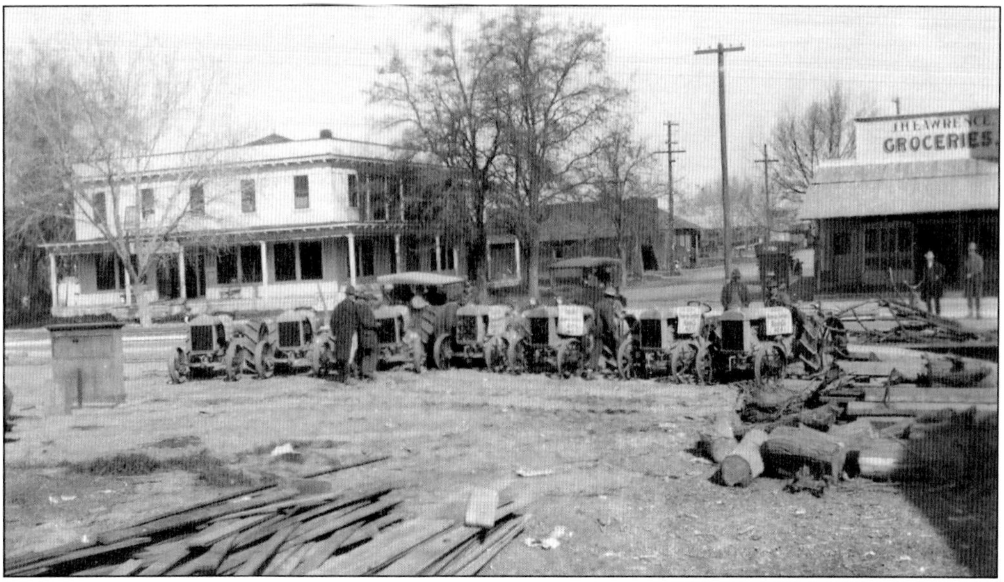

Gentlemen attend a used farm equipment sale in the late 1910s or early 1920s. The Lawrence Grocery Store was bought in 1917 from the Williams family. This was the only building to survive the fire of 1912 that devastated the business district on Front Street (Atwater Boulevard). However, this building met the same fate in 1922, and Lawrence built a new store in 1923 on Cedar Street and Winton Way. Also visible in this photograph is the Atwater Hotel.

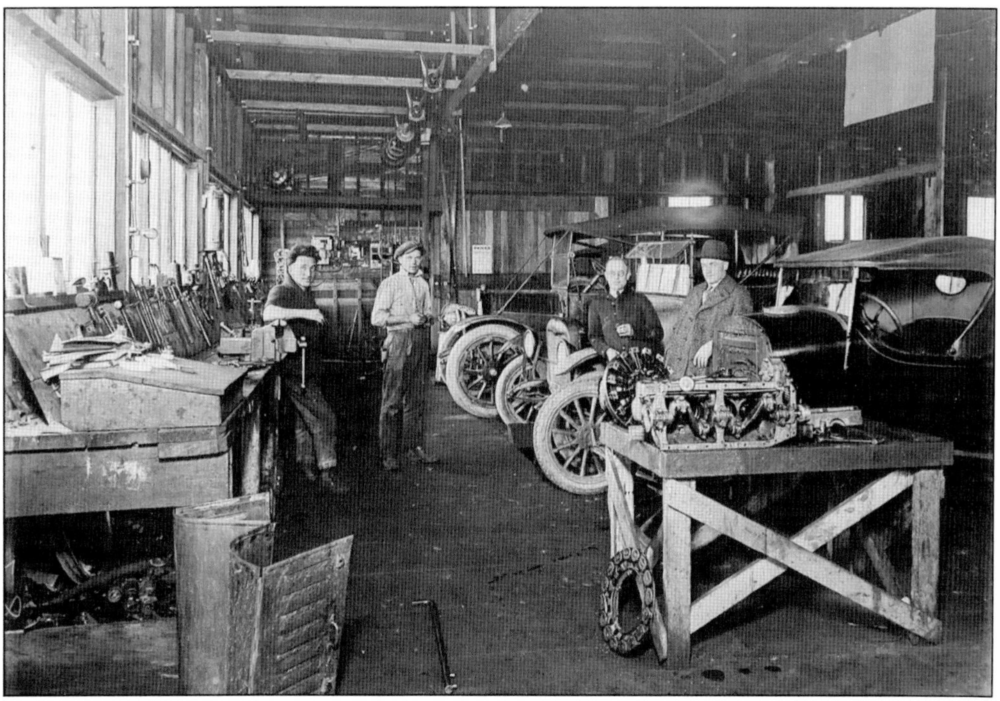

Mike's Garage, a typical garage of the period, was located on the corner of Winton Way and Front Street (Atwater Boulevard). Pictured, from left to right, are Mike Dellesio (owner), Walt Thompson, E. L. Walter, and a visiting salesman. A Signal service station was operated by Dave Silva in the front part of this building.

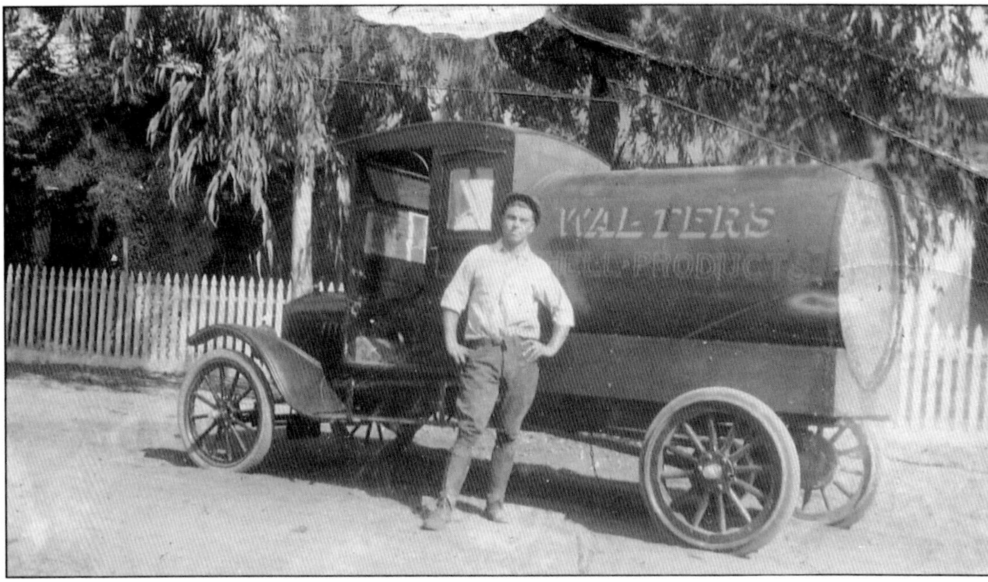

Louis Frago poses with the Shell Products truck that Walter's used for local deliveries to farms and businesses.

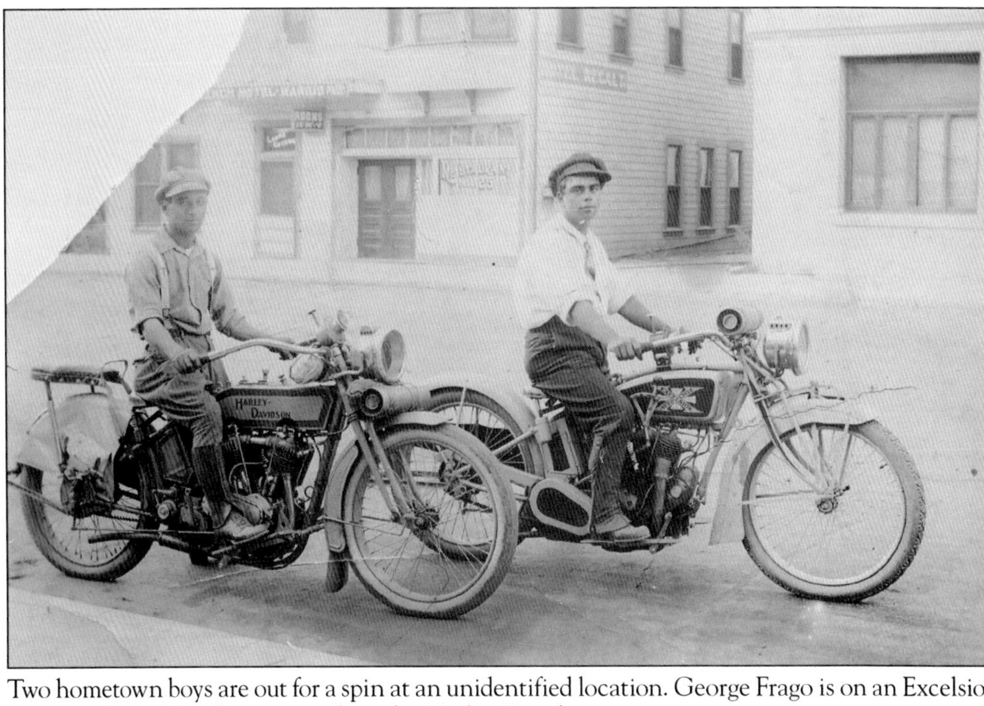

Two hometown boys are out for a spin at an unidentified location. George Frago is on an Excelsior motorcycle, and Joe Duarte is riding the Harley Davidson.

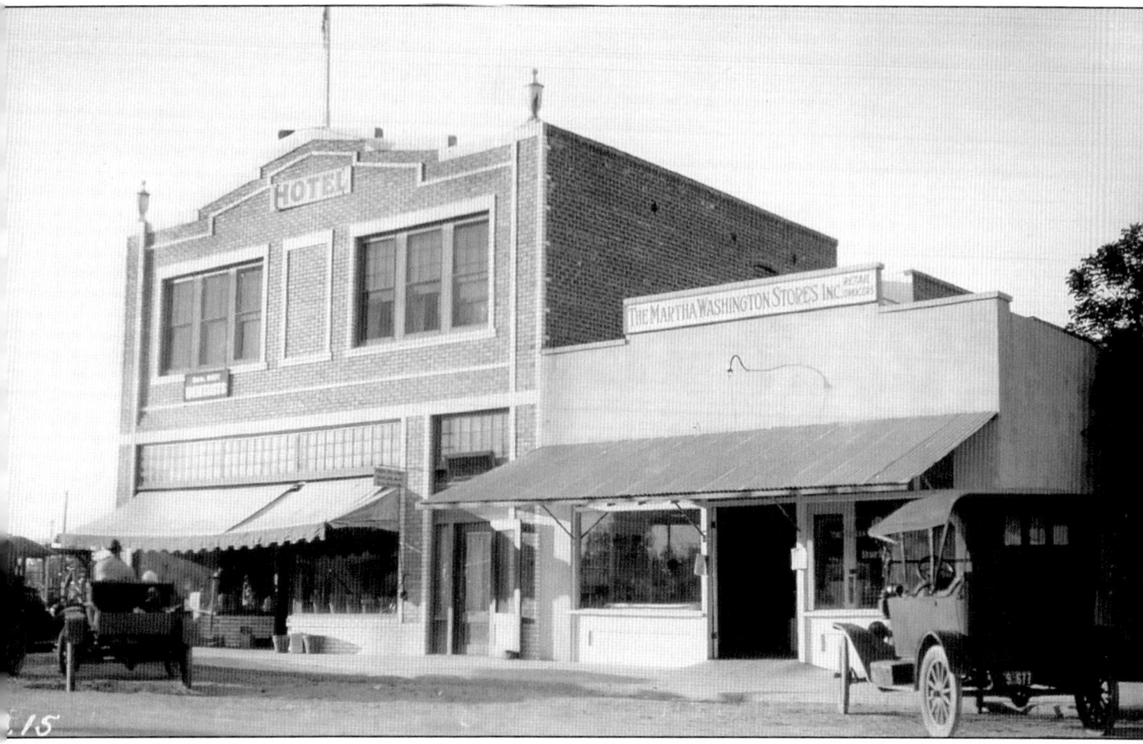

A. I. Rodrigues built this two-story building in 1922. It was located on Broadway next to the Martha Washington Stores, Inc. When C. J. Pregno moved his grocery and hardware business from Front Street into this building, his nephew, Louis Passadori, bought him out. Joe Rodgers had built a store across the street from the Rodrigues building. Louis moved his grocery business into the Rodgers building, where Rodgers already operated a butcher shop, and left the hardware store open in the Rodrigues building. There were also rooms on the second floor that were rented out. At one time, there was a beauty shop on the second floor. The first floor of this building was used for various businesses over the years. At one time it was used as a doctor's office and later by the Ivers and Alcorn Mortuary. The Rose Bud Antique Shop now occupies this site.

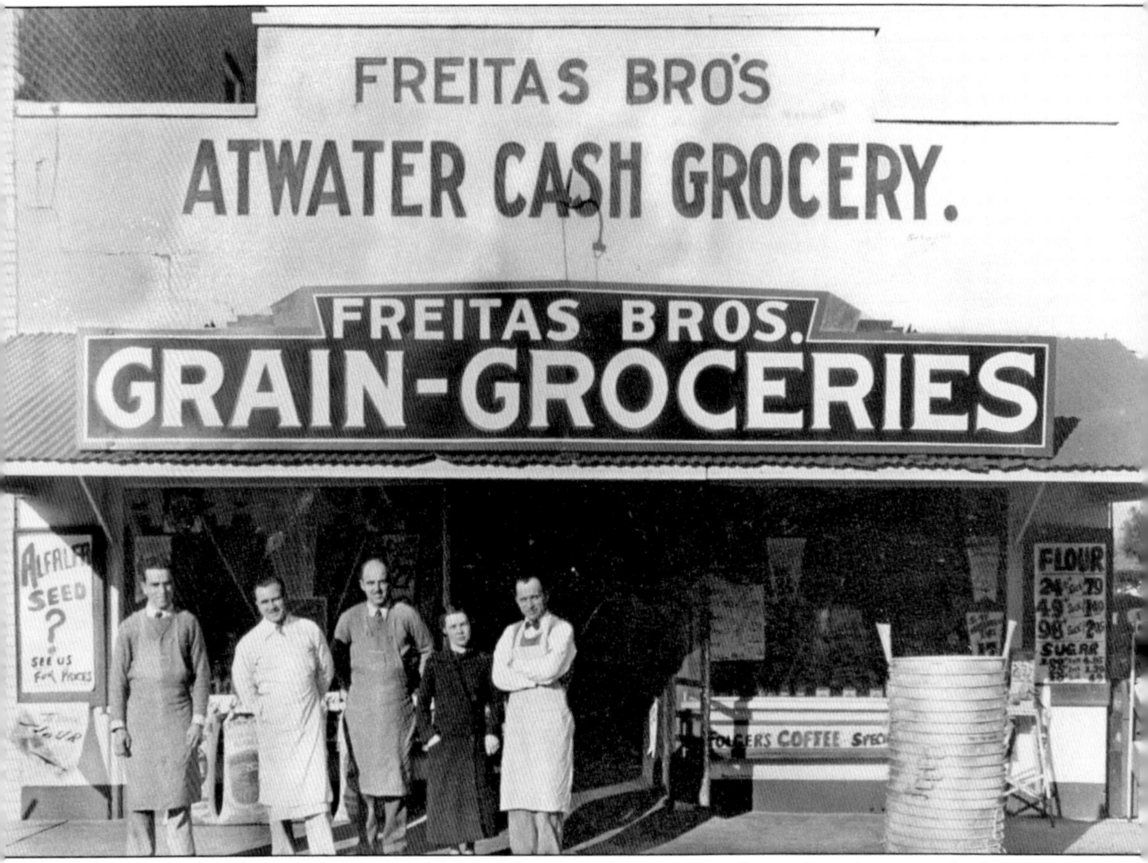

Built in 1917 by Joseph Vierra Alves and operated as a general merchandise store by Mr. Vierra and Mr. Areaga, this building later became part of the Martha Washington grocery chain. In 1923, the Freitas brothers (Frank L. and Tony L.) purchased it and operated a cash grain and grocery store until 1940. For part of this time, the meat-market section was rented to Manuel Caton Jr. In 1940, Art Vierra purchased the property and operated the Red and White Grocery Store until 1947, when he sold out to Mr. White. Shown in this 1929 photograph, from left to right, are Charles Hendricks, Manuel Caton Jr., Art Vierra, Elsie Freitas, and Tony Freitas. Today this building is a restaurant called Granny's Pantry.

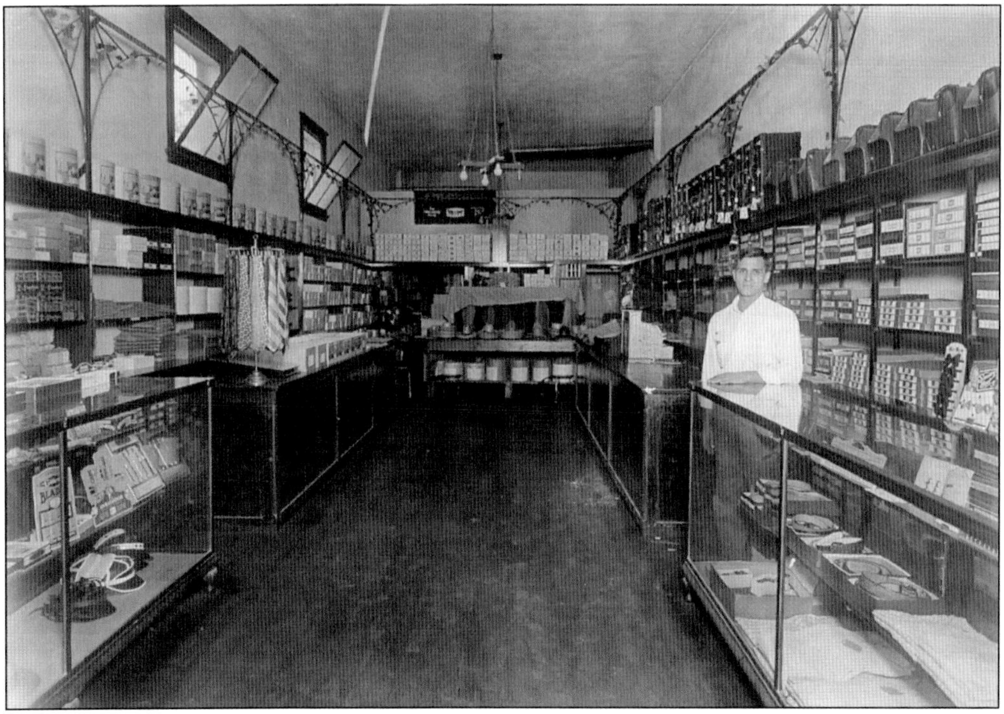

Located in the Bloss Block building, the Valladao and Corvelo Store was a men's, ladies, and children's store. At the end of the aisle is a table filled with men's hats. Suitcases and travel bags line the wall, bowties are on a card behind the counter, and razor blades and visors are in the other display cabinet. One of the owners, Frank Corvelo, poses behind the counter.

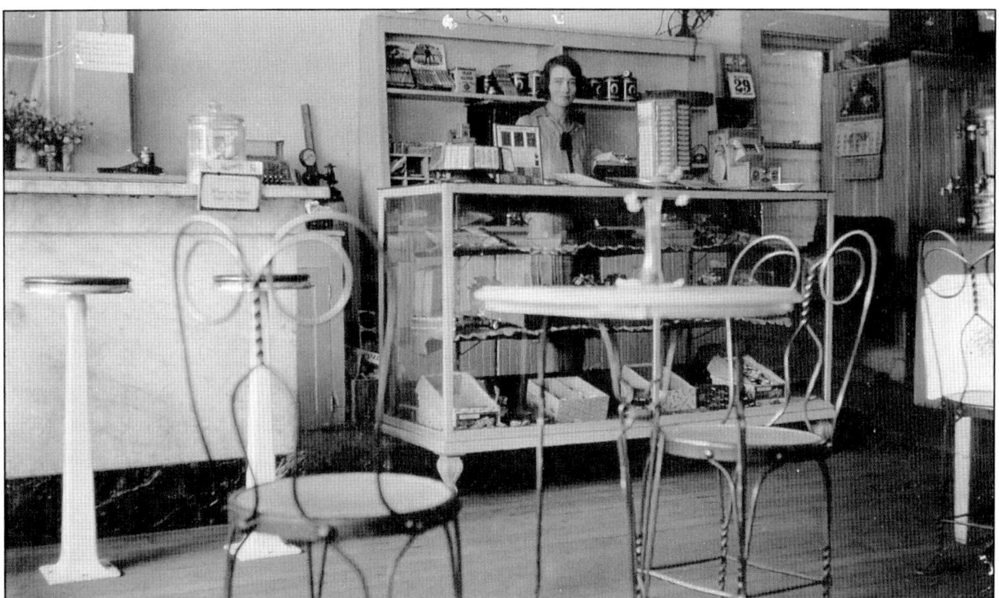

Charles Osborn erected a building in 1920 on Third and Front Streets for the purpose of having an ice cream parlor. It proved to be such a popular place with the townspeople that they gave it the name Pleasant Corner. Bert Ralston owned this business.

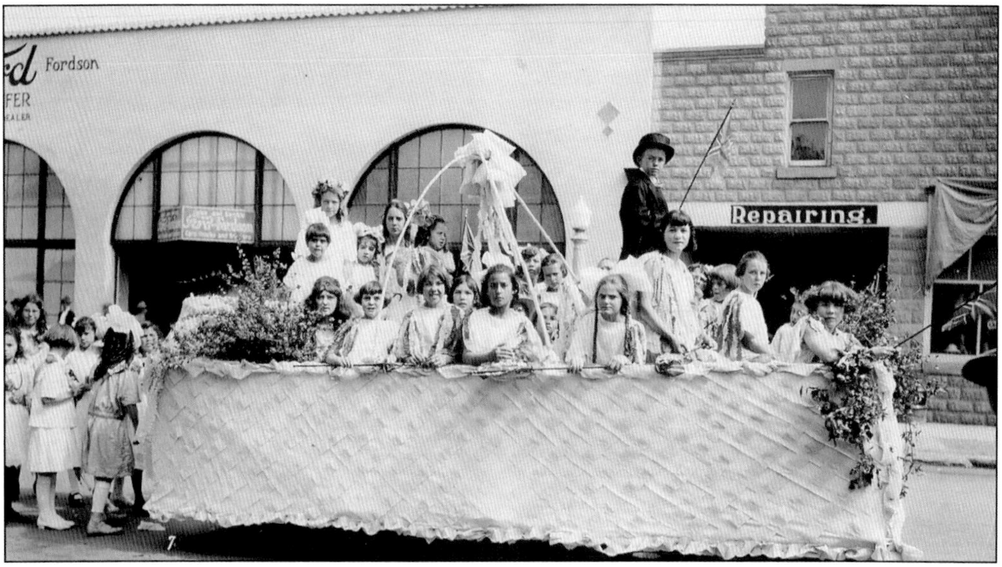

This is a float filled with Atwater children at the Nation Pageant held in Merced on April 20, 1923. From left to right are Sarah Fagundes Hendricks, Sylvia Galarin, Rosalie Heller, Dorothy Sutherland, Clara Fernandez, Muriel Wassum, Mildred Wayne, Betty Howard, Doris Crookham, Elsie Goularte, Alice Owen, Wanda Houser, Marjorie Thompson, Ethel Wayne, Archie Hinds, Edith Pregno, Leta Wayne, Marcella Prine, Edna Kitterman, Genevieve Owen, Ellen Osborn, and Alverna Phillips. Obscured behind the flowers is Carmel Hinds.

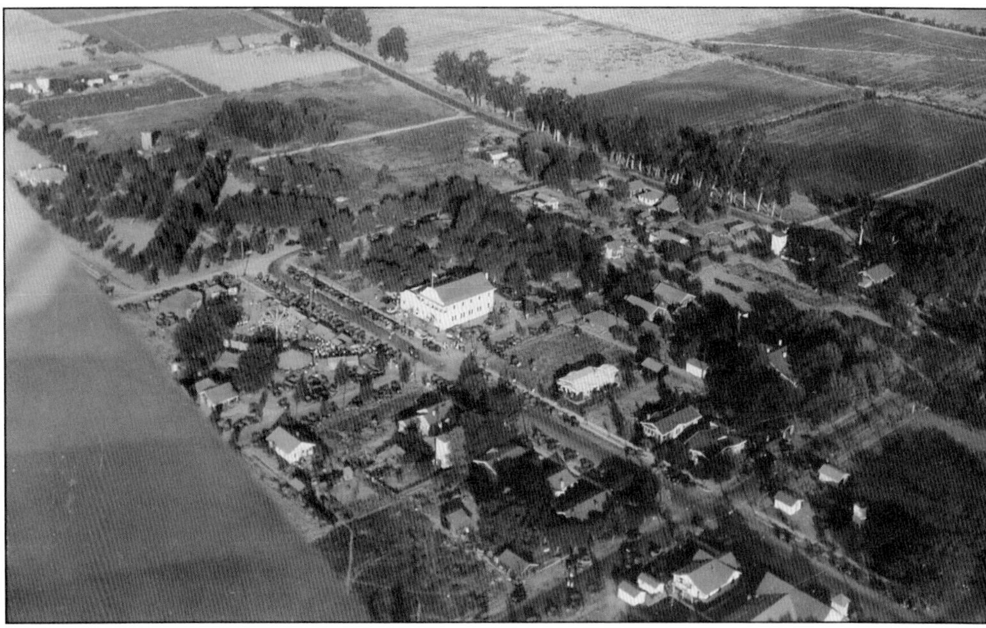

This aerial view of Atwater shows how sparsely developed the community was in the 1920s. The big building close to center of the picture is the APC (Atwater Pentecost Club) Hall. It became the center of many activities, and the Atwater Pentecost Festival was held there annually. It also served as a theater and roller rink. The building was demolished in 1972 and replaced by a more modern facility. The large number of trees is where Ralston Park is today. Third Street now divides this park.

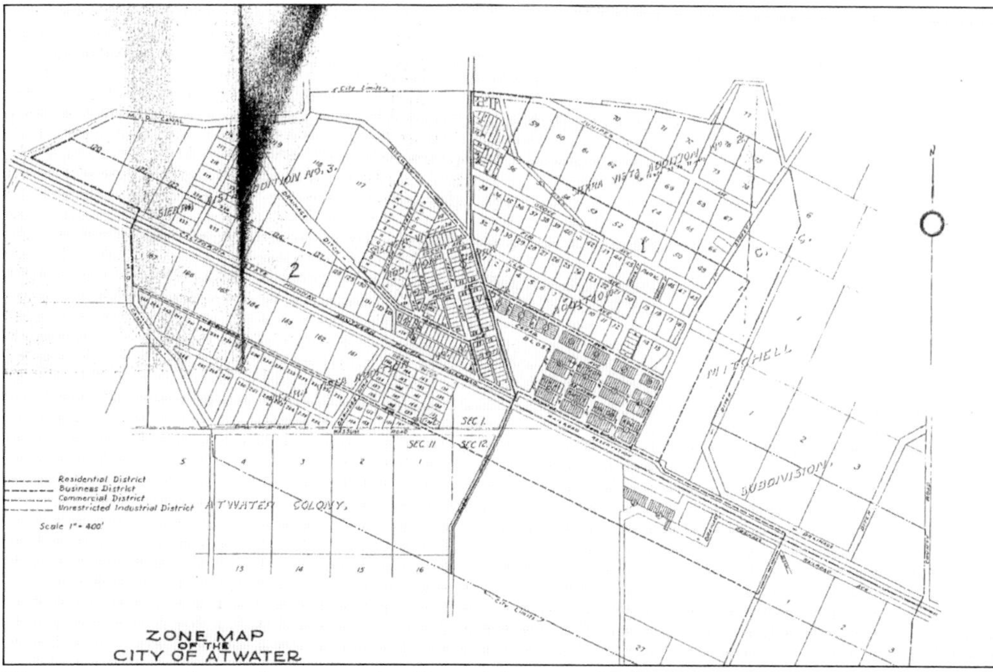

This is a proposed map for zoning the City of Atwater, filed in Merced County, in 1927. With the exception of the addition on the south side of the railroad and Highway 99, the map basically shows how Atwater developed.

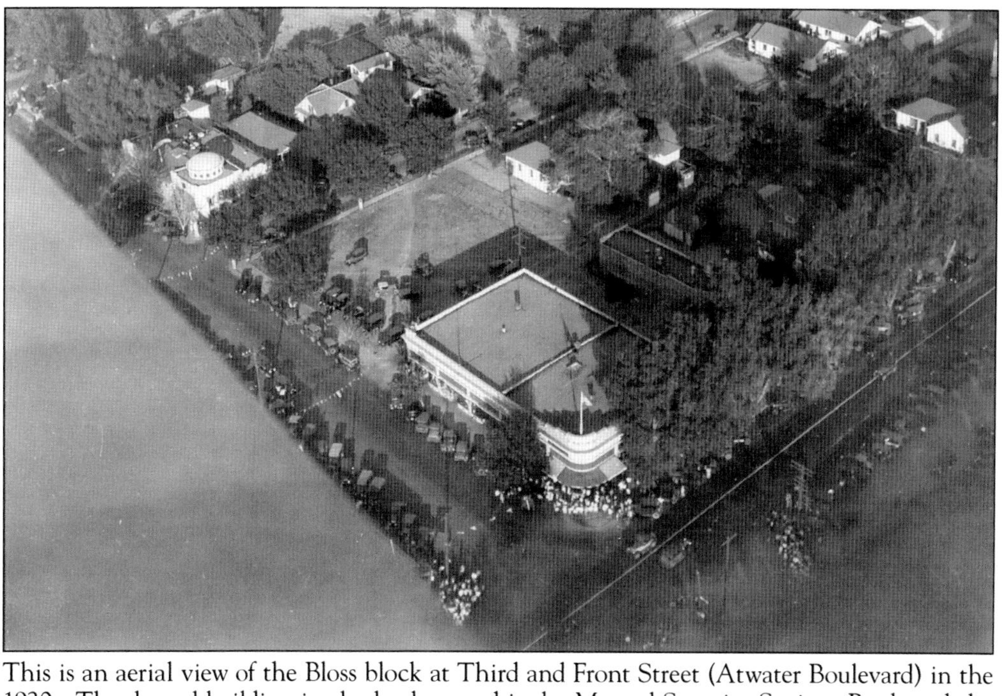

This is an aerial view of the Bloss block at Third and Front Street (Atwater Boulevard) in the 1920s. The domed building in the background is the Merced Security Savings Bank and the empty lot between is where Dr. Jackson would eventually build his professional offices.

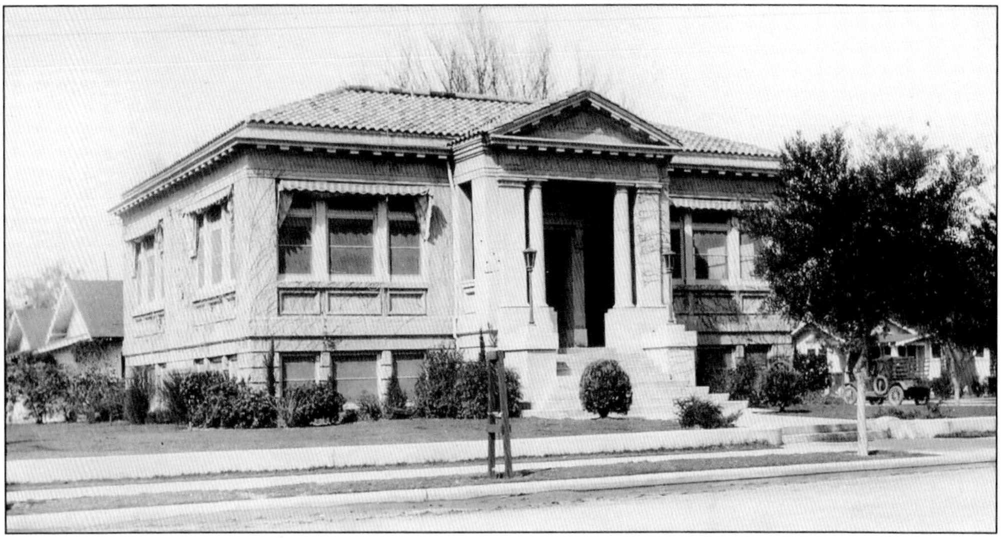

In 1925, George Bloss Sr. built the library on the corner of Third Street and Cedar Avenue in memory of his grandson, George Thompson Bloss. The basement of this building also served for many years as city hall and council chambers. Today it is used as a meeting place for the Boy Scouts, and the Atwater Chamber of Commerce utilizes the basement.

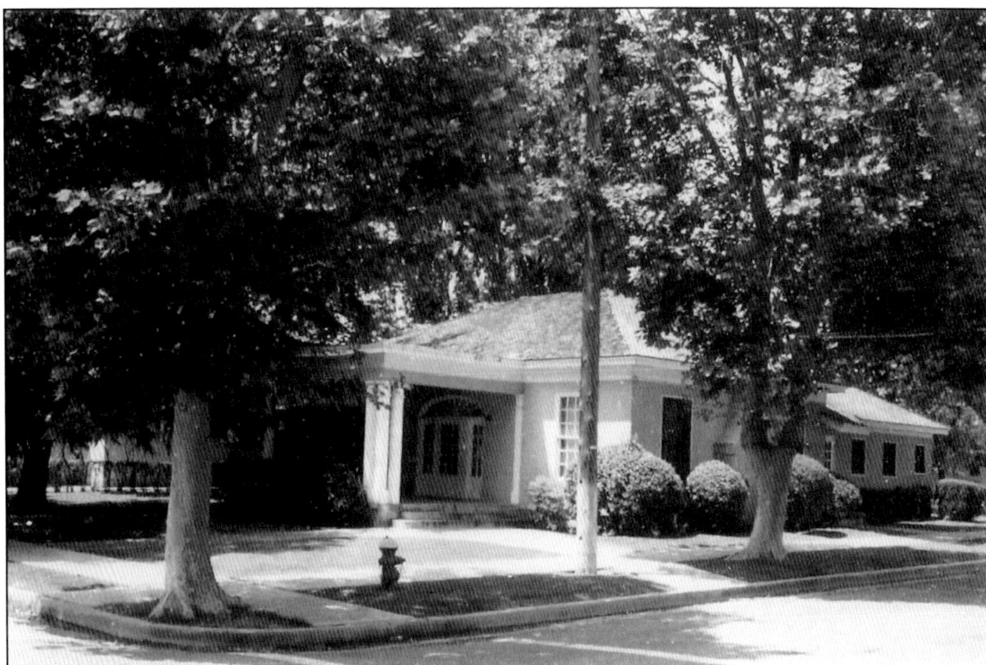

The Atwater Women's Clubhouse was built on Third and Grove Avenue in 1926, after Edna Thompson Bloss donated the lot. In the 1890s, Mrs. Clark Ralston helped form the Atwater Women's Club, which still functions today. With the encouragement of this club, Mitchell Hall was built in 1892. In 1907, the ladies of Atwater gathered at the home of Charles Shaffer and decided that the club would have the objective of improving the town of Atwater. When Atwater incorporated, the first city council decided that the women should name the streets. The Atwater Women's Improvement Club received the honor.

Three

Fire, Police, and Public Works

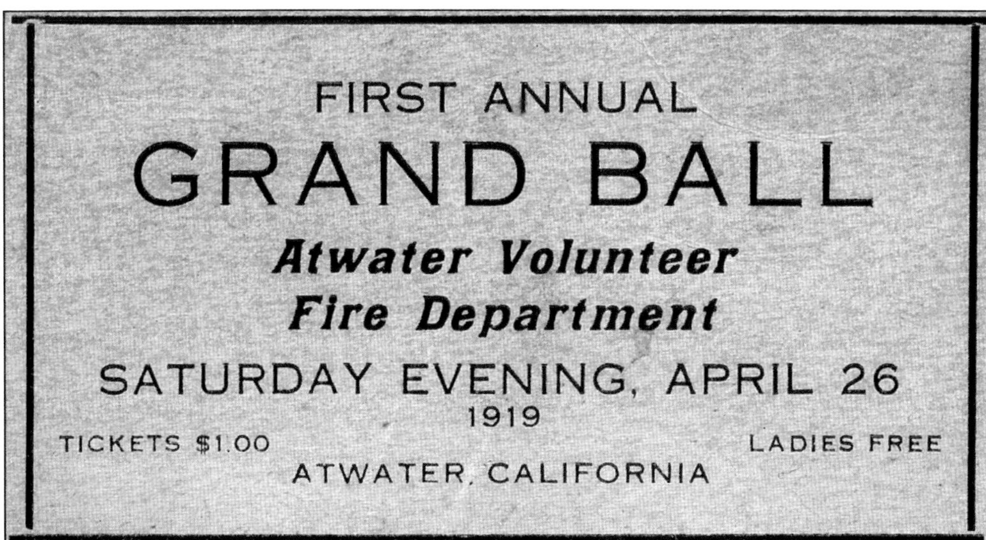
FIRST ANNUAL

GRAND BALL

Atwater Volunteer

Fire Department

SATURDAY EVENING, APRIL 26

1919

TICKETS $1.00 LADIES FREE

ATWATER, CALIFORNIA

The first Atwater Volunteer Fireman's Ball was held on April 26, 1919. Admission was $1 for men and free for ladies. Tom Margaretic donated this ticket to the historical society.

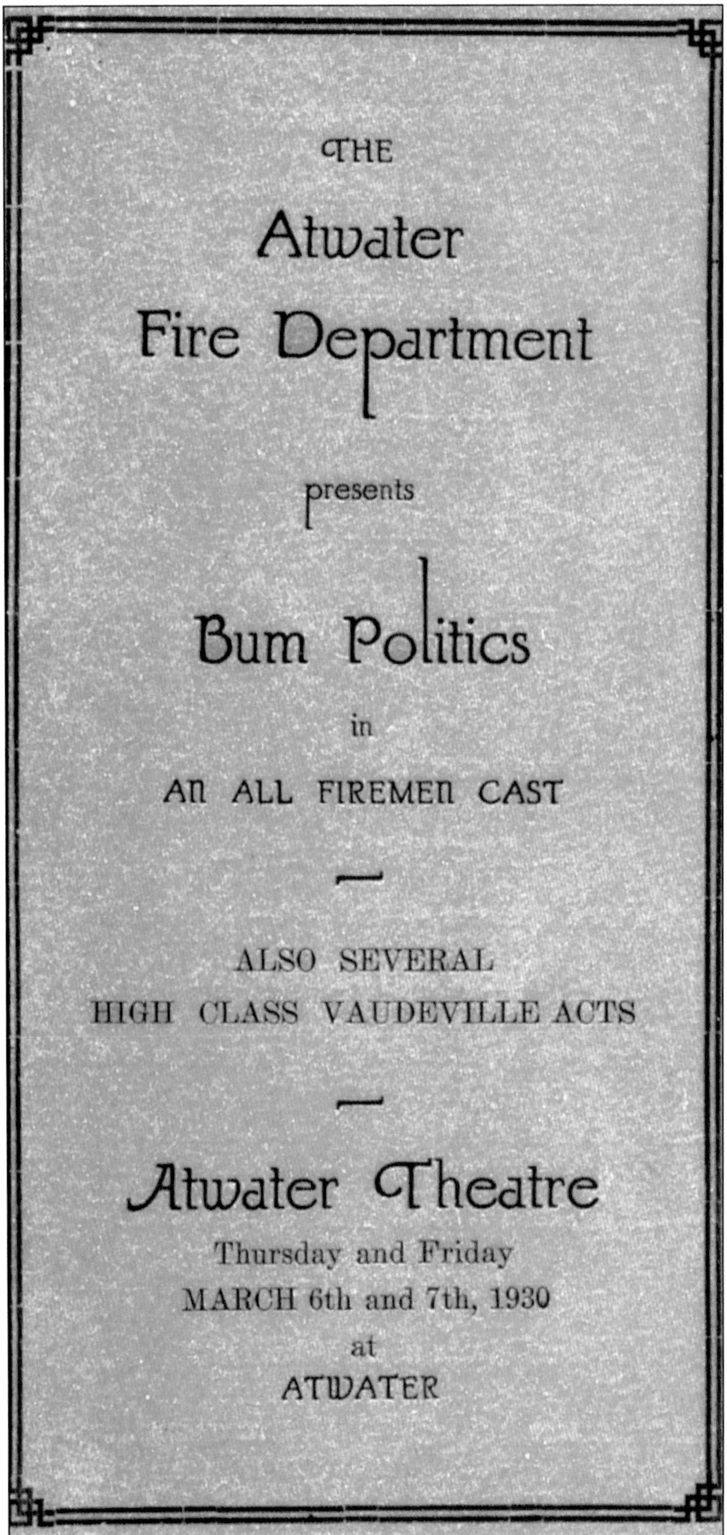
THE

Atwater

Fire Department

presents

Bum Politics

in

AN ALL FIREMEN CAST

ALSO SEVERAL

HIGH CLASS VAUDEVILLE ACTS

Atwater Theatre

Thursday and Friday

MARCH 6th and 7th, 1930

at

ATWATER

On March 6 and 7, 1930, the Atwater Fire Department presented a play called *Bum Politics*, put on by a cast of volunteers. An orchestra played, and the first number was a song sung by Jack Noonan of the American La France Company out of San Francisco. He also sang popular ballads with the Smith sisters, with Peggy Ralstini as chorus. A specialty dance was also put on by the students from Miss Signa Oust's dance class. The program featured advertising from all the local merchants. The actors were Elmer Hurd, Si Howard, Bert Ralston, Charles Kelber, Dade Osborn, Jimmie Herrod, Charles Osborn, E. L. Walter, and R. E. Waltamath.

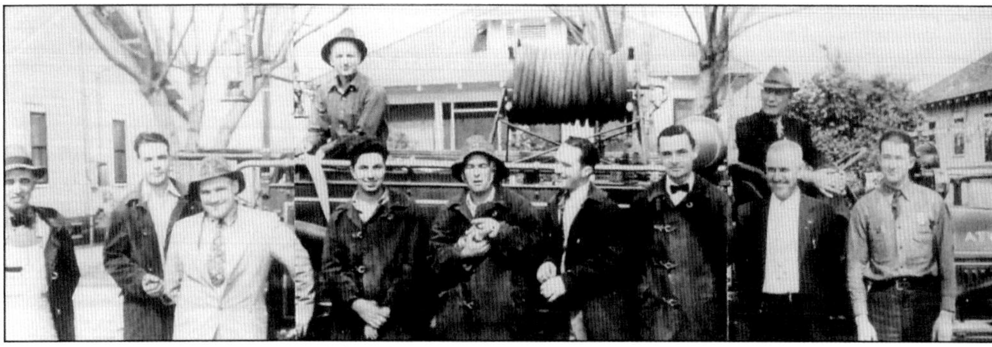

Pictured on the street in front of the old firehouse (not visible) are Atwater volunteer firemen, from left to right, Raleigh Galeria, Paul Crookham, Louis Passadori, Dade Osborn (above), Harry Neves, Charlie Vierra, Louis Weston, Frank Smith, Charles Osborn (front seat), and Paul Owen.

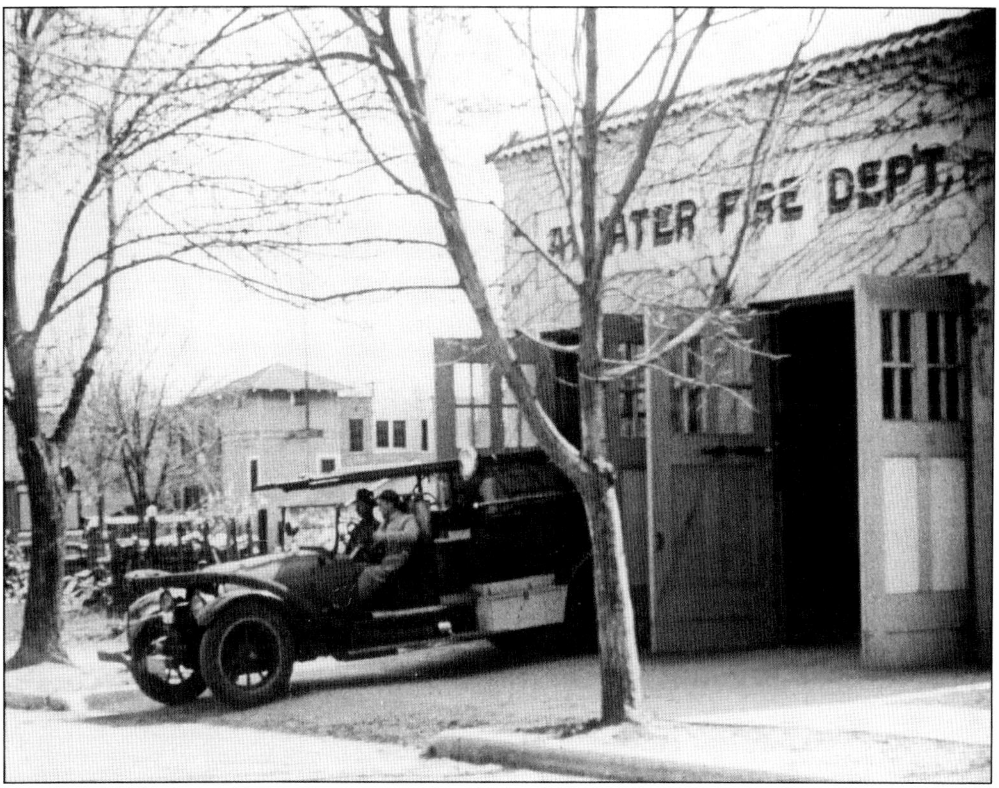

In this 1936 photograph, firemen Louis Passadori and Raleigh Galeria sit in the 1918 Cadillac fire engine outside the first fire station. Before this station was built, the fire engine was kept in the garage of the Bloss home. The 1918 Cadillac touring car was donated to the fire department after George Bloss Jr. became upset with a San Francisco car salesman because he would not give Mr. Bloss the trade-in value of what George thought the car was worth. George Bloss said he would as soon give the car away than accept the pitiful amount offered him. This fire truck is kept in pristine condition and is used annually for parades and other Atwater functions.

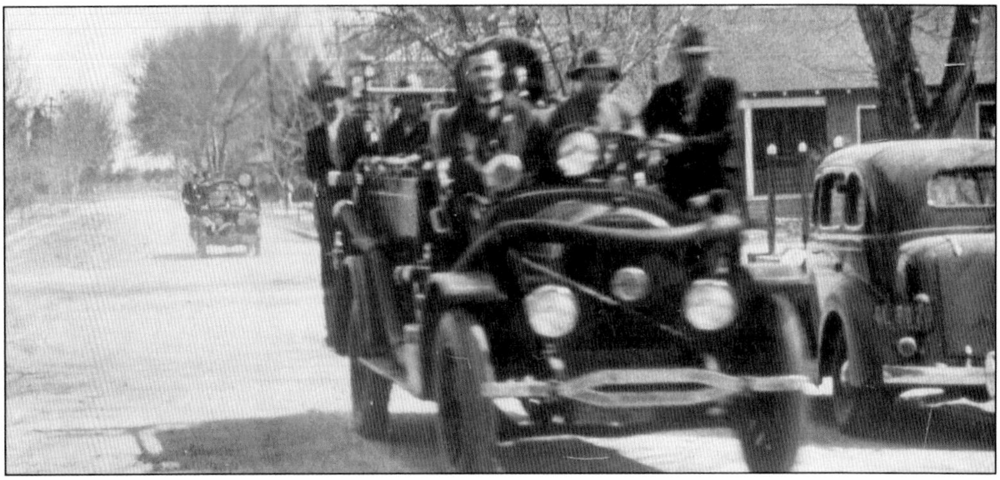

The volunteer firemen are seen here returning from a call. The fire alarm was a shotgun that was kept handy by the kitchen door, and if there were a fire, whoever discovered it would go outside and fire three rounds as fast as they could reload. If they did not have a gun, they would just go outside and holler as loud as they could. When the first fire siren was installed, the townspeople had trouble with birds and bats nesting in it. A practice was started to sound the siren every day at noon and to keep the creatures out of the siren.

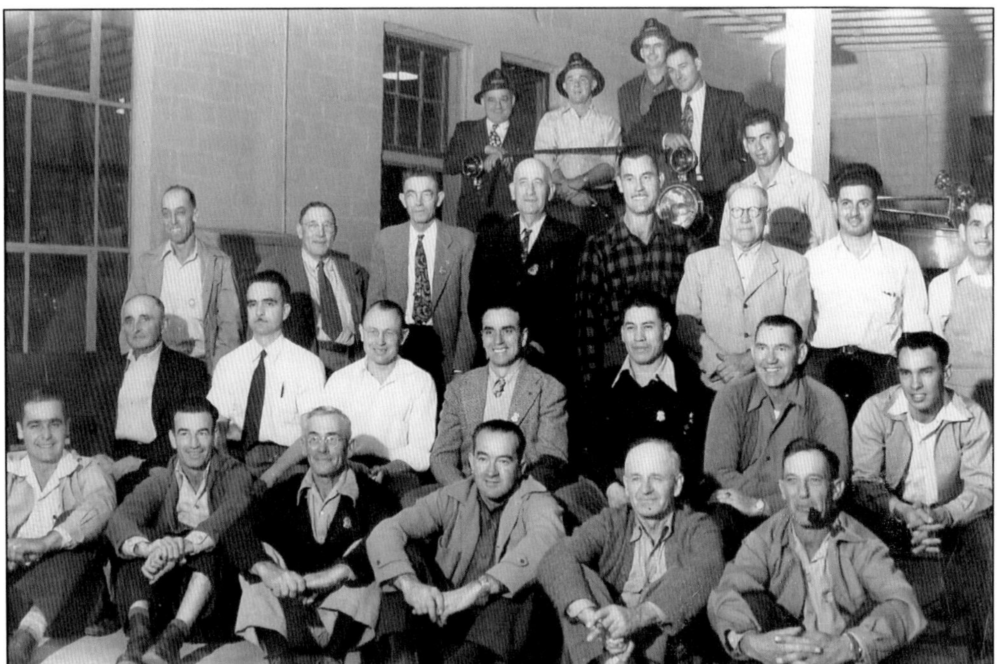

This is an image of the volunteer Atwater Fire Department in 1948. Pictured, from left to right, are (first row) Dave Silva, Paul Stanton, Ernest Harrod, Paul Owen, Dade Osborn, and Charlie Kelber; (second row) Vic Baptista, Jim Hickman, Bill Crews, Charlie Hendricks, Tony Arries, Hank Jensen, and Jimmy Ligena; (third row) Frank Fagundes, John Colburn, Elmer Hurd, Charlie Osborn, Ed Wilhoite, George Bloss Jr., Harry Neves, and Frank Perry; and (fourth row) Louis Passadori, Norman Weston, Milt Hogancamp, Bill Rose, and Franklin Gonzales. Not pictured is Paul Crookham. The firemen said they didn't save any buildings, but plenty of valuable lots.

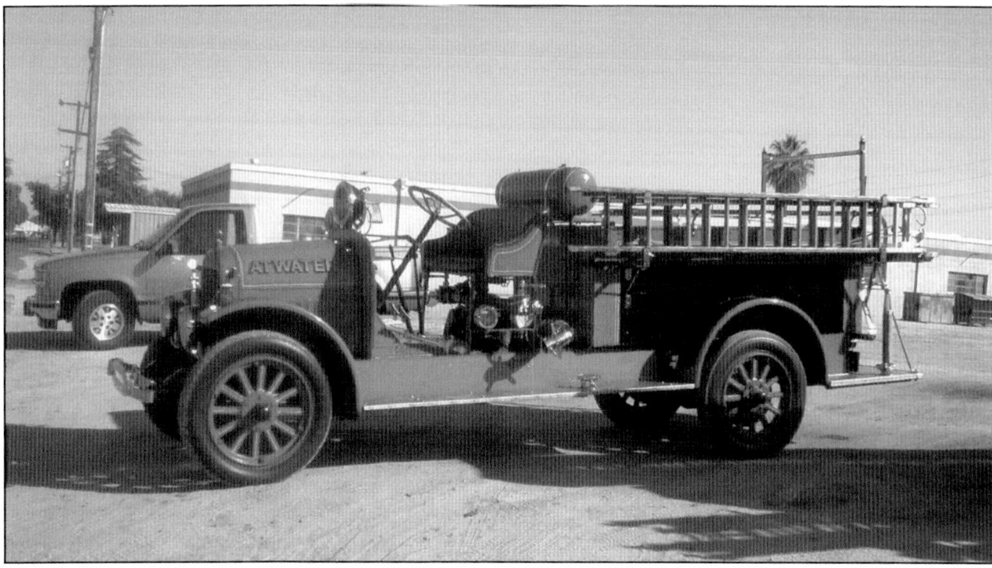

This is one of three antique fire trucks kept by the Atwater Fire Department. This old charmer is a 1924 Brockway Torpedo manufactured by the La France Company.

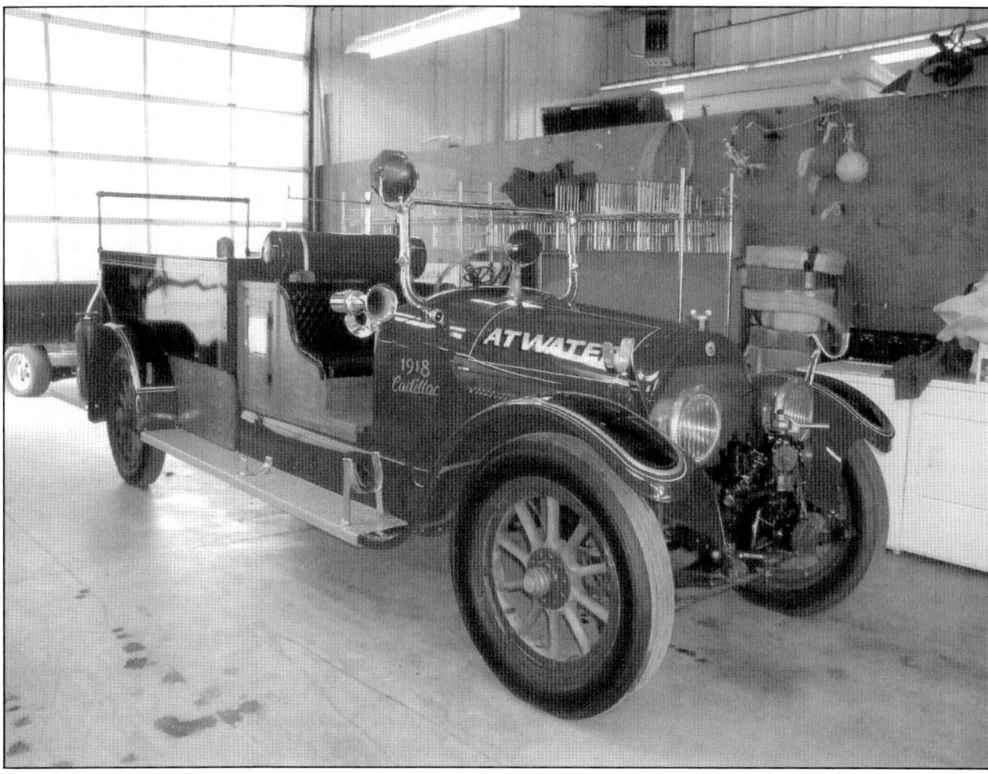

This 1918 fire truck has been called "Old Bess," the "Caddy," and is the number two engine for the Atwater Fire Department. She's an old Cadillac touring car converted with the money, ingenuity, and sweat of the volunteer firemen who turned her into the first fire truck put into service for any part of Merced County. Donated by George Bloss Jr., the car was converted in the early 1930s. Early-timers claim she had plenty of "hiss."

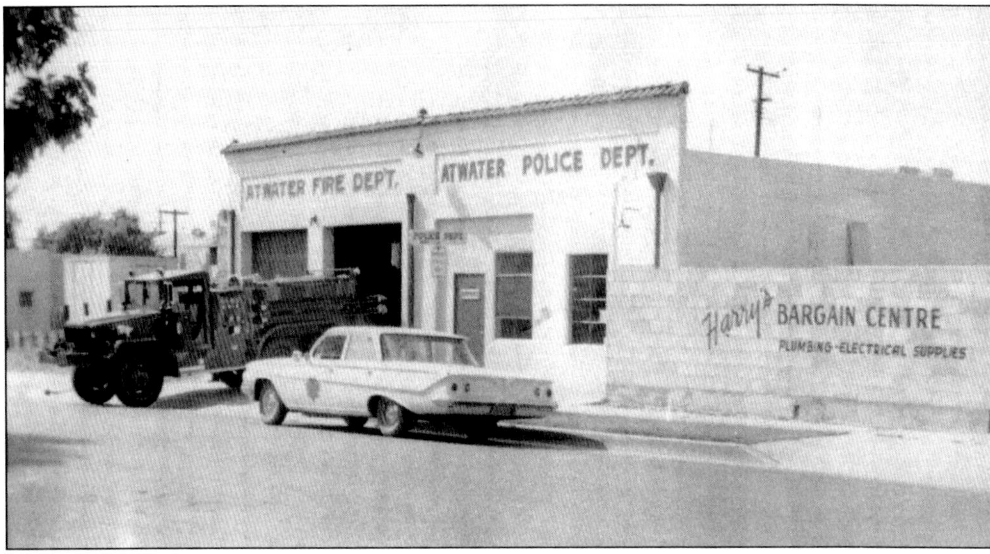

Prior to sharing one-half of the fire station building, the police were housed behind Justice Court on Third Street. Later they moved to Bellevue Road into a facility in the new city hall.

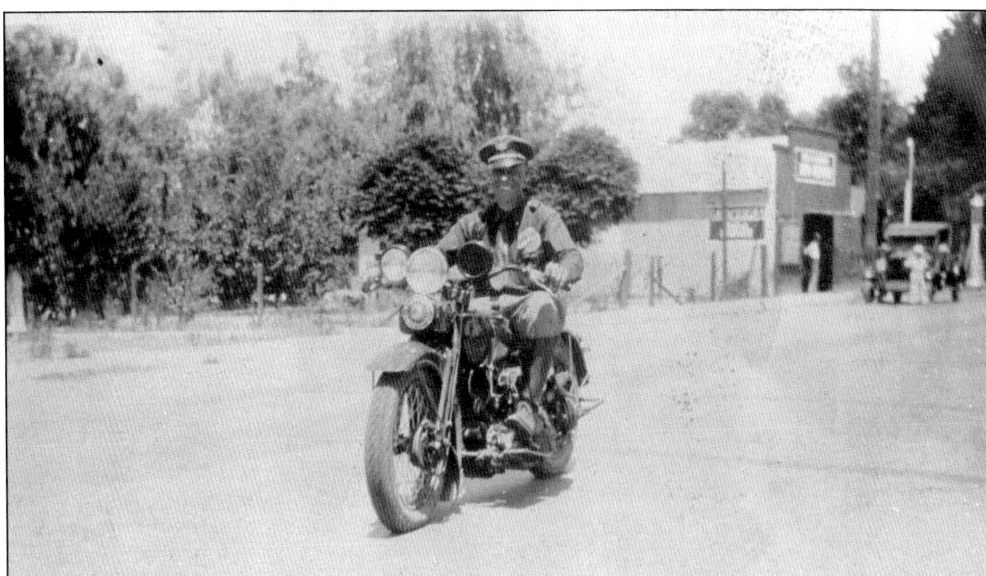

Atwater's first chief of police was William Randol, pictured riding his motorcycle. Prior to the city having a police chief, the top law enforcement officer was the city marshal. Sometime in the 1920s, all communities reaching a certain population made the transition to police chief.

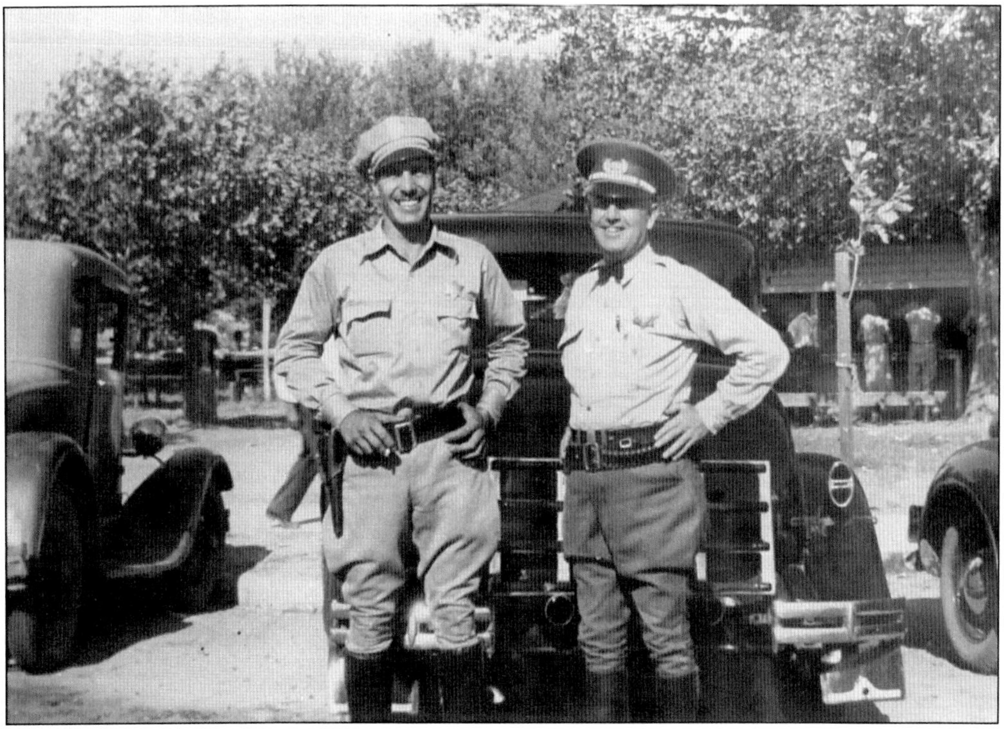

Two members of the Atwater Police Department, Chief E. L. Walter (on the right) and patrolman Ted Souza, pose in 1937. The officers are standing in front of a Ford police car by Ralston Park. A park on Linden Avenue in Atwater is named for Chief Walter.

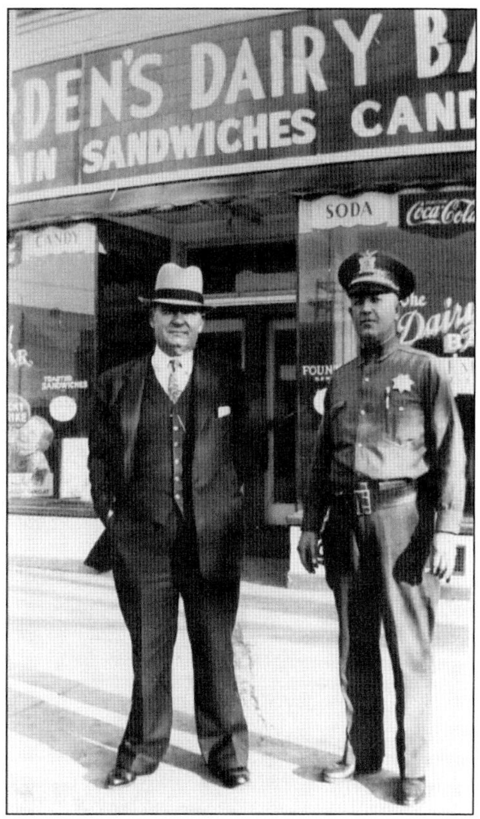

Joe Pimentel was appointed to the city council and then became mayor of Atwater. At the time of his death in 1947, he was the city clerk, however he was also one of the "big four" of the California Pioneer Sweet Potato Shipping enterprise headquartered in Atwater. E. L. Walter was appointed chief of police in 1933, and he became justice of the peace in 1943. Besides their homes in Atwater, both Judge Walter and J. J. Pimentel had homes in Pacific Grove, California, that their families enjoyed.

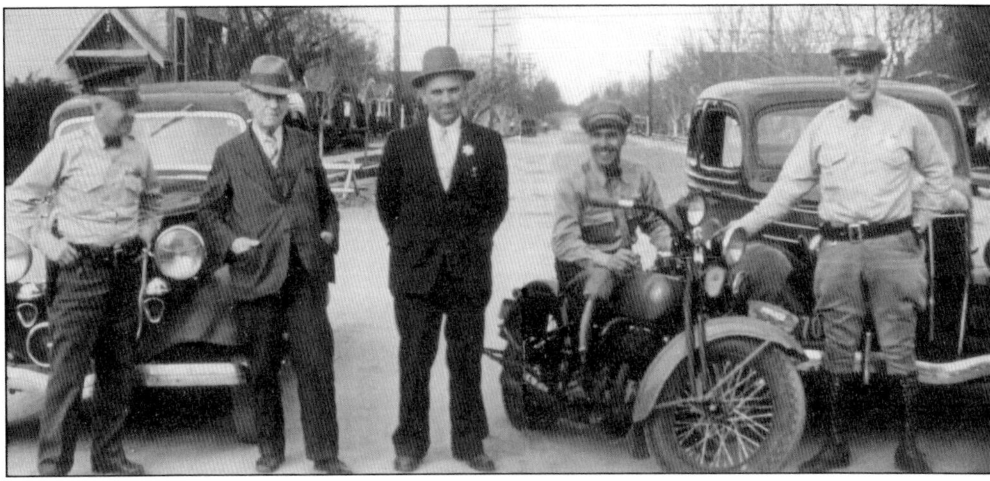

Pictured here, from left to right, are E. L. Walter, Frank Pebley, Frank Valladao, Ted Souza, and Bill Carlon. Mr. Pebley was elected Merced County Supervisor for the Third District (including Atwater) in 1914 and served the people for 28 years. Bill Carlon was appointed chief of police following E. L. Walter.

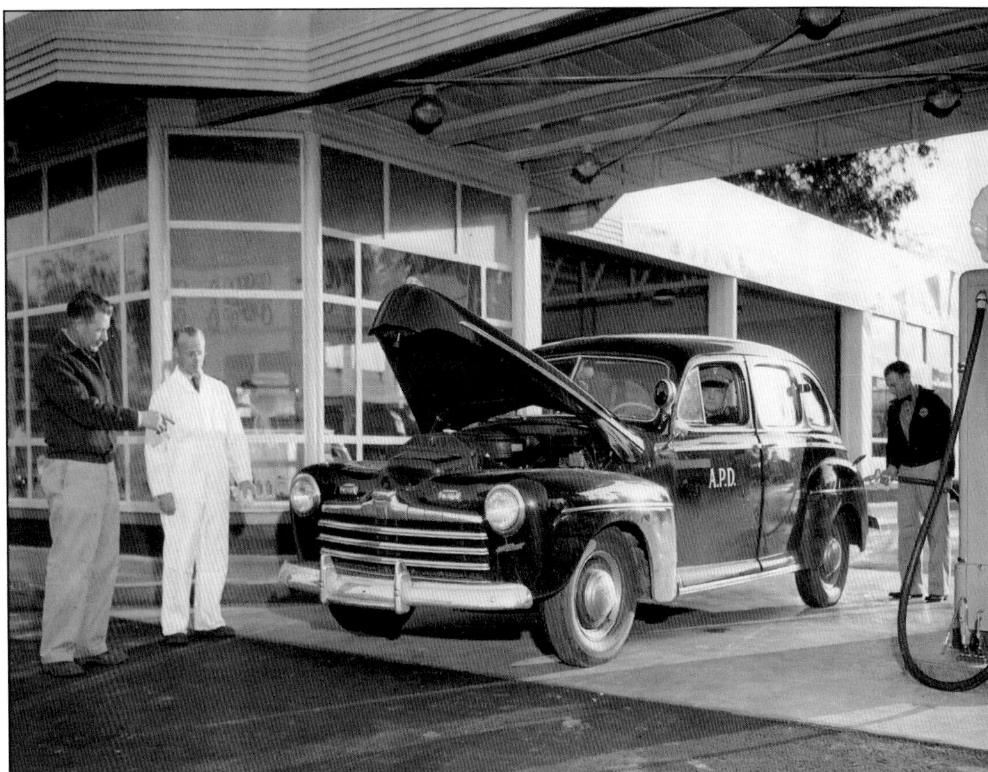

The image was taken in 1947 at the Shell Station located at Fifth Street and Highway 99 (Atwater Boulevard). The police officer in the car is Bill Carlan. Also pictured, from left to right, are Tom Bicker, Shell Oil instructor; Walt Boyer, station salesman; and Waite Paul, local resale representative for Shell Oil, pumping gas.

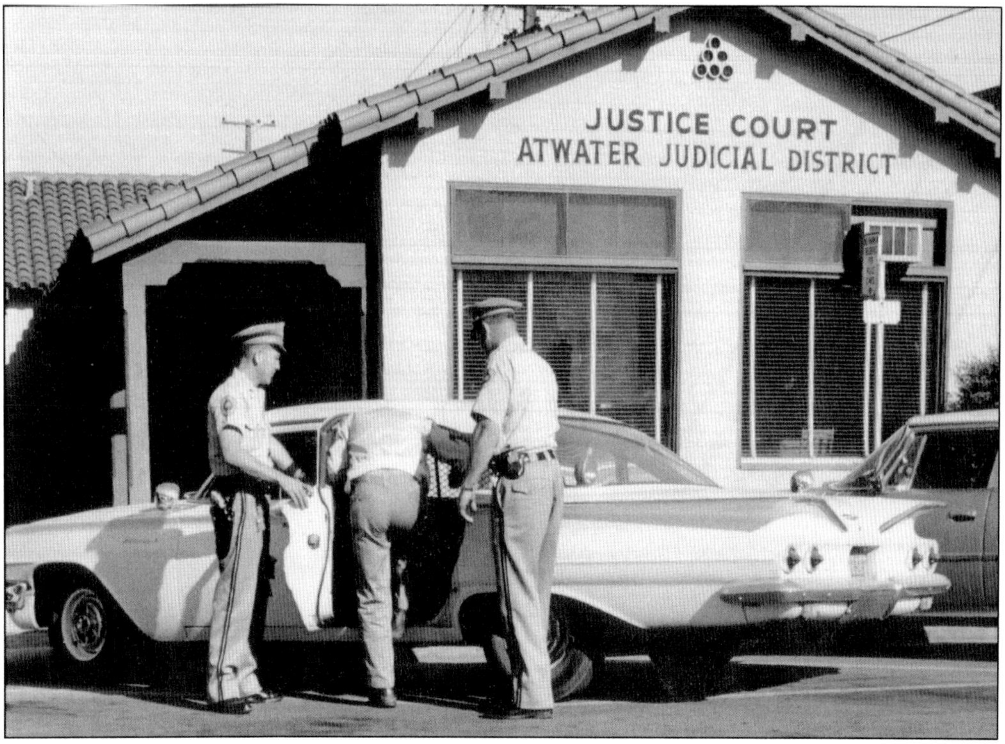

The Atwater Justice Court was located on Third Street, adjacent to the Bloss Block. Dr. Edward A. Jackson had this building erected in 1940 as an additional business area next to the building he had built in 1936 for his practice. The post office moved into the front of this building in 1941. The Atwater Justice Court moved into the room just behind the post office.

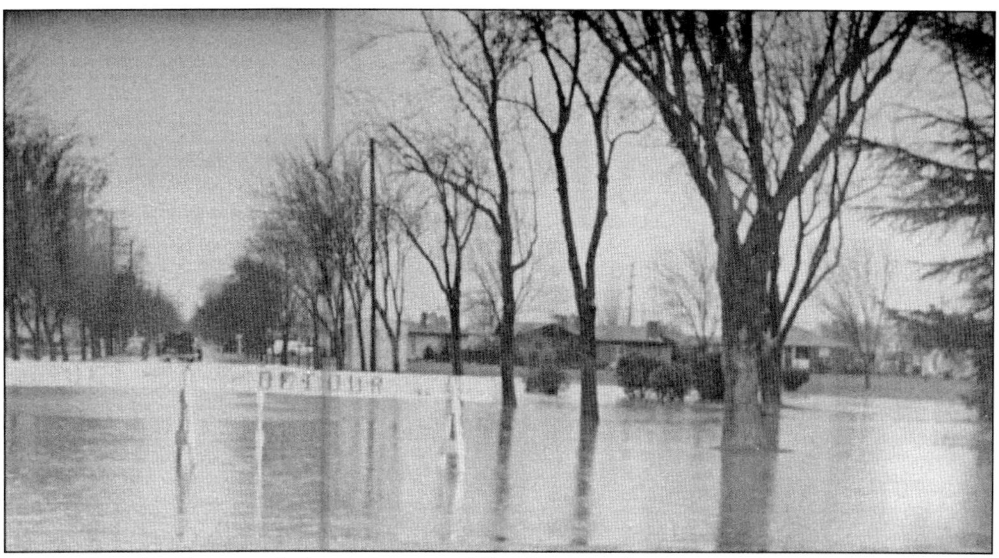

This early 1950s photograph shows the typical flooding after heavy rains, before the city installed more adequate drainage. The Atwater Public Works Department had a great deal to clean up in the town after each flood.

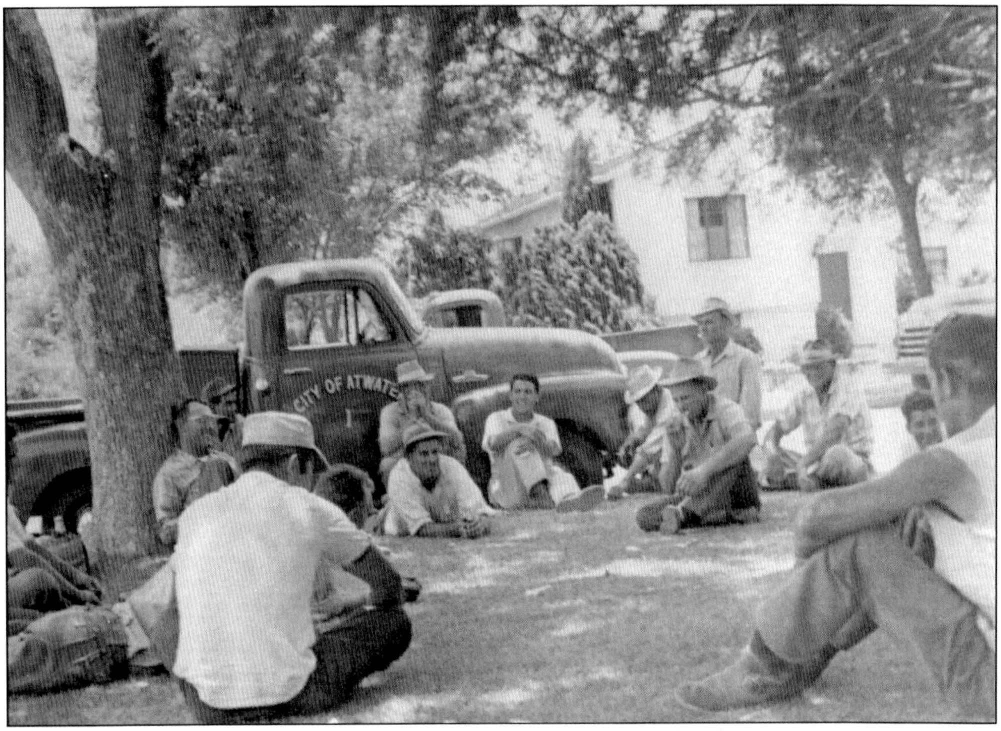

City of Atwater employees are seen here taking a well-deserved break. These men are responsible for general clean up of the city, its streets, and the public buildings in the city, as well as maintaining all the public parks and downtown.

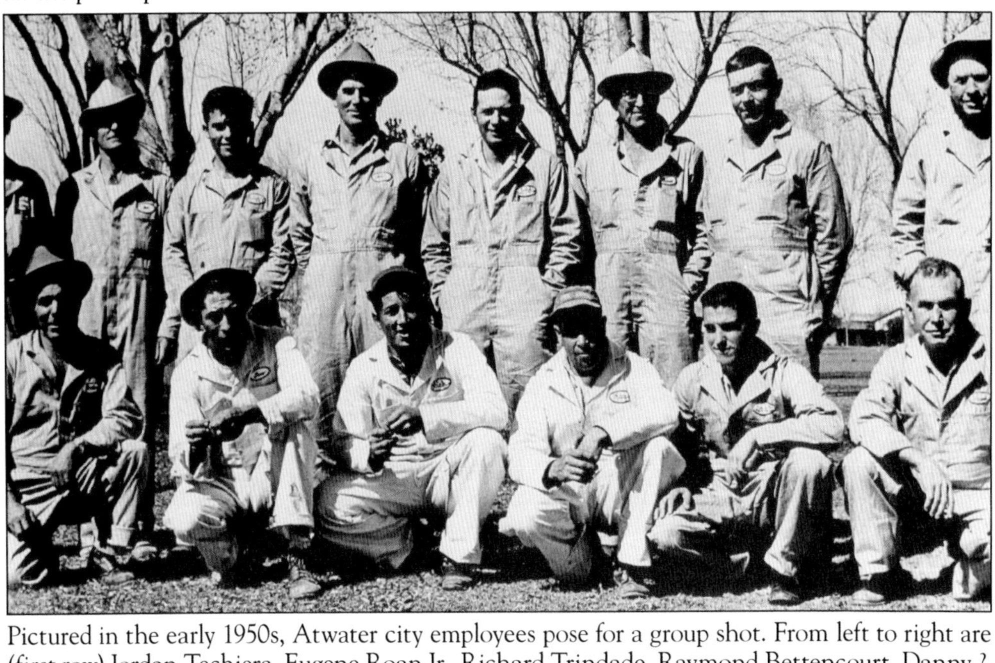

Pictured in the early 1950s, Atwater city employees pose for a group shot. From left to right are (first row) Jordan Techiera, Eugene Roan Jr., Richard Trindade, Raymond Bettencourt, Danny ?, and Frank Perry; (second row) Coy Oneal, Joe Pimentel, Danile F. Caton, John Trindade, Charles A. (Todd) Branco, Manuel Mancebo, Clinton Jones, and Louie Jewall.

Four

School, Churches, and Surrounding Colonies

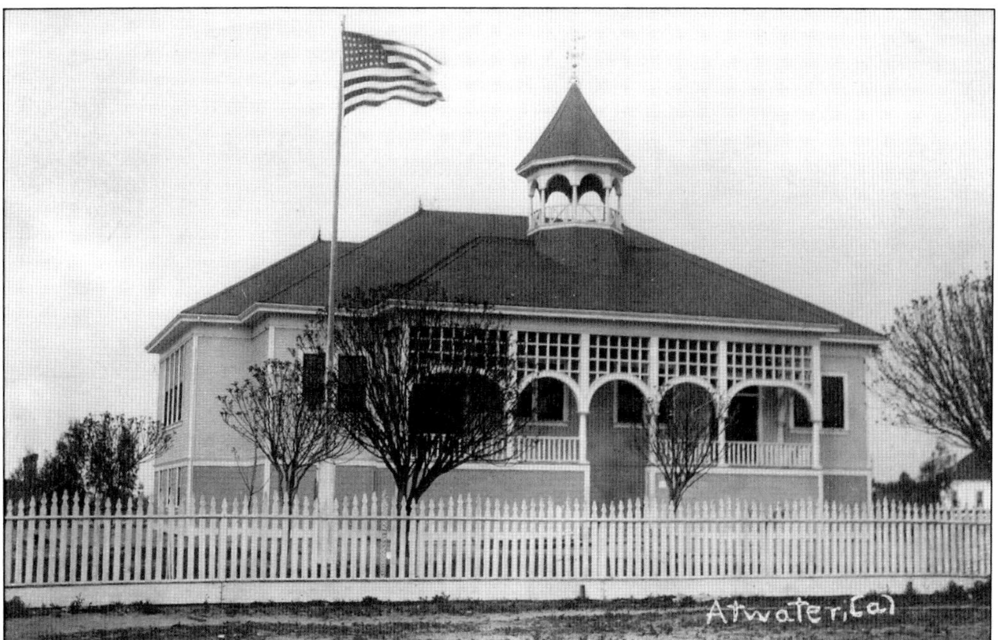

Built in 1903, this school was occupied in January of 1904. It was the first two-room school in Atwater and was located on the corner of Jones Road (Winton Way) and Front Street (Atwater Boulevard). By 1913, another schoolhouse was needed and a two-room stucco building was erected on the school property facing what is today Broadway Avenue. The flag that is flying in this picture has 40 stars on the blue field.

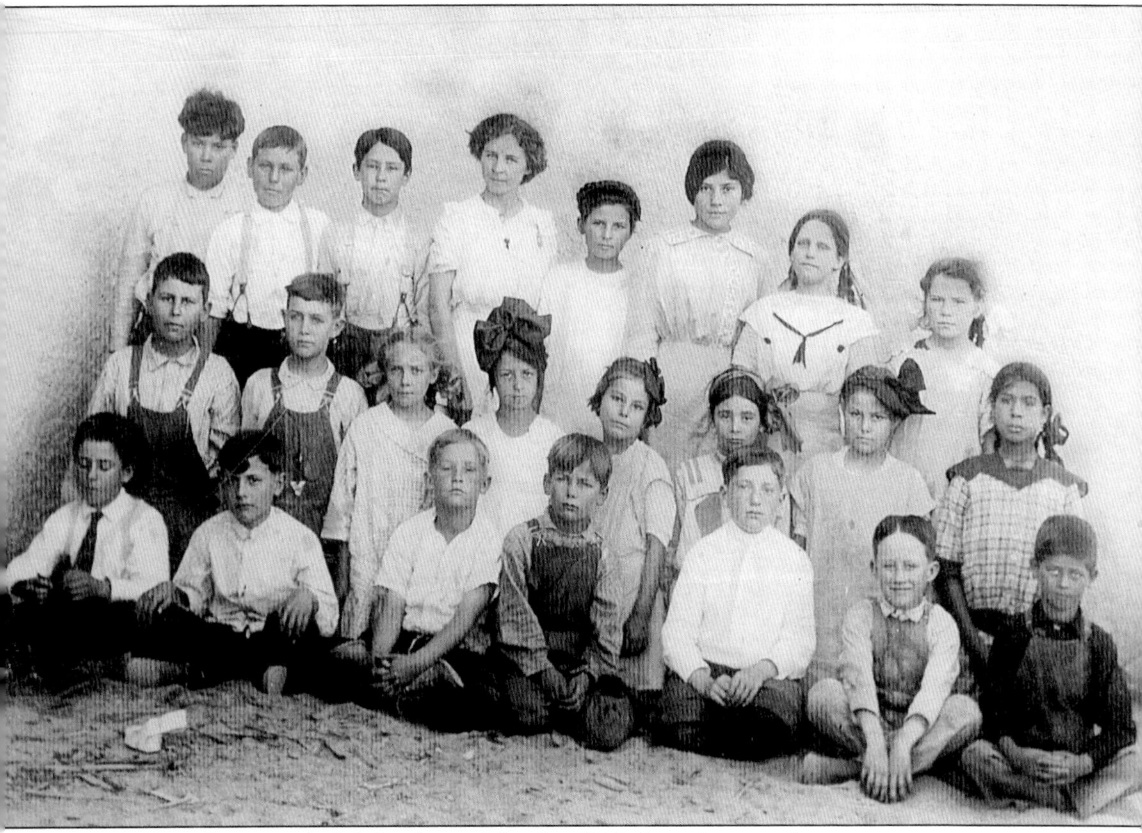

Children from Mitchell School posed for this 1913 class photograph.

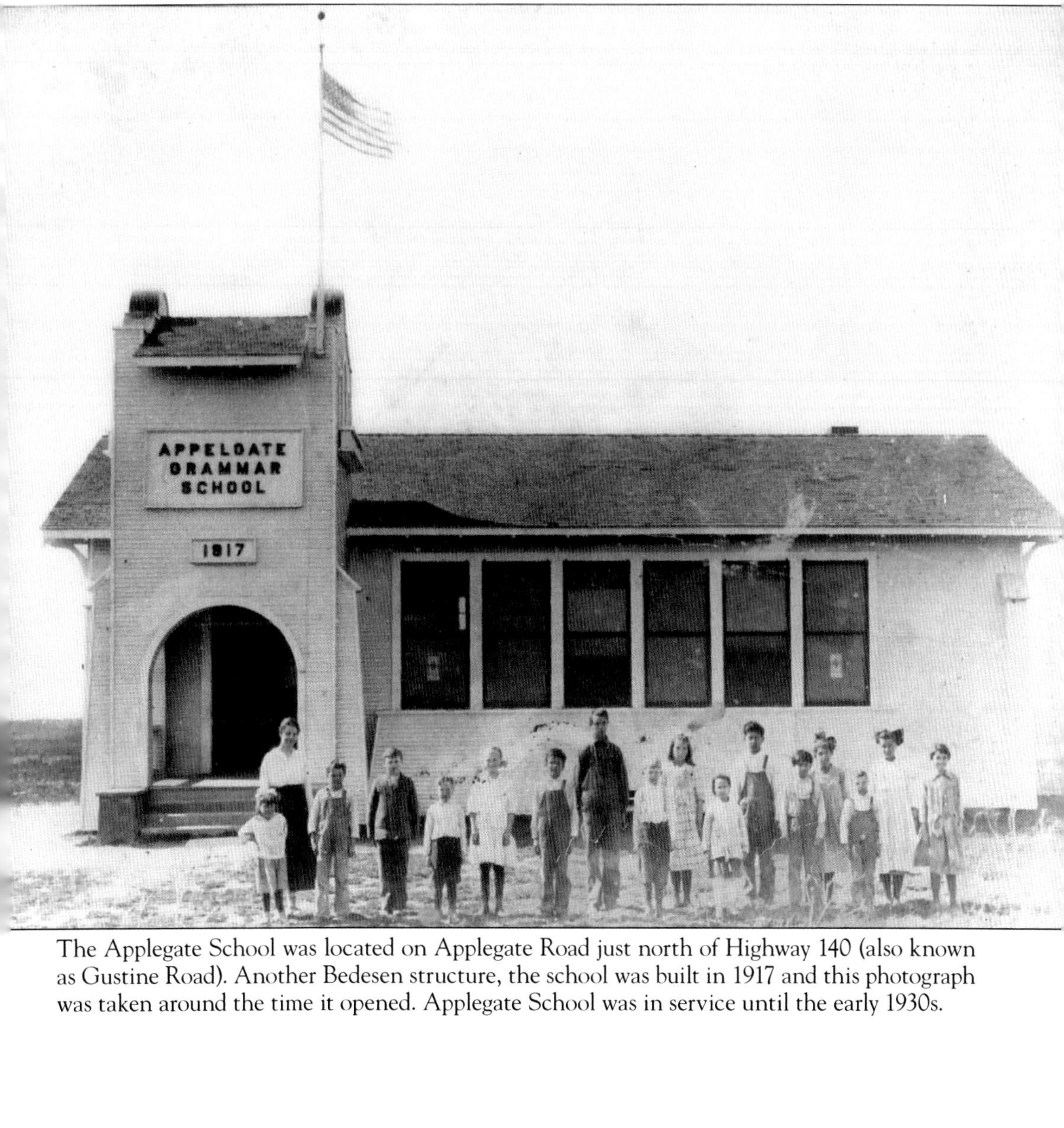

The Applegate School was located on Applegate Road just north of Highway 140 (also known as Gustine Road). Another Bedesen structure, the school was built in 1917 and this photograph was taken around the time it opened. Applegate School was in service until the early 1930s.

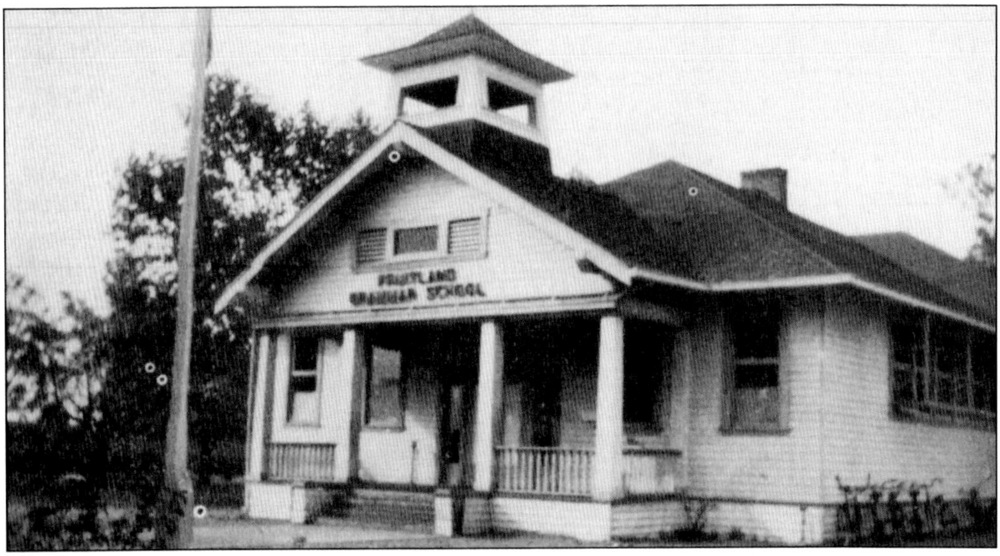

Early in 1913, after a series of meetings were held, the Fruitland School District was organized and a two-room school was built. George Parr donated two acres of land for educational purposes and Miss Janes was the first teacher. In December 1945, due to decreasing enrollment, an election was held for the unification of Arundel, Mitchell, and Fruitland Schools. The action carried, and on July 1, 1946, the three districts became one. This school is still standing in the original place but is now a private residence.

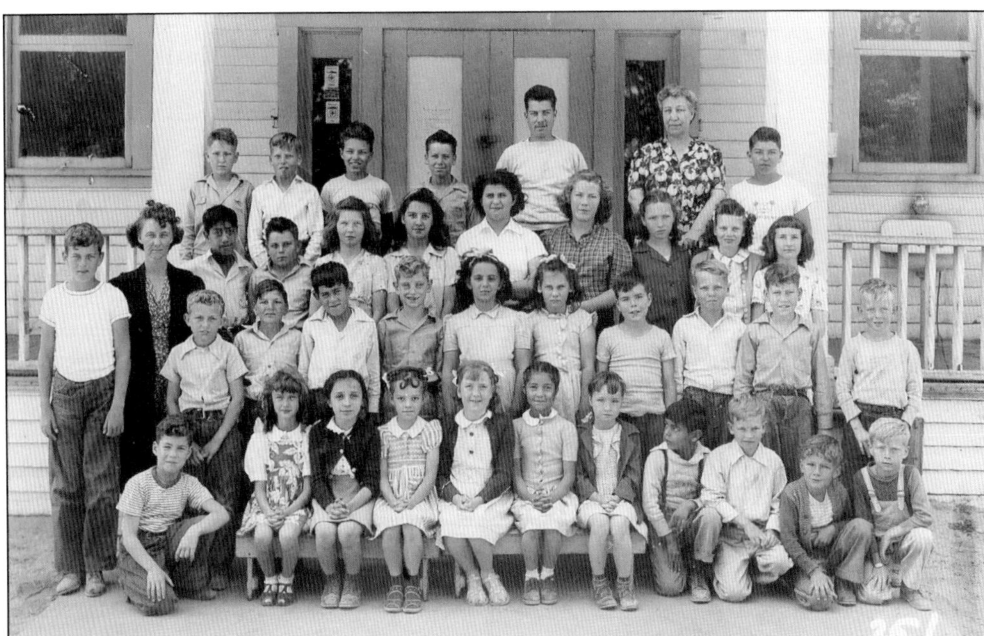

Pictured here are the classes of Fruitland School in 1946.

In this image, Joseph Saca, the son of John and Adeline Saca, is at his eighth-grade graduation. The Sacas arrived in the Fruitland Colony in 1928 after immigrating from the Island of Pico in the Azores with their two young sons, Joe (age 7) and John Jr. (age 6). Joe, who spoke no English, originally attended Mitchell School. In 1929, he entered Fruitland School still in the first grade, but was only there a short while before being advance to second grade. John also attended Fruitland School and graduated from Livingston High School. He entered World War II in 1943 and died at San Lo, France, in 1944. Joe remained in the area and married Laura Maciel. They have three children: Kathy (Jansen), Ron, and Alan.

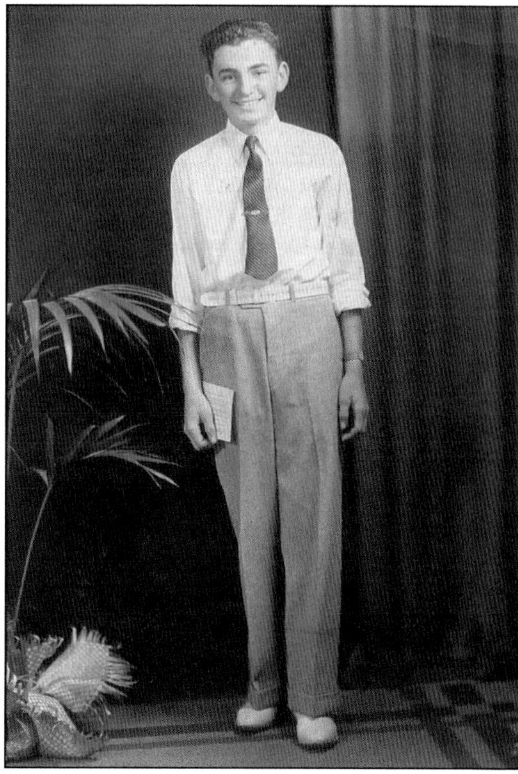

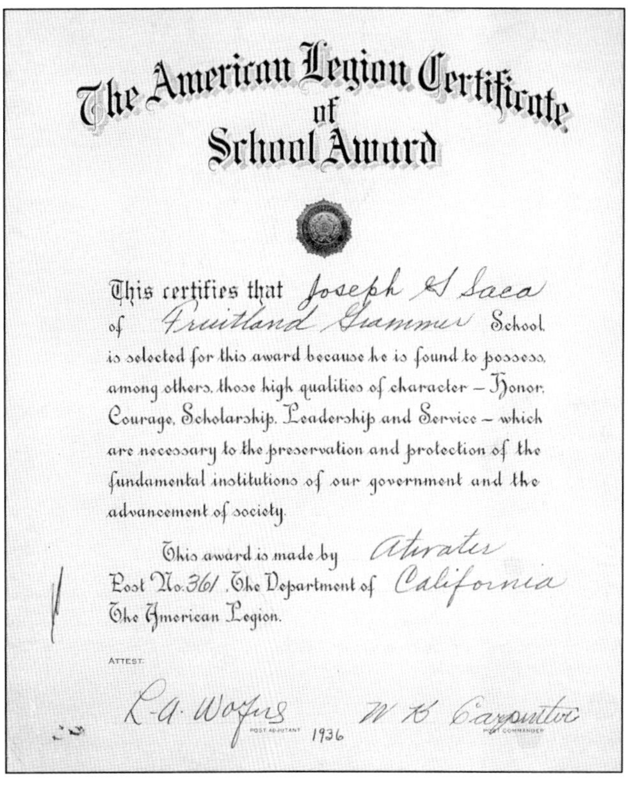

The American Legion Certificate of School Award

This certifies that Joseph G Saca of Fruitland Grammer School is selected for this award because he is found to possess, among others, those high qualities of character – Honor, Courage, Scholarship, Leadership and Service – which are necessary to the preservation and protection of the fundamental institutions of our government and the advancement of society.

This award is made by Atwater Post No. 361, The Department of California The American Legion.

ATTEST:

L. A. Wofers POST ADJUTANT 1936 W K Carpenter POST COMMANDER

Joseph Saca received the American Legion Certificate of School Award when he graduated from eighth grade in 1936. The award was for "Honor, Courage, Scholarship, Leadership and Service." He also had a perfect attendance record at Fruitland Grammar School.

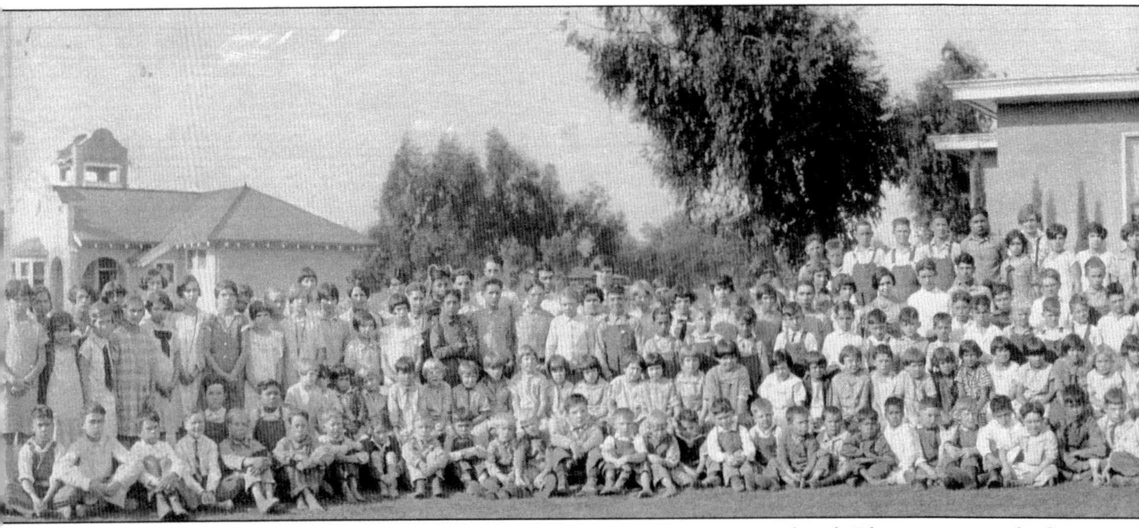

After World War I ended, Atwater had outgrown its grammar school. Plans were made for a much larger building, and in 1921 a four-room school with an auditorium was built. The teachers were Mrs. Ruth Culbertson, principal; Ruth Elliot (Harrison); Jesse Peck; Mary Fitzgerald; Mary

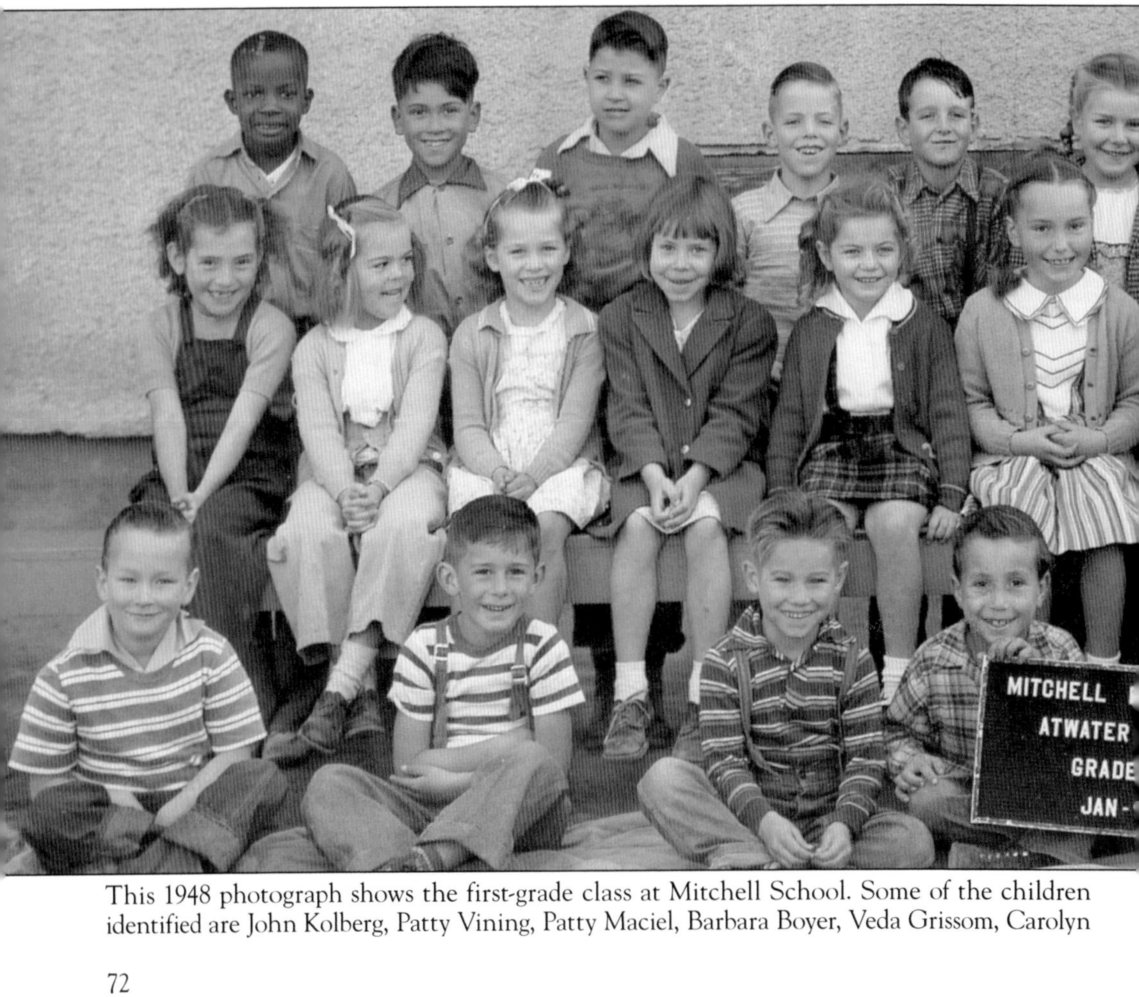

This 1948 photograph shows the first-grade class at Mitchell School. Some of the children identified are John Kolberg, Patty Vining, Patty Maciel, Barbara Boyer, Veda Grissom, Carolyn

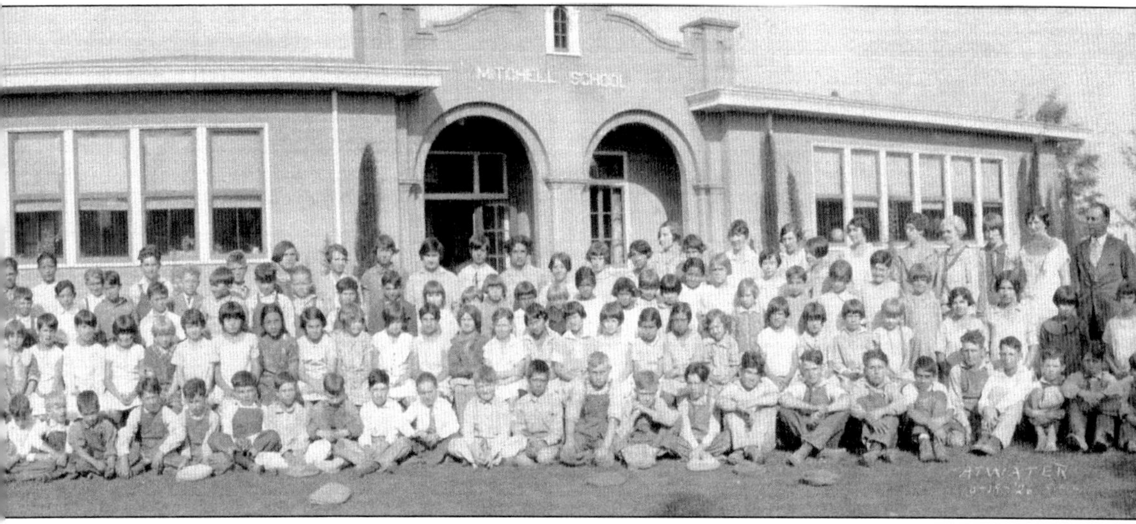

Stanfield; and Olive Peck. Steady growth made it necessary to add more rooms to the new school. The building was on the corner of Fifth Street and Cedar Avenue. In the photograph, the 1913 stucco building is on the left.

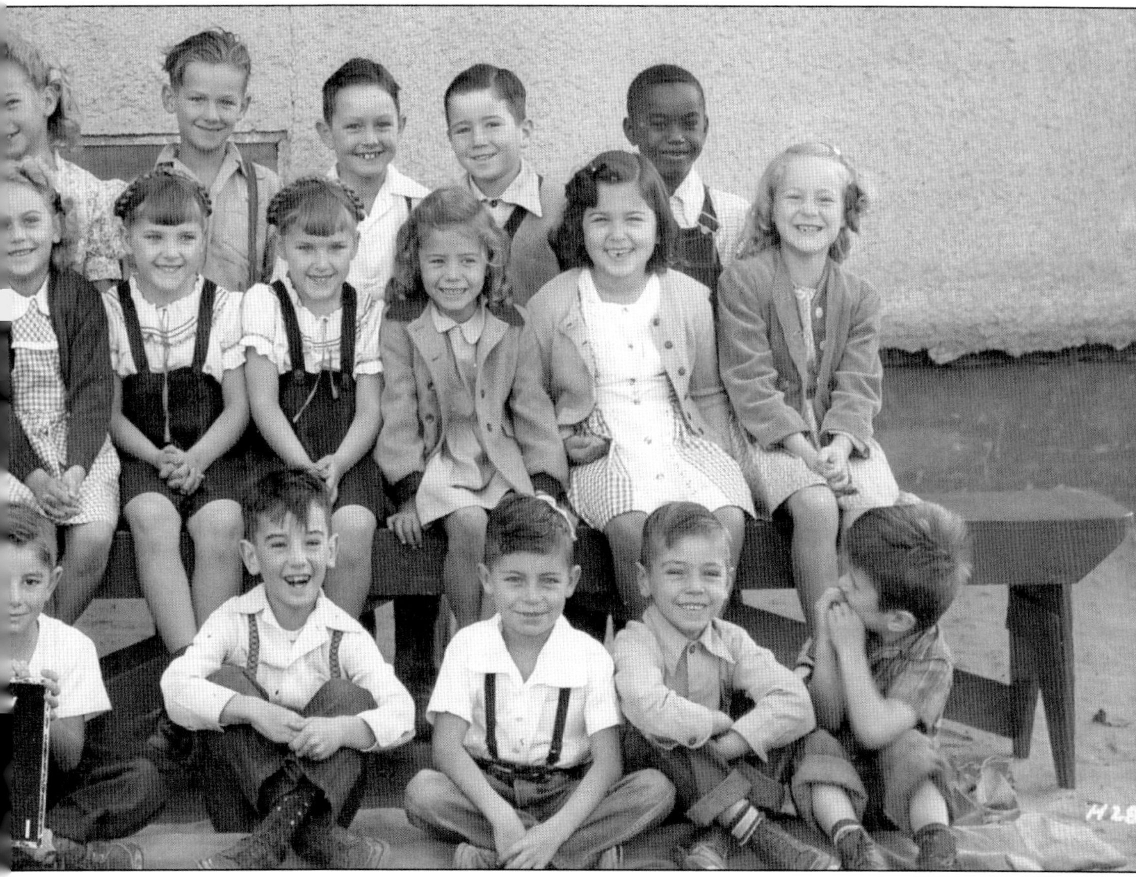

Rose, Sharon Hanson, Milford Machado, Bobby Vierra, Ronnie Adams, Bill Moraine, Louis Texeira, and Jay Baldwin. The teacher was Jessie Peck.

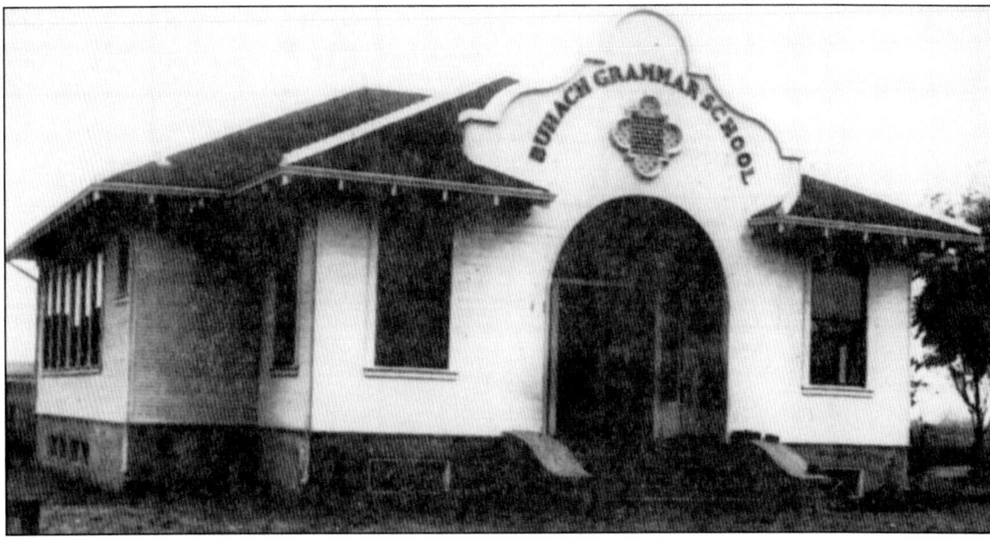

Built in 1900, the Buhach Grammar School served the Buhach Colony community until it closed its doors in 1953. The school building has since been used as a residence and for a while as a storage area for sweet potatoes. In January 1982, Greg and Betty Lema purchased the building and restored it to its original condition. Located on Buhach Road just south of Atwater, the school today is used, along with other restored buildings, as a preschool.

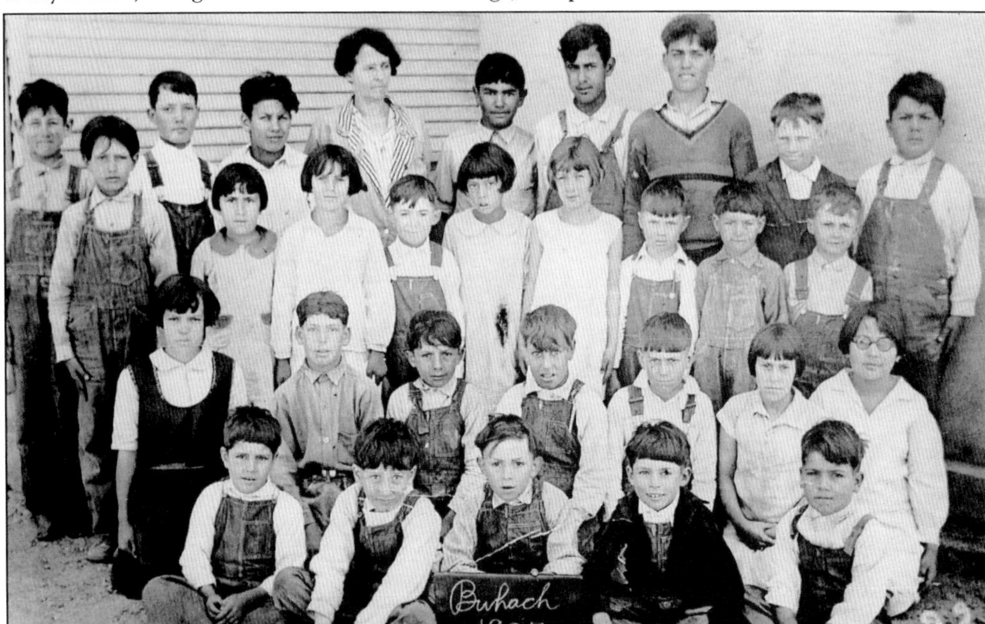

These are the school classes of Buhach in 1927. Pictured, from left to right, are (first row) Isaac Bill, David Branco, Clarence Silveira, Harold Dutra, and Leonard Mello; (second row) Cecilia Cardoza, Claude Gonzales, Art Caton, Dennis Costa, Elmer Machado, Viola Belloli, Genevia Mello; (third row) Albert Valladon, Anne Silveira, Janette Silva, Dave Pacheco, Helen Gulart, Margerite Pacheco, Henry Damos, Manuel Gonzales, and Richard Pacheco; (fourth row) Billie Pedros, Alfred Valladon, Don Machado, Miss Miller (the teacher), Laverne Calderia, Eugene Costa, Johnie Avela, Lee Ellis, and Bernard Mello.

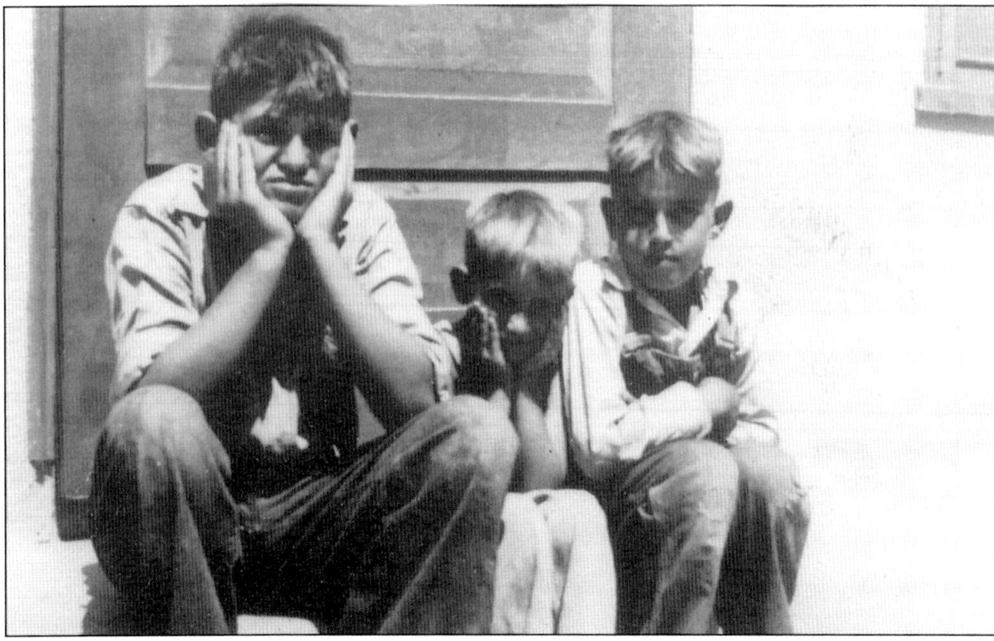

Pictured, from left to right, are Donald, Marvin "Mike," and Eugene LaManna. This May 2, 1937, photograph shows how the boys feel about school not quite being over for the year.

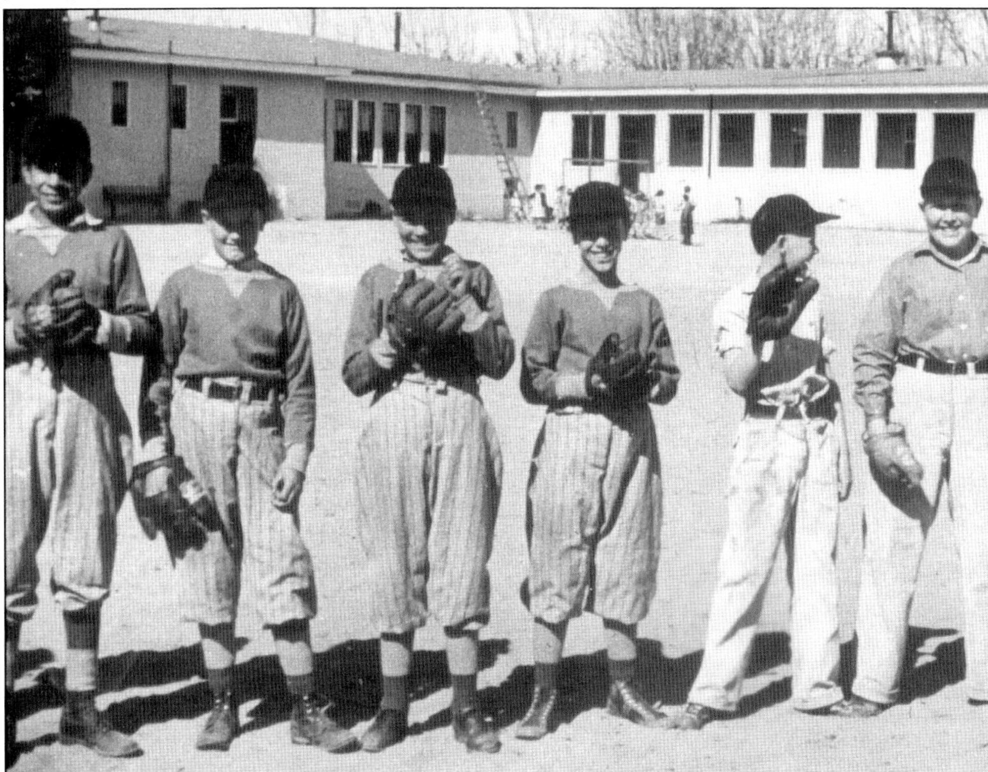

The boys look ready for a good game of baseball. This photograph shows how the original 1921 building was added to by building more rooms in an L configuration down Cedar Avenue.

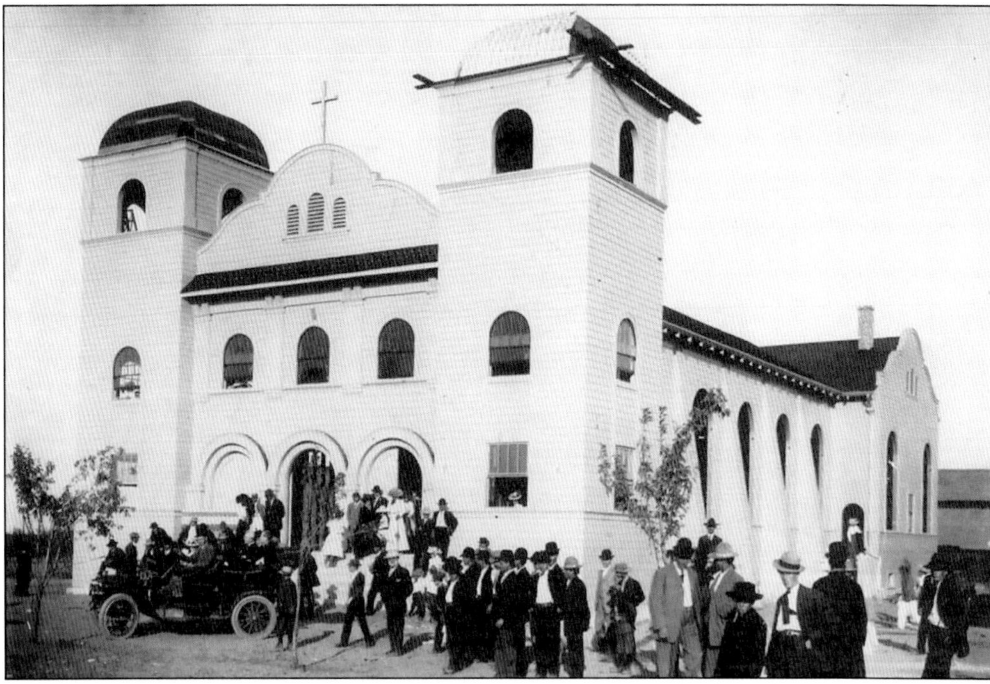

The first Catholic Church in the area was built in 1909 in the Buhach Colony. Frank Souza and Jose F. Freitas donated the land. Known as the Buhach Church, it was consecrated by Bishop Dom Enrique da Silva of Fraganoplois, Portugal, on October 17, 1909. This imposing structure could seat 400 parishioners.

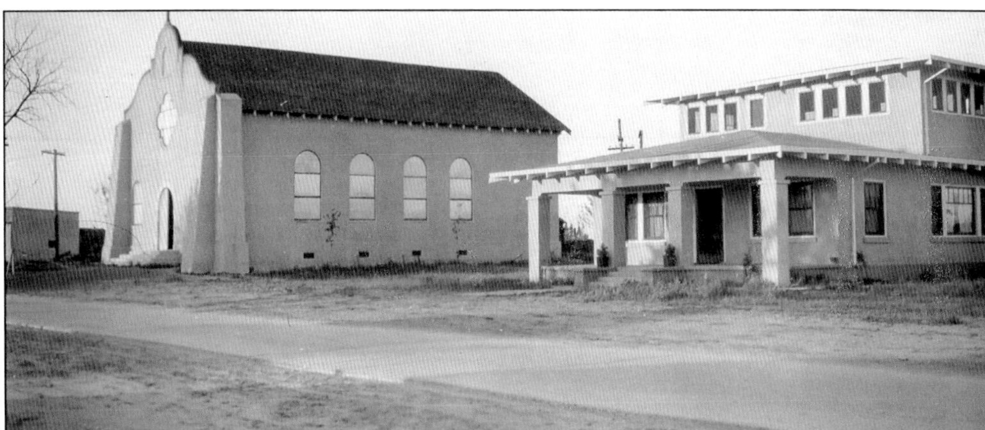

In 1913, Father Cunha built the Atwater Catholic Church. In 1918, the rectory was built on the south side of the church. In 1922, the new diocese of Monterey-Fresno and Father Cordeiro renamed the Atwater Church to St. Anthony's and the Buhach Church Immaculate Conception as a memorial to Bishop Henry da Silva. After 1958, plans were made for a new parish church in Atwater. This was built on the grounds where the Catholic school and convent were erected. A quote by a member of the parish today is "St. Anthony's is so blessed to have a beautiful school, hall, and convent; and our wonderful priest Father Tom Timmings."

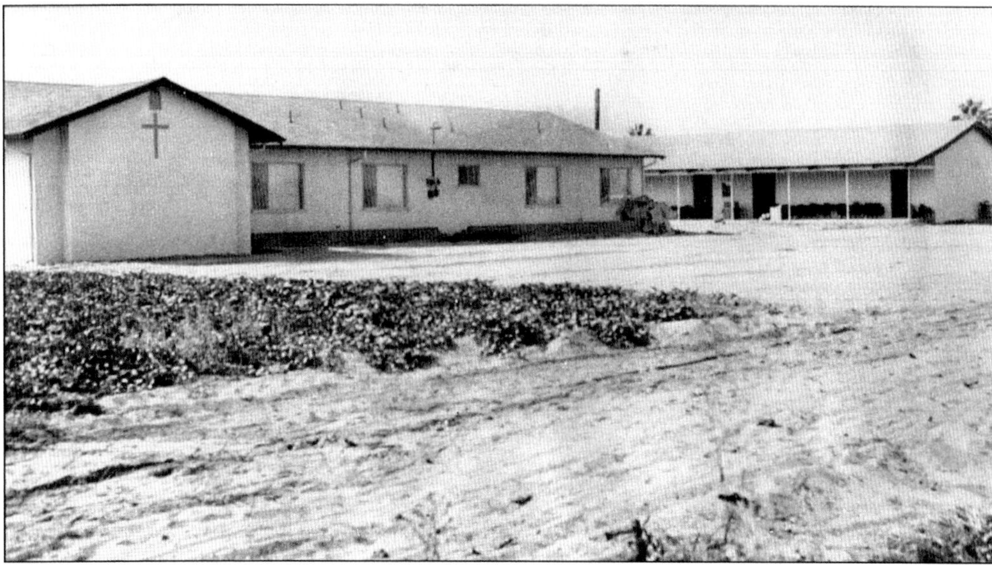

In 1950, Rev. William O' Shea was the promoter of the St. Anthony's Parochial School and Convent. The school is located near the corner of Winton Way and Juniper Avenue. Arden Hutchins, a Merced contractor, and Warren Miller, a masonry contractor, were the builders. Louis Passadori was general chairman of the building and finance committee, and was assisted by Joe Enos, Joseph Trindade Jr., and Alex Klimas. The committee purchased 10 acres for the school grounds in 1952, and classes began on September 21, 1953. The convent has 14 rooms and covers 3,500. It was built at the cost of $40,000 and an addition was added in 1955. The Sisters of the Sacred Heart of Jesus and Mary arrived from England in 1953 to take charge of the school.

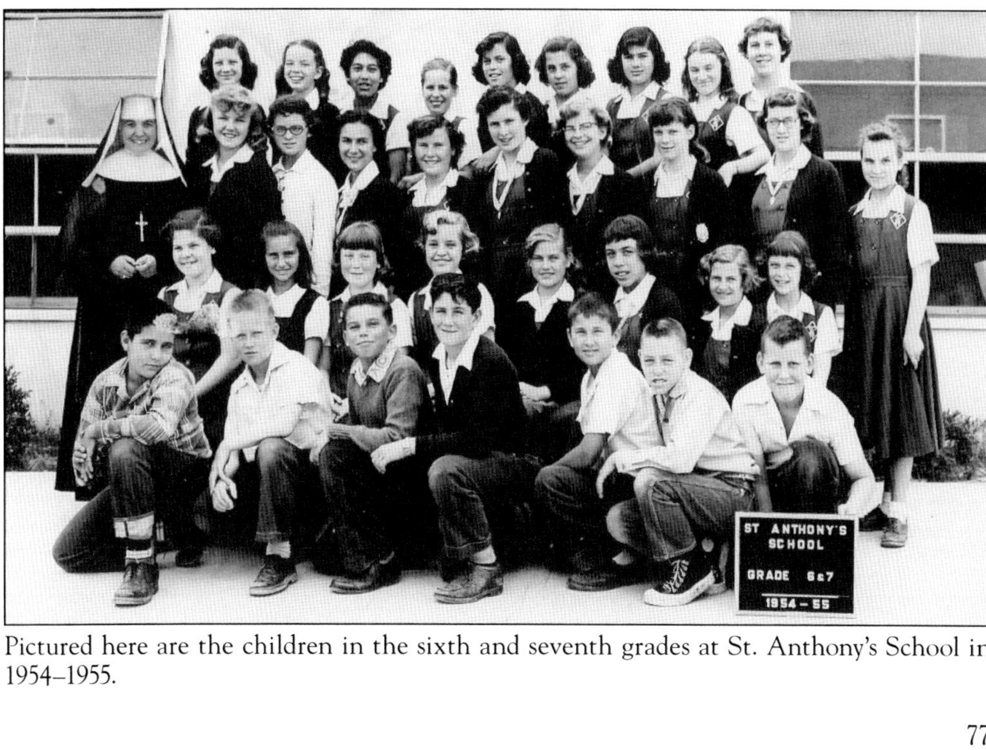

Pictured here are the children in the sixth and seventh grades at St. Anthony's School in 1954–1955.

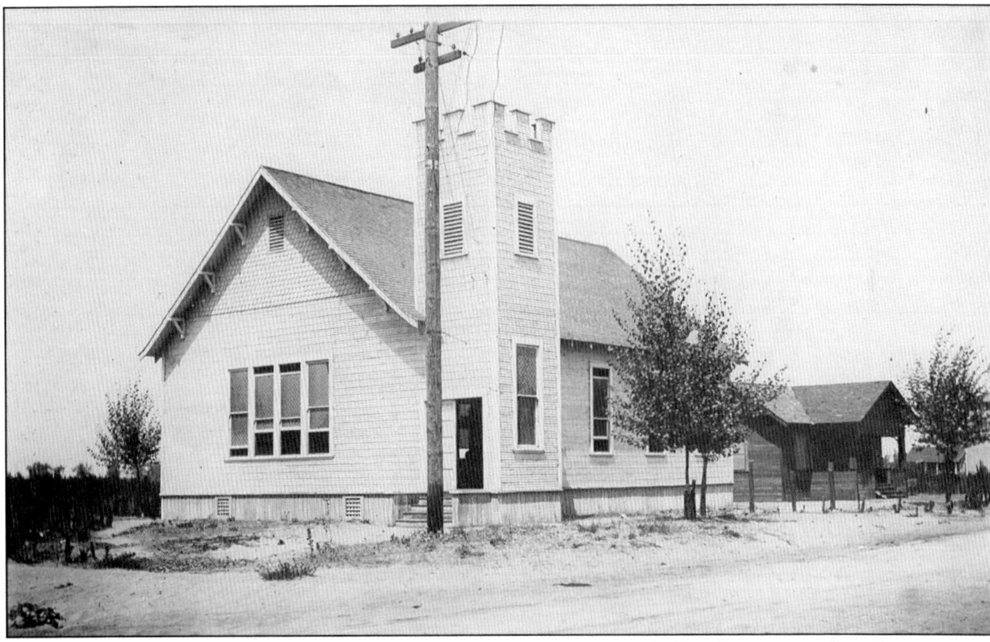

The First Methodist Church was built in 1910 on the corner of Third Street and Cedar Avenue. Rev. George Steed originally organized the church in 1908 and George Bloss Sr donated the lots. This building was dedicated in September 1910 by presiding elder H. W. Peck.

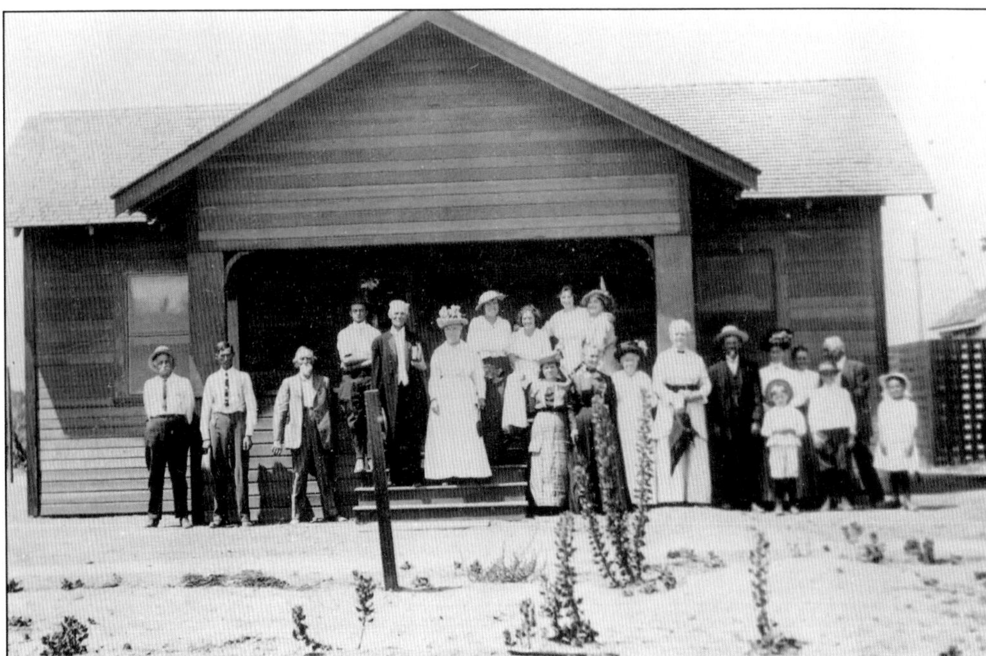

The parsonage for the Methodist Church was built in 1912, right behind the church building on Drakeley Avenue. The pastor was A. P. Peel. The small boys pictured are Stanley and Earl Almquist. Judge William H. Osborn and Mrs. Osborn are standing in the center of the second step. This building no longer exists, and the area where it stood is now a commercial building.

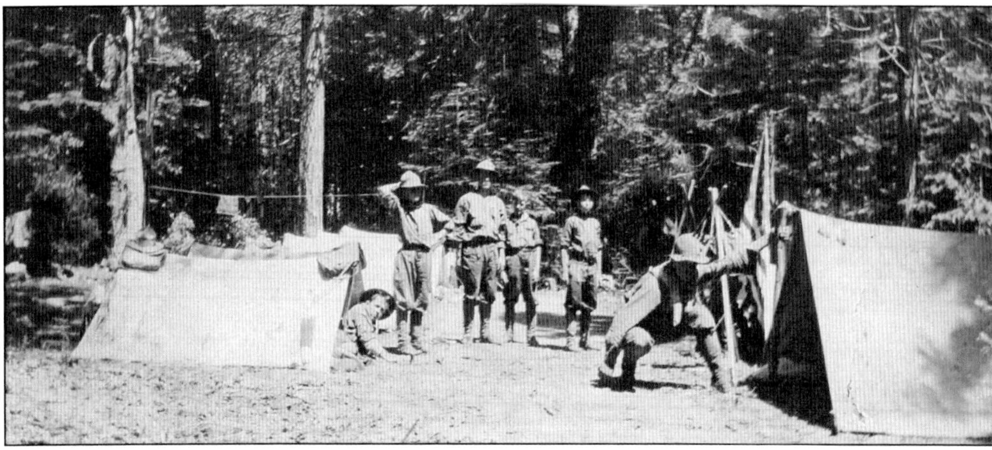

The Atwater Boy Scout Troop No. 1 camps in Yosemite National Park. Rev. Earl Dexter, who was then the pastor of the First Methodist Church, organized the troop in 1914. The scouts did not have a building where they could meet, so most of the meetings were held in the parsonage. Their activities included a couple of trips to Yosemite Valley, traveling by horse and wagon. The first trip by wagon, which carried their supplies and clothing, made it necessary for the boys to travel on foot. It has always been considered an honor for a boy to be a scout, for through its training a boy will be admired for the strong character he will acquire.

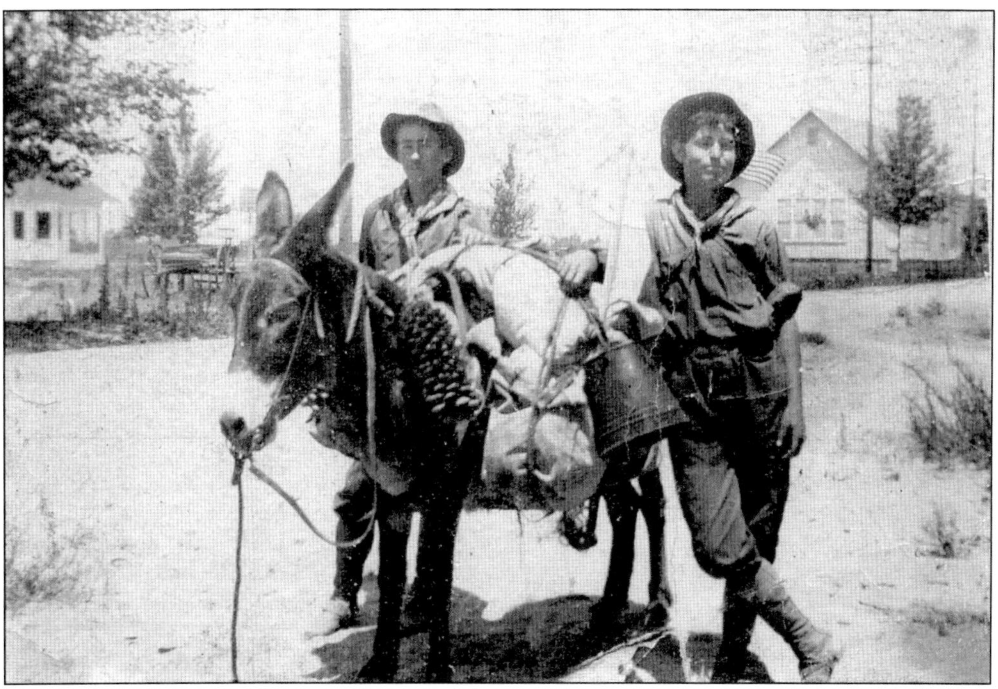

Scouts Olin Thomas and Brent Kirtley return from a camping trip to Yosemite in 1914. The donkey is the famous "Posy Hinds," who had a partner named Rosy. These donkeys, owned by the C. E. "Pete" Hinds family, were often used to carry packs for trips made by the scouts.

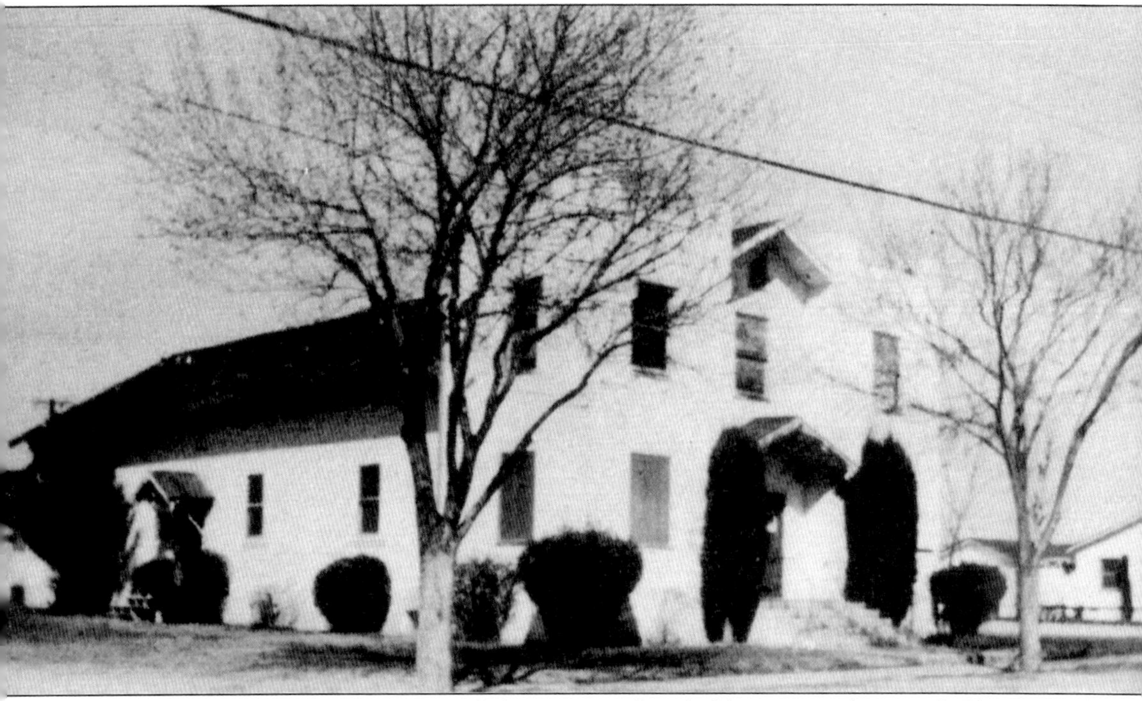

In 1923, Manuel B. Sequeira rented the APC Hall to hold a two-week revival. This revival meeting included plans for a new church and an unknown donor gave land on the corner of Fifth Street and Grove Avenue. The Assembly of God church was finished and dedicated in July of that same year.

The Buhach Colony was famous for producing Buhach Powder, which was an insecticide. Pyrethrum is a small bush-like plant that grows 8 to 10 inches tall. It has a daisy-like flower that when harvested and dried can be ground into a powder. This image is of an actual can that was found in a café in Alaska by Ed Mendes. The people that owned the can would not sell it, but they allowed Ed to photograph it. Fortunately for the historical society, Mr. Mendes shared this photograph.

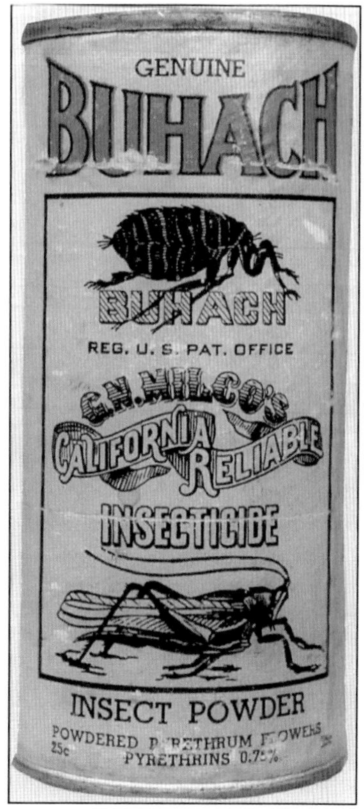

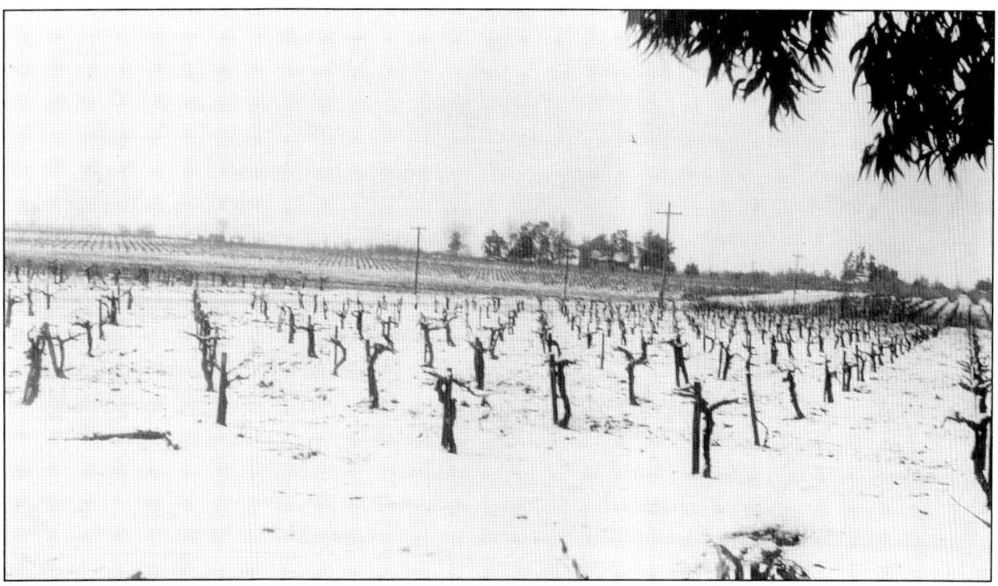

In 1905, the Merced Land and Fruit Company planted the first vineyard (Malagas) south of the original town site. This became known as the Giannini Vineyard. The land was so open and unprotected from winds that rows of bamboo were planted every half-mile or less to serve as windbreaks. Unfortunately, this was the year it snowed and everything froze.

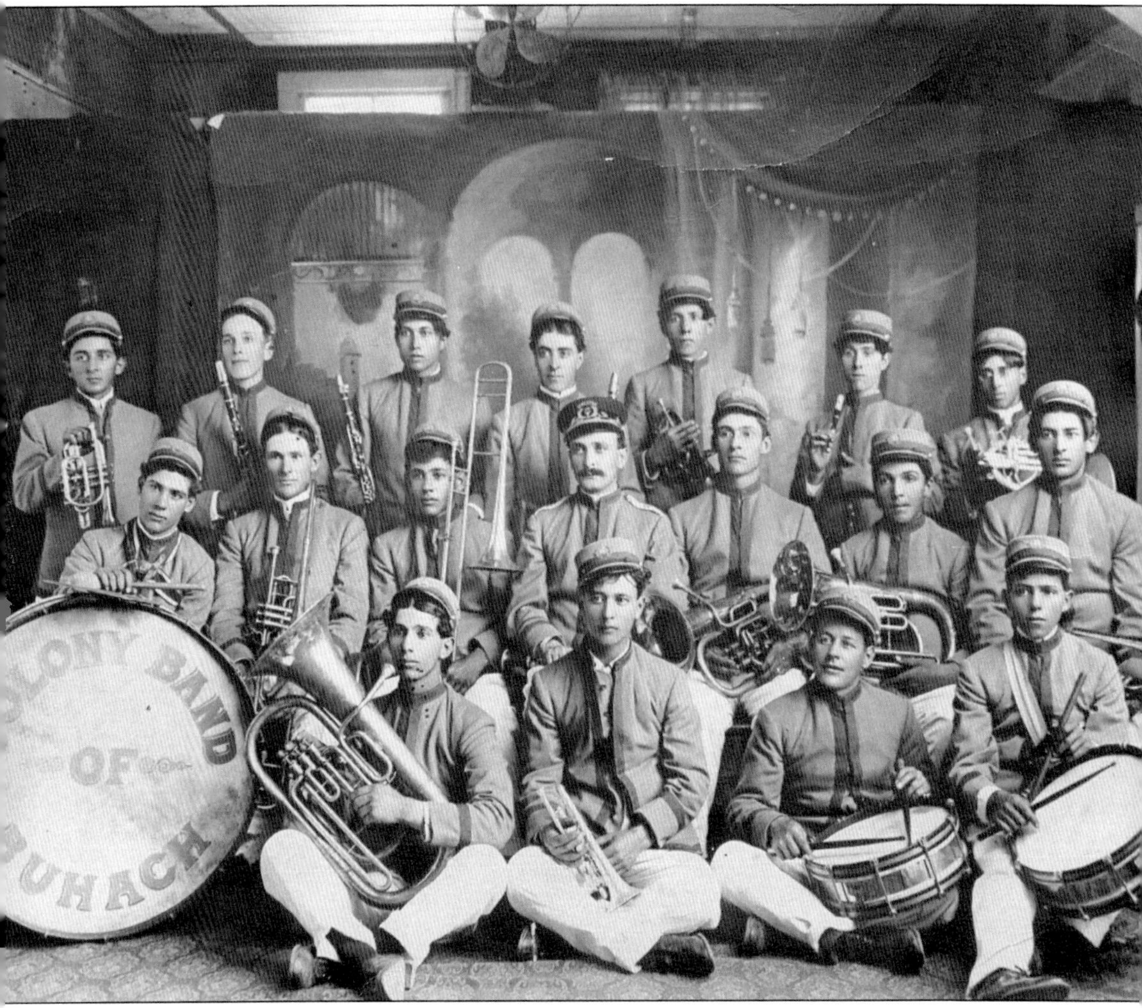

The Colony Band of Buhach was quite prominent in the area at the turn of the century. They appeared in many of the parades and played for the townspeople. Pictured here in 1908, from left to right, are (first row) Joe Silva, Joe Duarte, Paul Thorn, and Frankie Armas; (second row) Anthony Gonzales, Lee Mitchell, Fred Silveira, J. P. S. Costa (director), Frank Pimentel, Joe Mello, and John Baptista; and (third row) Vic Baptista, Dave Rossi, Joe Rogers, Tom Lopez, Tony Freitas, Joe Lewis, and John Duarte.

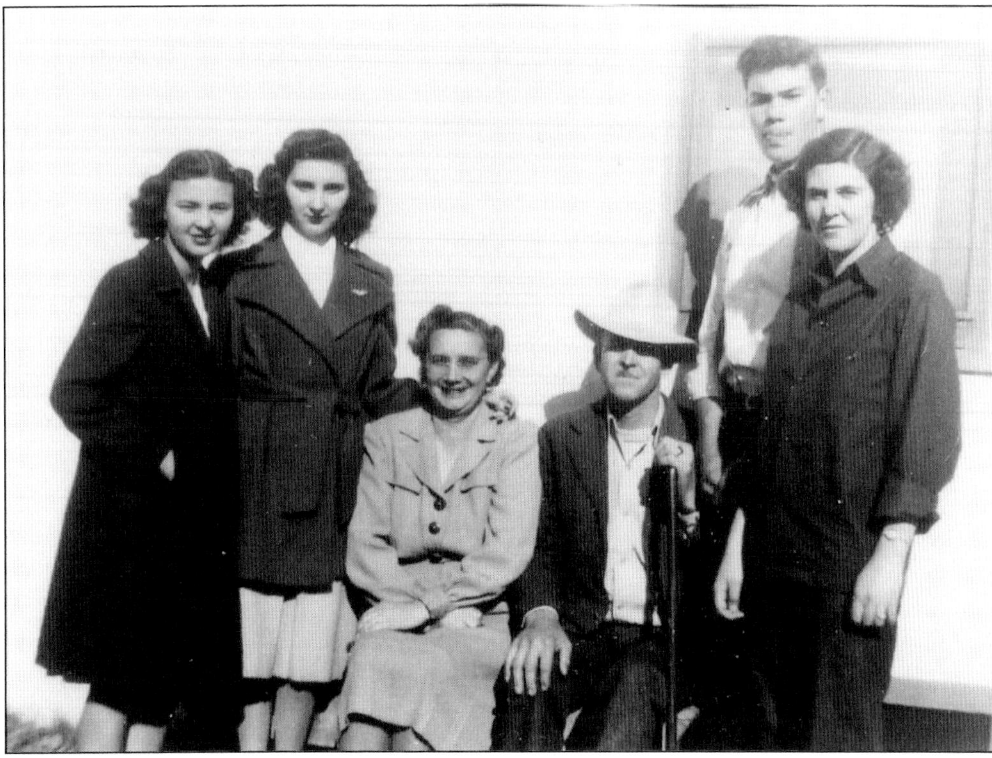

This is the Silveira family of Buhach Colony. Pictured, from left to right, are Josephine (Trindade), Evelyn (Parzell), Mary, Tony "Slim," Fred, and Aileen (Secco). The Silveira's had a farm on Elliot Avenue. Both Mr. and Mrs. Silveira were born in the Buhach Colony.

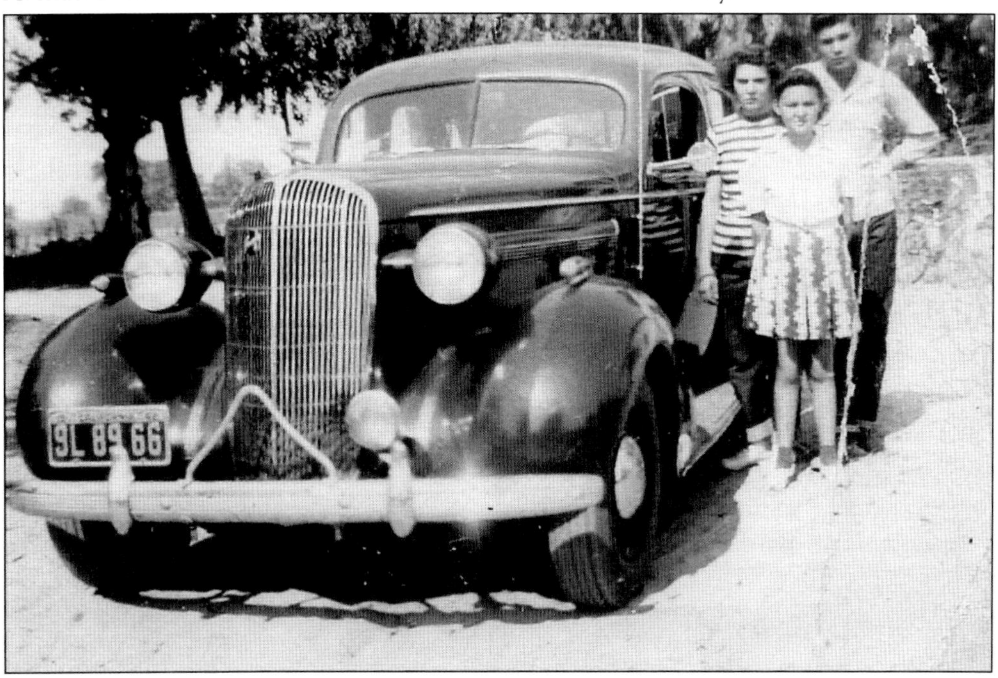

Josephine, Aileen, and Fred Silveira pose with their parent's new 1936 Buick.

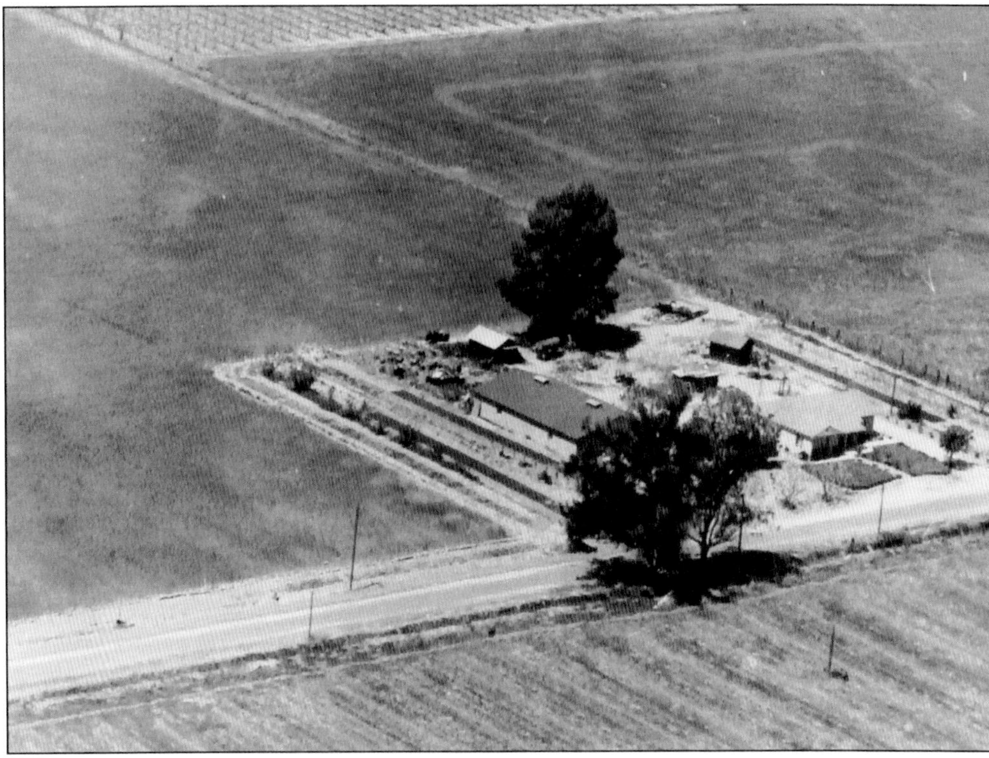

This property that belonged to the Espinola family on Sultana Drive, southwest of Atwater, was part of the Jordan Colony. The Espinola children walked to the Jordan Grammar School just about a half-mile east of this land.

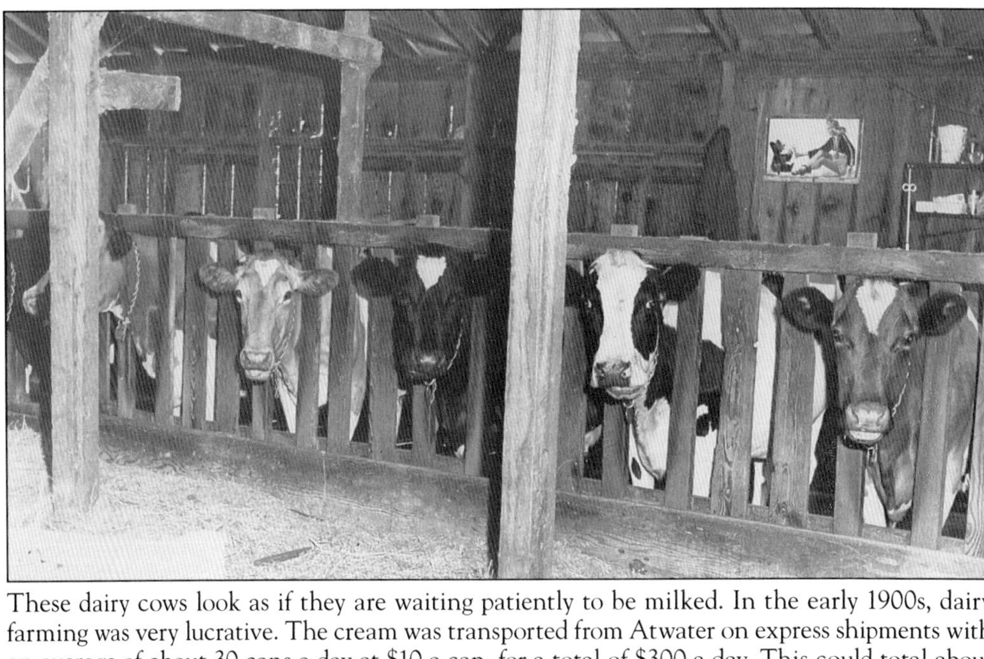

These dairy cows look as if they are waiting patiently to be milked. In the early 1900s, dairy farming was very lucrative. The cream was transported from Atwater on express shipments with an average of about 30 cans a day at $10 a can, for a total of $300 a day. This could total about $9,000 per month for the farmers.

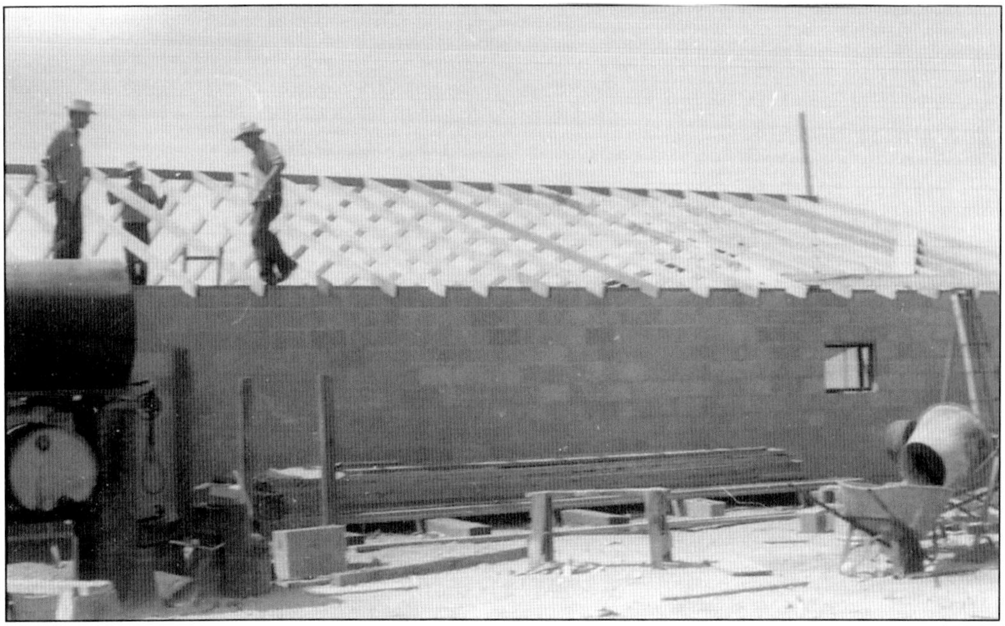

This building on the Espinola farm was once a dairy barn. When William Espinola decided to farm sweet potatoes, this barn was converted to become storage for the harvested potatoes.

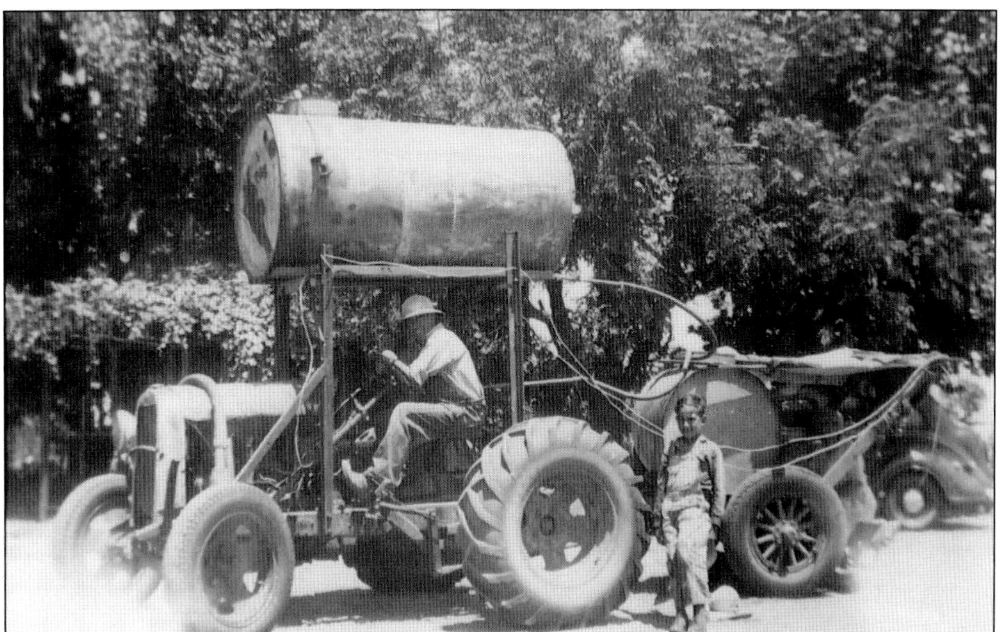

In 1941, William "Bill" Espinola converted a GMC truck into a tractor with a water tank attached. This made growing sweet potatoes much easier as each plant could be watered at the time it was put into the ground. Mr. Espinola was renowned for his inventions.

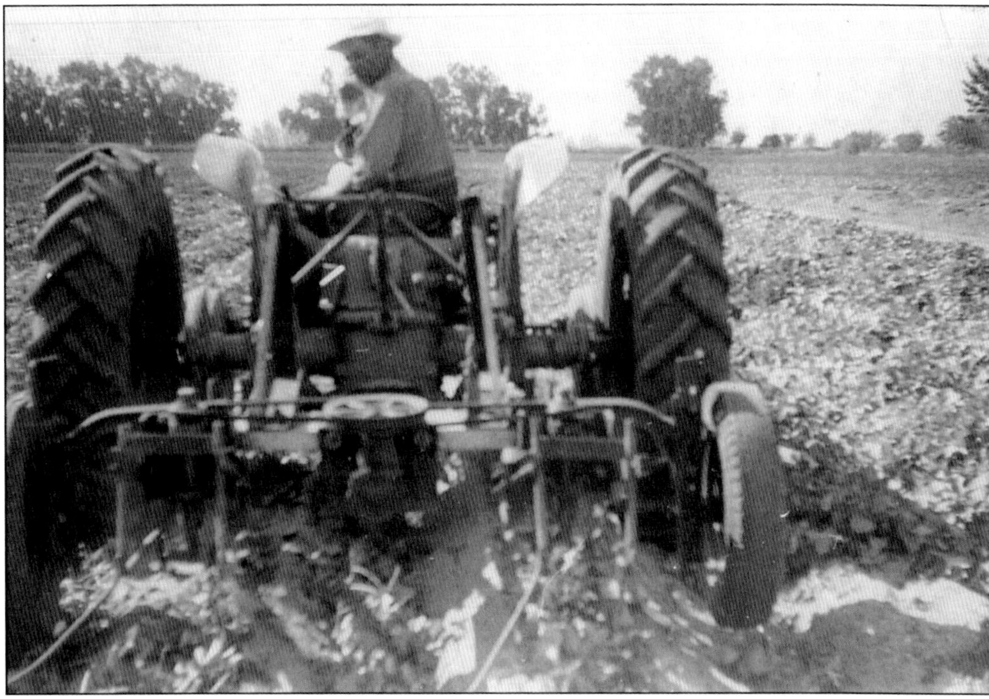

Invented by Bill Espinola, this machine for cutting vines from sweet potatoes before harvest was a true time- and labor-saving device.

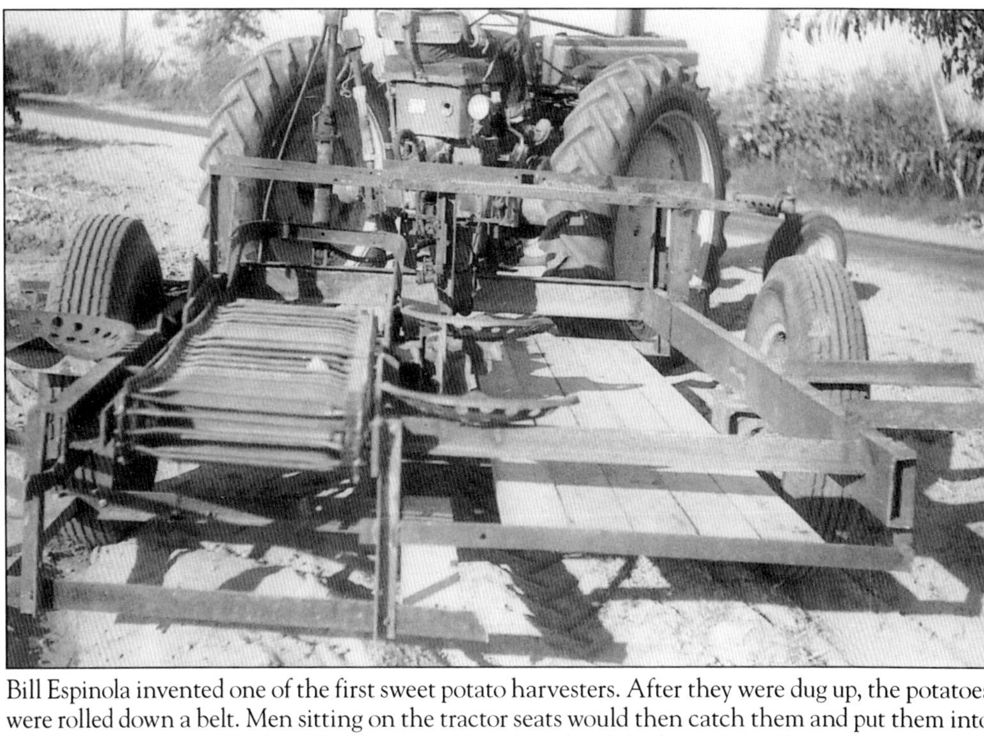

Bill Espinola invented one of the first sweet potato harvesters. After they were dug up, the potatoes were rolled down a belt. Men sitting on the tractor seats would then catch them and put them into boxes, which were carried on the irons on the right side of the harvester. This was just another efficient innovation from Bill's active imagination.

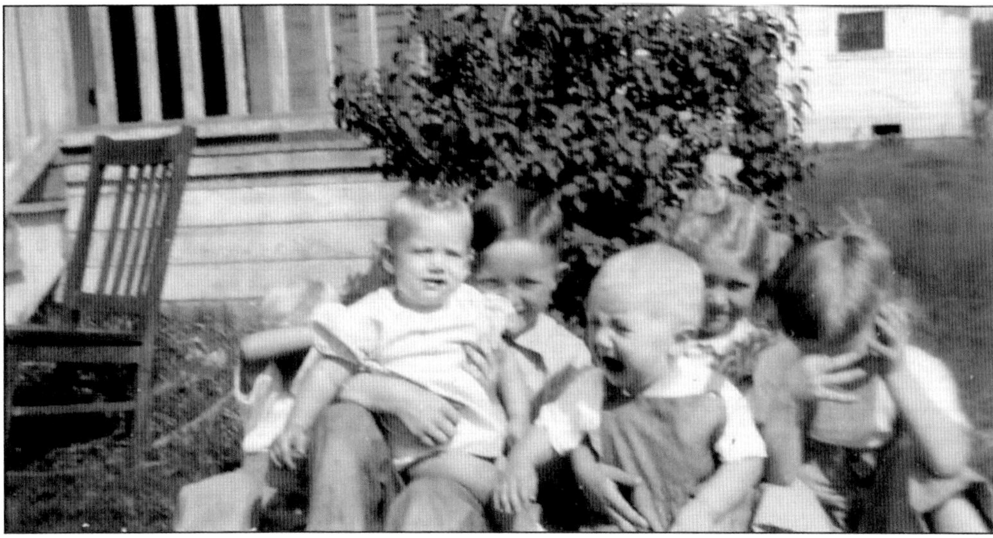

Pictured in the 1940s, the Dixon children, from left to right, are Ronnie, Linda (Coppedgel), Pete, Mike, Eva May (Rampy), and Anthony. The Dixon's lived in the Jordan Colony and the children attended Jordan School.

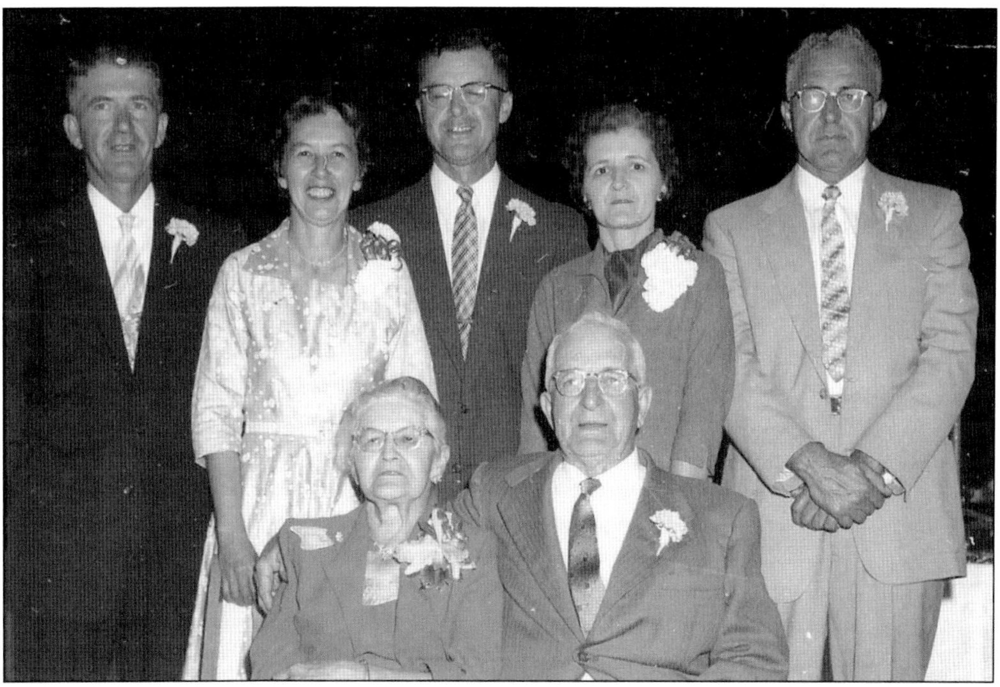

Laurence Arnold came to California from Pittsburgh, Pennsylvania, in 1902 and went into the grocery business in San Francisco. In 1907, he went east and married Miss Clara Stiner of Bluffton, Ohio. In 1910, they decided to move to Fruitland Colony and farm. They had five children. Pictured, seated, are Mrs. and Mr. Arnold. Behind them, from left to right, are Howard (a Fruitland District rancher), Mae Dilley (of Sebastapol, California, Paul (Arnold Hatchery in Merced), Ruth Gill (secretary at the Unified School in Hilmar), and Frank (a realtor in Merced and also a past mayor of the town). Mr. Arnold was a Mason, and Mrs. Arnold a member of OES and a past president of the Women's Improvement Club of Fruitland.

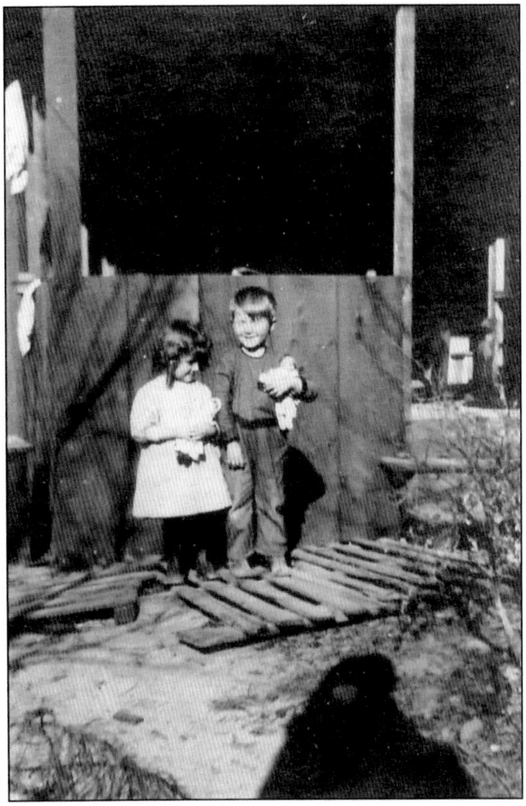

Ruth and Howard Arnold, the youngest children of Laurence and Clara Arnold, are pictured at home in the Fruitland Colony in 1918.

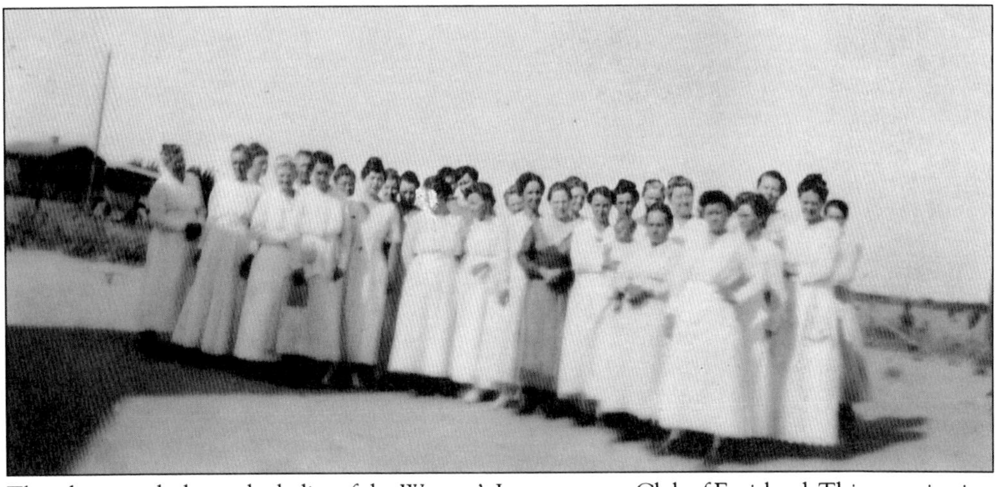

This photograph shows the ladies of the Women's Improvement Club of Fruitland. This organization was formed in 1913 for the specific purpose of maintaining Fruitland Grammar School. Mrs. Cronk and Mrs. Deming were the first presidents for the club. The ladies put together fund-raisers and socials, and with these funds they were able to buy many needed items for the school. The school was also used for community activities. This organization still exists and is one of the oldest women's clubs in the area. Though the school is no longer their specific purpose, the club still meets as a social group and gives donations each year to worthy causes.

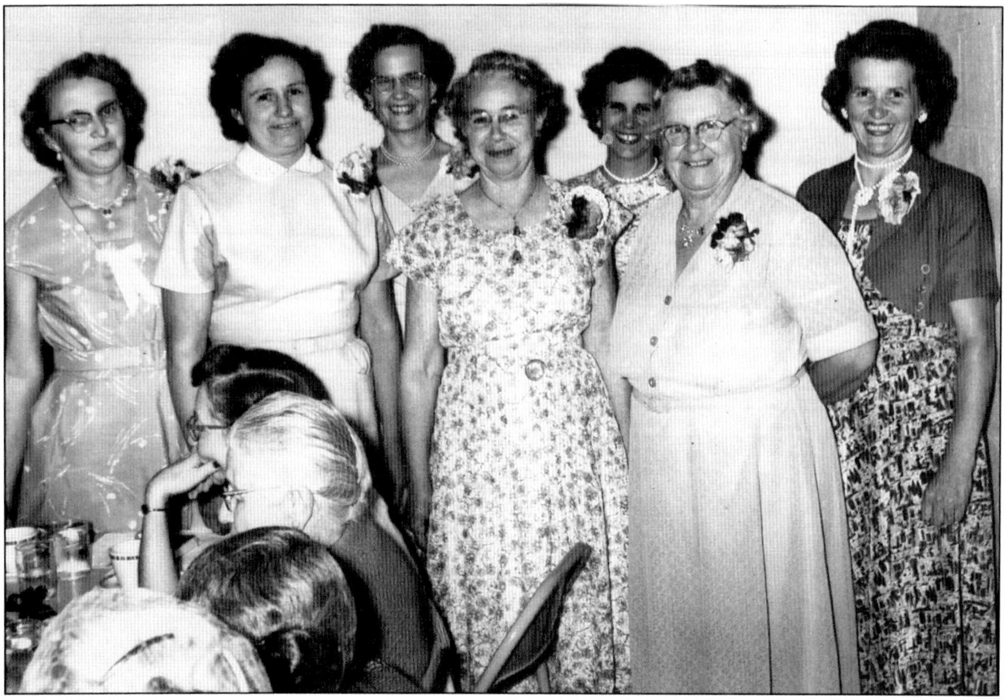

The Women's Improvement Club of Fruitland is shown here in 1957. The school has now been remodeled and is used as a community center (1955–1956). The ladies, from left to right, are (first row) Lois Downey, Mina Rogers, and Marguerite Nielsen; (second row) Agnes Klien, Pam Peterson, Veva Downey, and Mary Lohman.

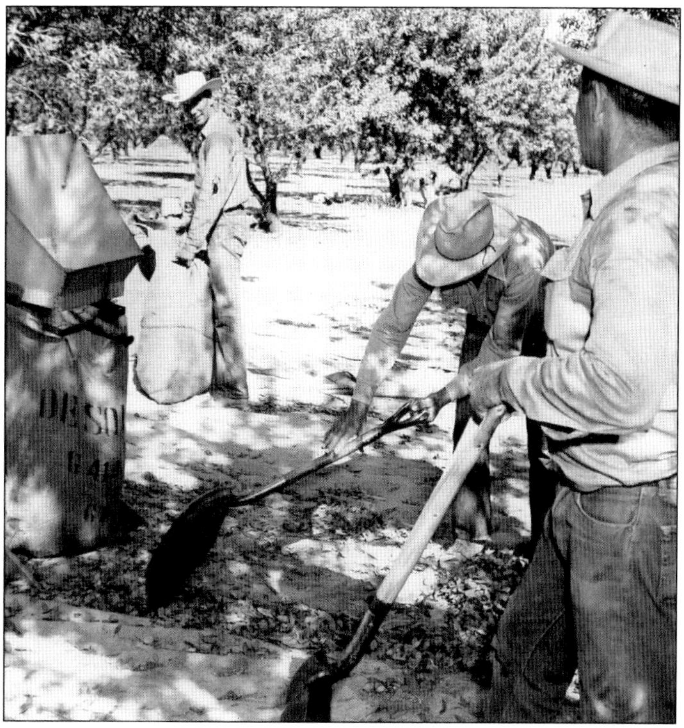

Many acres of land were planted with almonds trees in the Atwater area. This photograph depicts a typical harvest of the nuts, before machines were invented to make the work less labor-intensive.

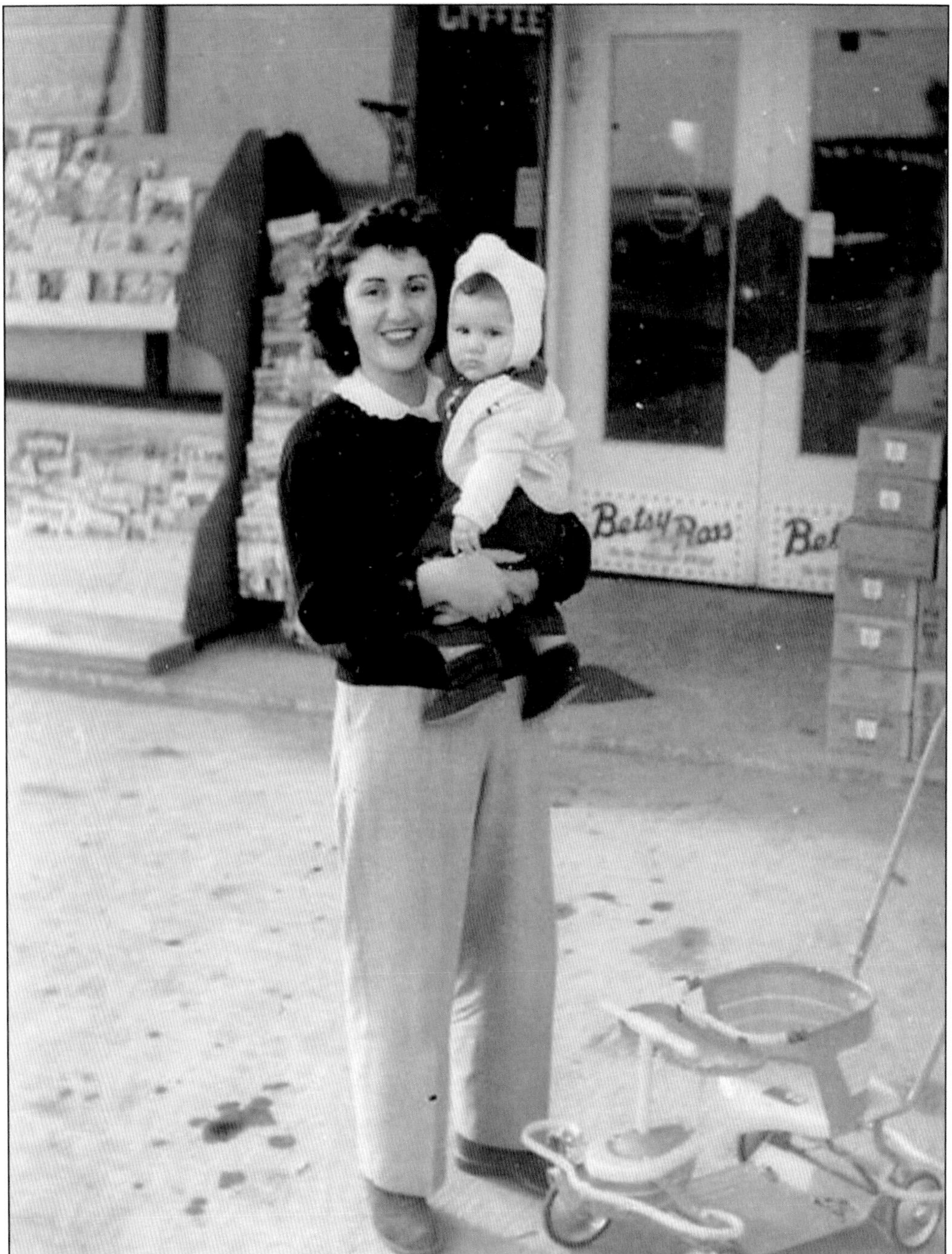

C. J. Pregno opened a small store in 1916 on Arena Way and the north side of Highway 99. In 1948, when the building had to be moved to make way for highway widening, Dan Trindade sold the store to Joe Saca. Joe Saca's in-laws, Joe and Mary Garcia, owned a piece of property on the south side of the highway and agreed to move the building there. Joe and his wife, Laura, ran the business until 1954 when they leased it out and moved into Atwater. In the early 1960s, the store was sold to Chet and Lois Downey. Pictured in front of the store are Laura Saca and her first child, Kathy.

Five

ATWATER'S PROGRESS

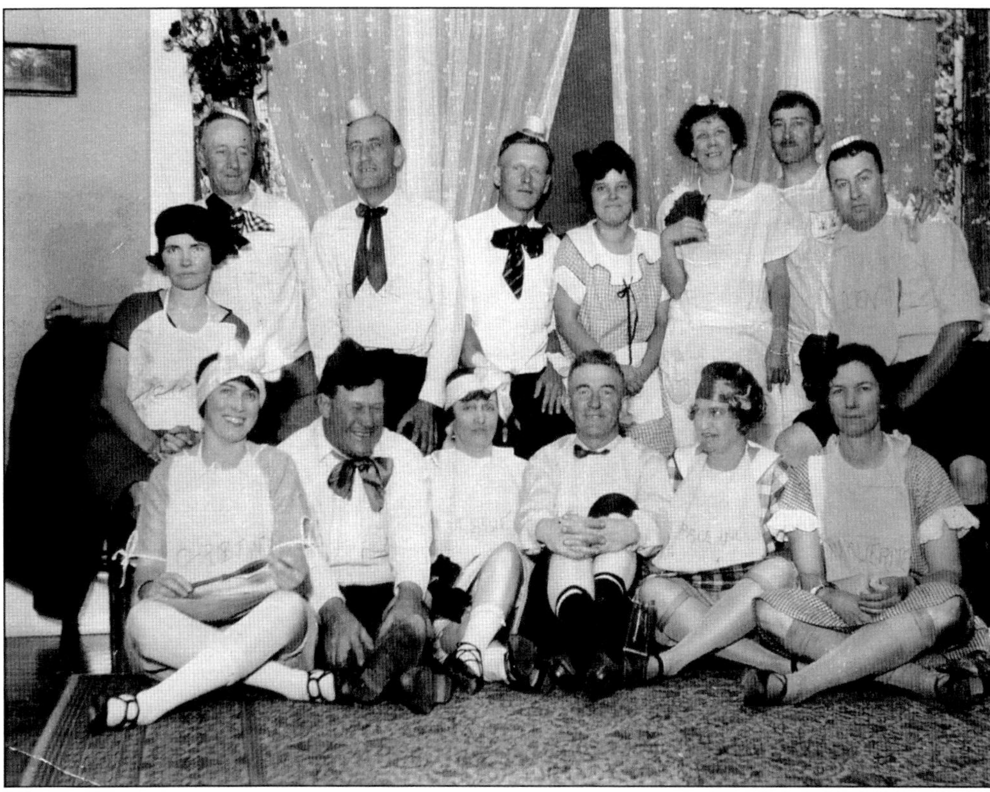

George and Christine Bloss entertain at home. Pictured, from left to right, are (first row) Christine and George Bloss Jr., Jessie Parr, unidentified, Pauline Reed, and Marguerite Heller; (second row) Mae Osborn, Ed Parr, Charles Osborn, Elmer and Dorothy Wood, Dr. and Mrs. Cotton, and E. Allen Heller. No one now living can tell us what this event was; however, it is quite apparent that the adult's are dressed as children, and the hats may indicate that it was a birthday party.

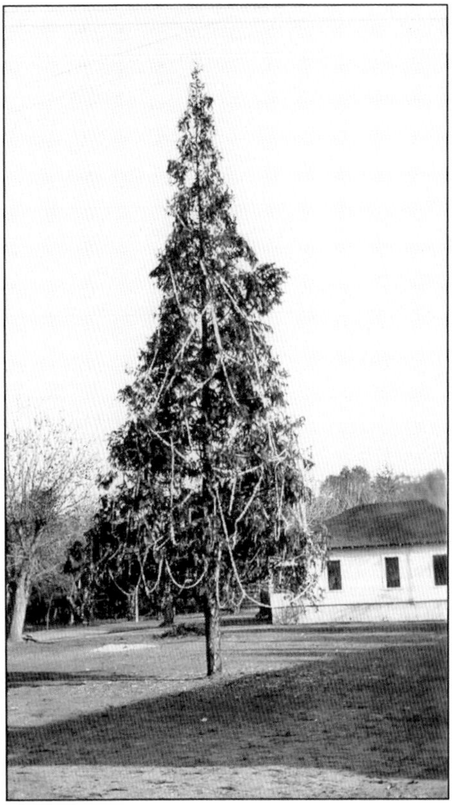

This tree was brought from the mountains and decorated as the town Christmas tree on December 7, 1941. The house in the background was located on Broadway near Second Street. Frank and Mary Fagundes occupied this home for about six years.

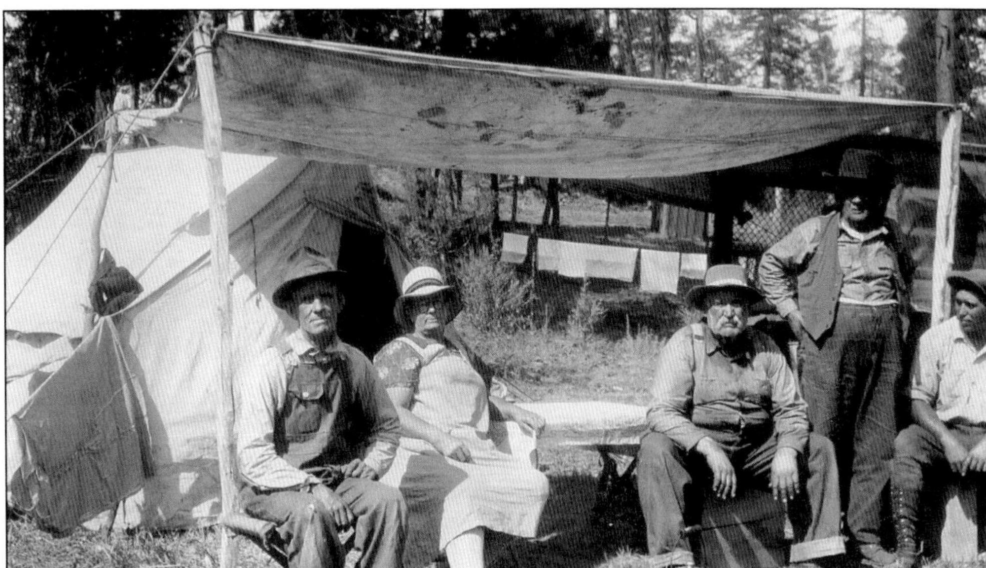

This photograph, taken near White Rock, Mariposa County, California, shows a group camping out. They may have been supplementing their income by gold panning, as many people did this during the Depression. Pictured, from left to right, are William Alexander Johnson, Verlie Mae Oxford Johnson (from Atwater), Uncle Bill Oxford, Berry Hill Oxford, and Joe Rodgers.

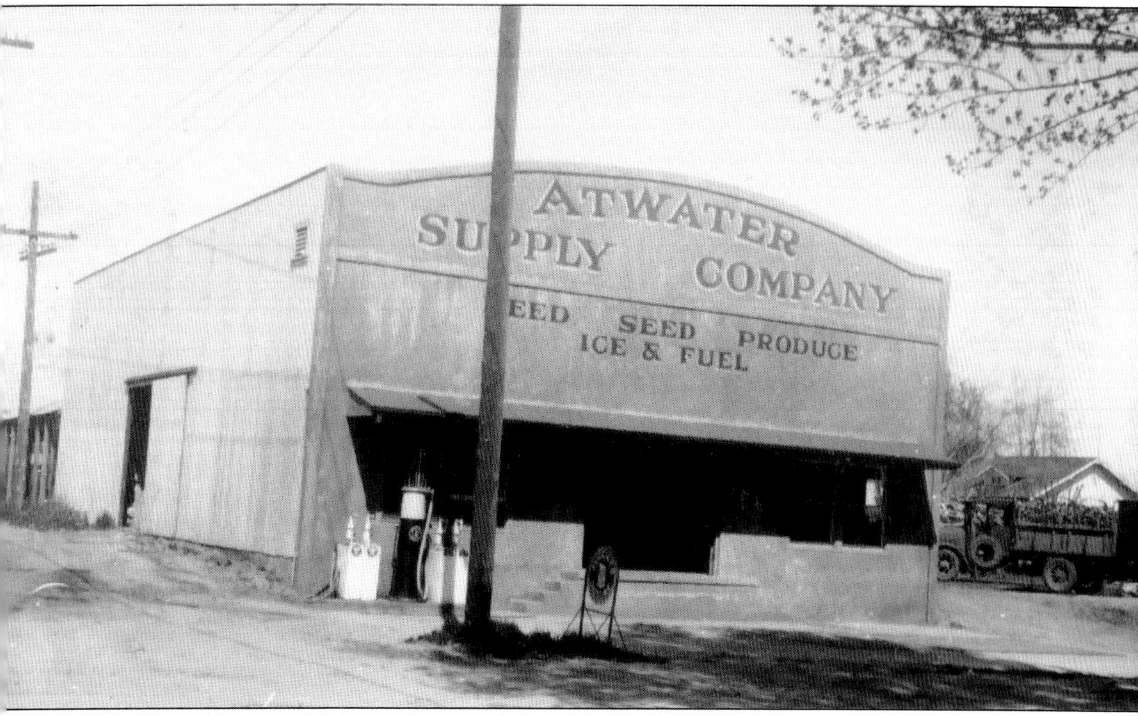

Joe Owen and Bennett Johnston entered into partnership in a feed store in 1918. The first business was at one end of the old Mitchell warehouse. When the building burned in 1920, they moved into a small building on Broadway where Joe remained until 1926, then moving into the building pictured above on Fourth Street, close to Cedar Avenue. Paul Owen, Joe's son, ran the business until he retired and sold it to John Freitas. About 1985, Mr. Freitas moved the business into an old sweet potato packing shed on Atwater Boulevard, and two years later it was sold to the Fragulia family. Today it is the Atwater Feed store. The building on Fourth Street was demolished in the 1980s.

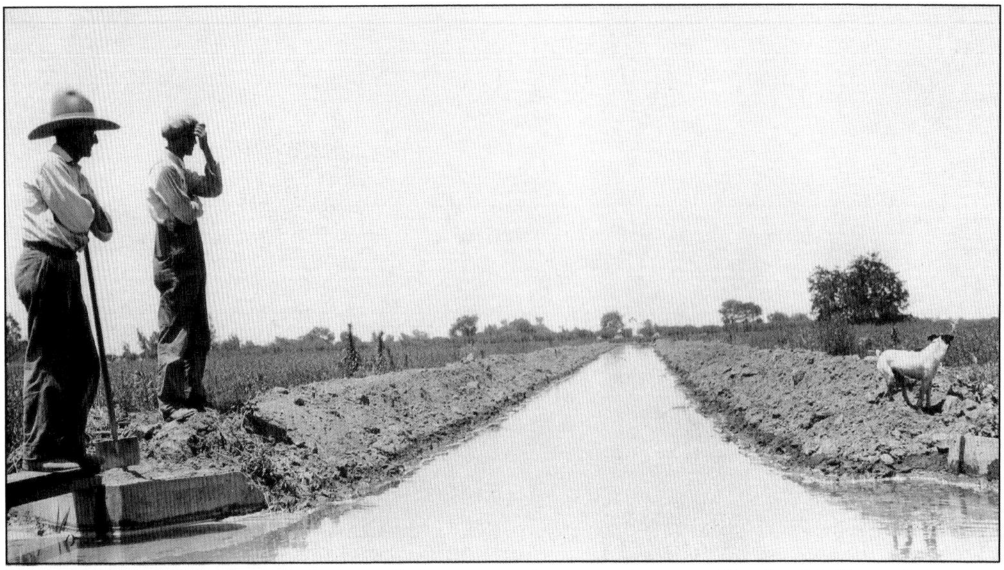

Pictured here is an early irrigation canal. Its source of water is the great Crocker-Huffman Irrigation System of Merced County, which covered the Atwater area and was eventually bought out by the Merced Irrigation District. The quantity and quality of farm goods would never have been produced without irrigation from the Merced River.

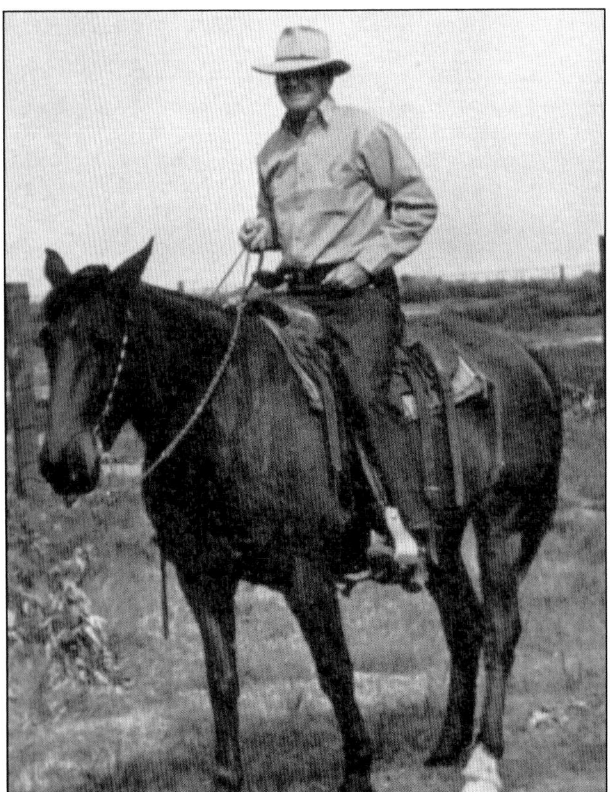

Even though Frank Furrer was born in the Mission District of San Francisco, he became interested in livestock as a very young man in association with his father, who was a cattle buyer. After serving in World War I, he joined his father as a partner in cattle buying, with their headquarters in Merced. Frank had a retail meat market there for many years. In 1934, he and his family moved to Atwater and bought the meat plant on Winton Way. It had been owned by Joe Mancebo but was originally known as the Baireuther Abattoir. In 1945, he sold the Abattoir to four employees: Tom Hallahan, Manuel Bolcao, Ed Pinheiro, and Joe Rodell, who operated under the name of the Atwater Meat Company. Frank continued to raise Hereford cattle on his two ranches south of Atwater, and the family lived in Atwater on First Street.

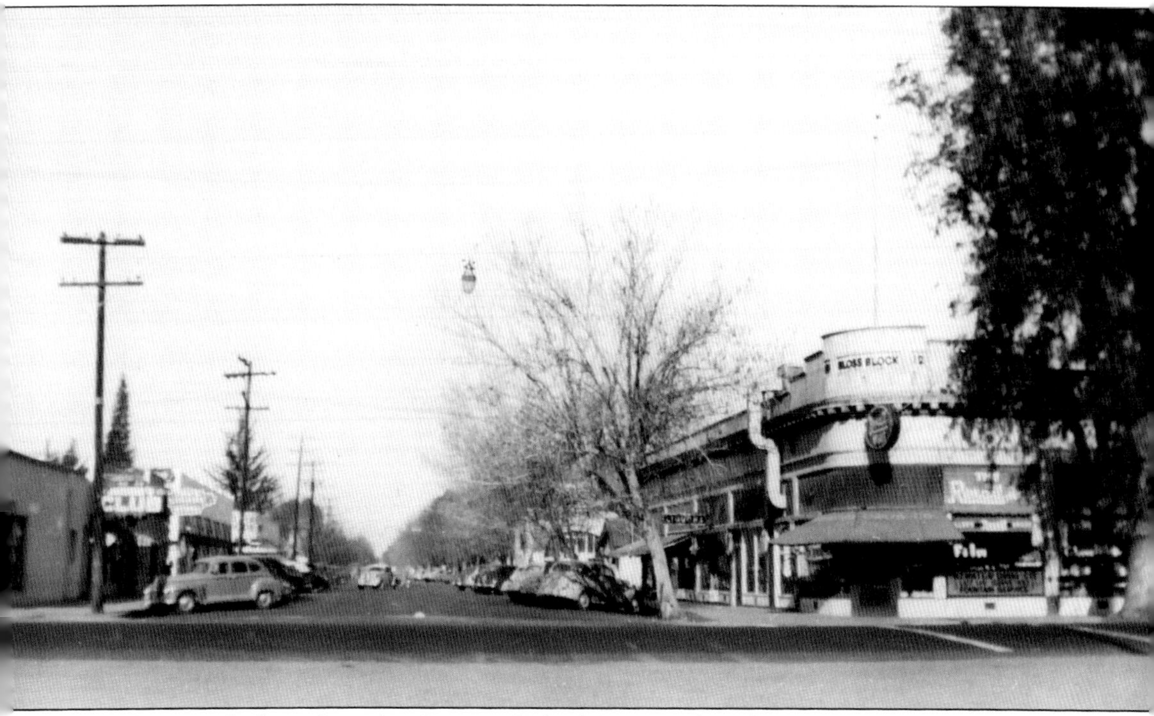

This photograph shows how the Corner of Third Street and Highway 99 (Atwater Boulevard) appeared in the mid-to-late 1930s. Heller's Drug Store still occupied the corner of the Bloss Block Building, but many changes have taken place across the street. Where there was once an ice cream parlor and a garage, there are now two bars. Passadori's new building is on the left side of the image toward Broadway. There appears to be a streetlight suspended from an overhead line in the center of Third Street.

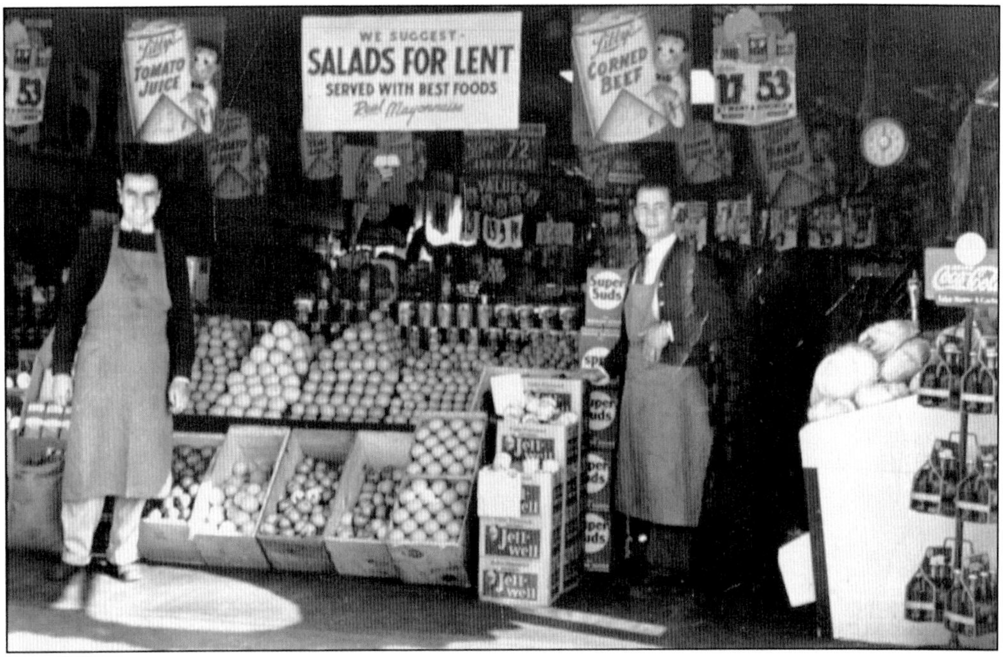

Charles Hendricks, on the left, and Louie Guveria clerked at the Atwater Cash Grocery in the late 1930s.

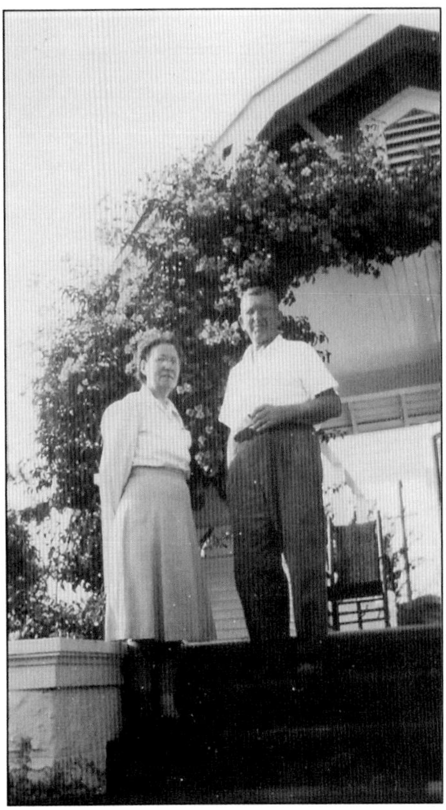

Mr. and Mrs. Gusinde operated a bakery on Highway 99 (Atwater Boulevard) from the 1920s to 1946. It was next door to the old Mitchell Hall, which was replaced by the Townsend building after Mitchell Hall burned. The Gusinde's lived in the house next to the bakery on the corner of Second Street and Highway 99. It was built and occupied by Dr. Kinney in 1910. The home is still on site. The building that was the bakery was rented to Mrs. Grissom in 1951, and she opened a second hand furniture store.

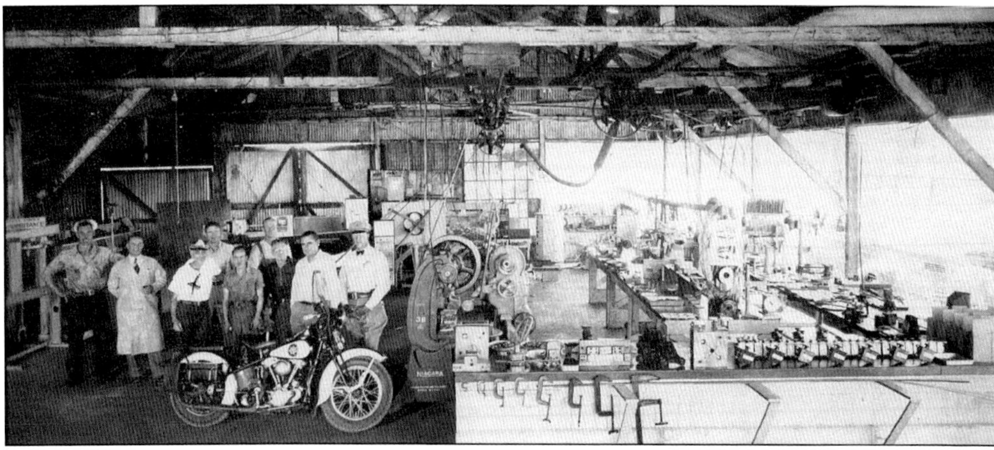

This c. 1939 photograph shows the interior of Waltamath's Machine Shop on Highway 99 and Sierra Vista Street. Pictured, from left to right, are Ed Wilhoite, Ray Waltamath, Vern Cassaretto, five unidentified people, and Chief of Police Bill Carlan. The motorcycle is a 1939 Harley Davidson, owned by the Atwater Police Department. Ed Wilhoite eventually went into partnership with his brother-in-law W. M. "Hogie" Hogancamp, and they formed E&H Garage at Highway 99 (Atwater Boulevard) and Fourth Street, in business until 1949. They then moved to the E&H Garage building, which is still in operation and now owned by Tony Pedro.

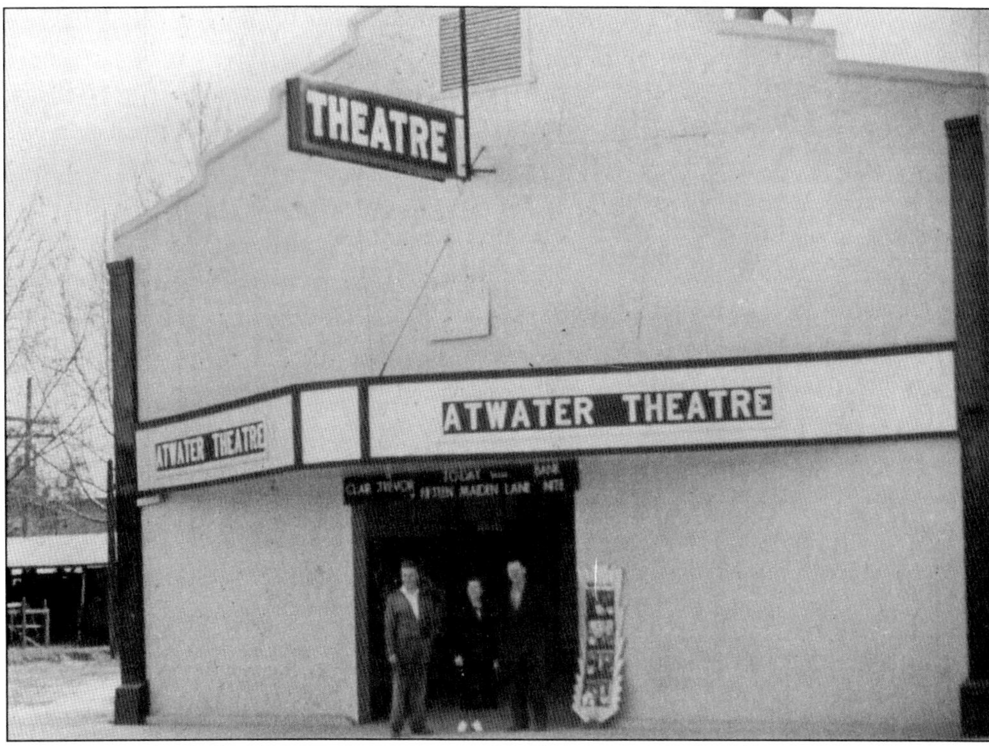

Mr. Serfuntes built this theatre at the corner of Cedar Avenue and Fifth Street in 1923. Movies had previously been shown at the old Mitchell Hall until it burned that same year. Several people owned the theatre in later years before Stanley Court Sr. bought it in 1936. His son Stan Court Jr. operated the business until it closed. Pictured, from left to right, are Frank Fagundes, Sarah Fagundes (Hendricks), and Stanley Court Sr.

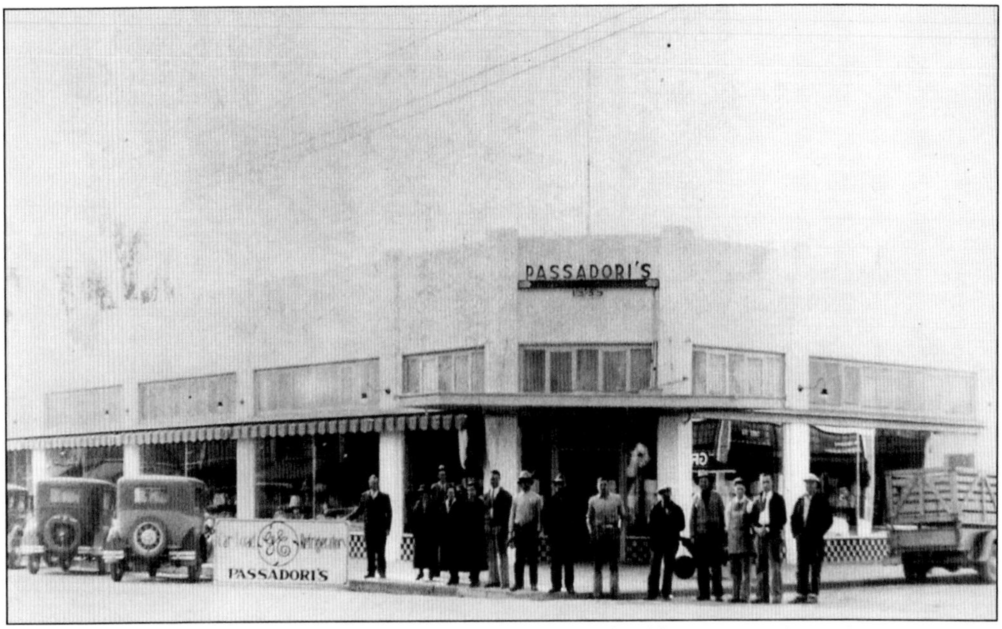

Louis Passadori erected this building in 1935. Passadori's had been a supplier of groceries and hardware for many years. This family-owned business is still in operation today, well known for the hardware store as well as their large inventory of fine furniture and appliances.

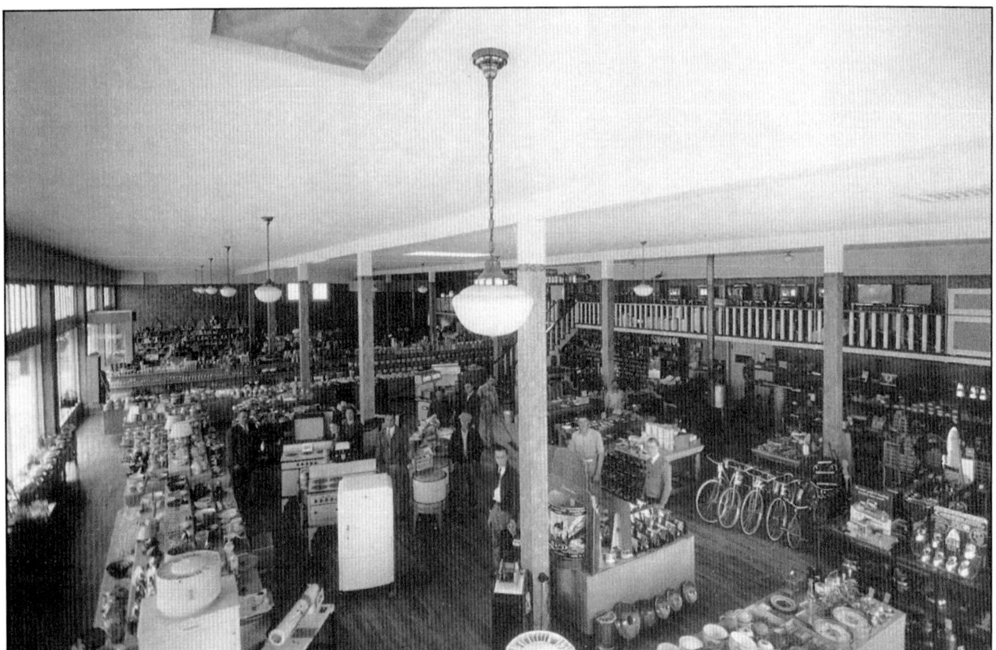
This inside view of Passadori's store in the 1930s, shows its typically diverse inventory: refrigerators, cook stoves, washing machines, dishes, bicycles, and many other items needed by a growing community.

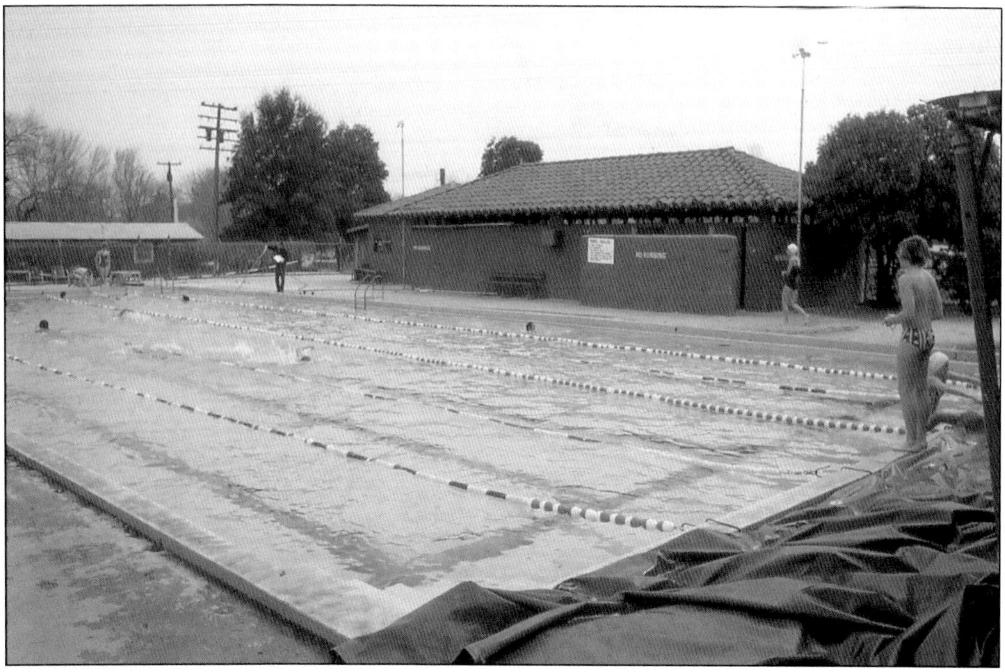

In 1935, the United States Works Progress Administration was set up to provide work for men and women during the Depression. Several projects in Atwater were completed by the WPA. One was the Atwater Plunge; the material was furnished by the late George Bloss Sr., and labor by the WPA. This public swimming pool was enjoyed by the community until it was removed in the 1980s. It was located where the branch of the Merced County Library is today, on the corner of Grove Avenue and Third Street.

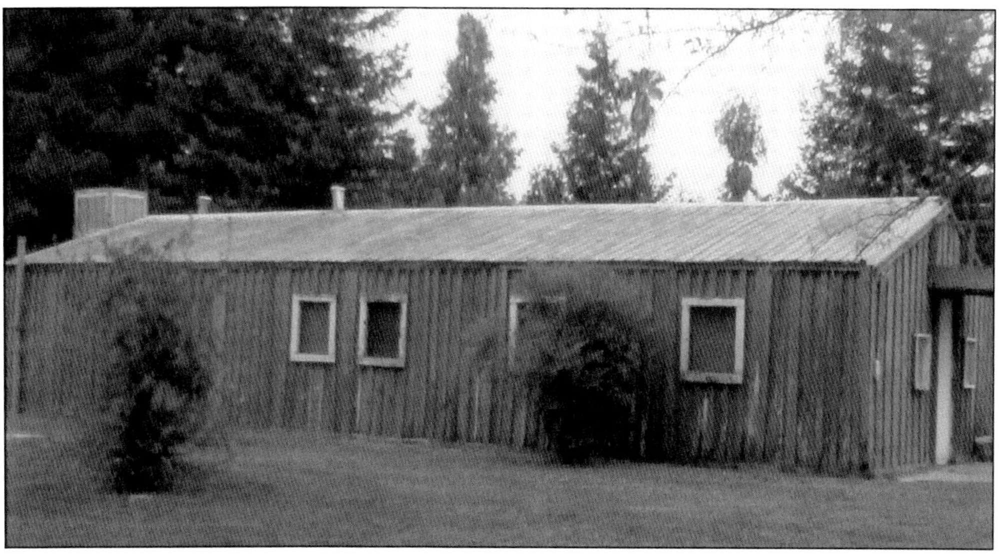

Adjacent to the Atwater Plunge is this building known as the "Scout Hut." Boy Scout Troop number 29 collected newspapers and sold them for the money to purchase this old building and have it moved to the site next to the Plunge. It originally was a fish market that was located on Highway 99 between Fourth and Fifth Street. It is not known what happened to the structure, but it was replaced between 1950 and 1954 by a Quonset hut that is still in use by the Girl Scouts.

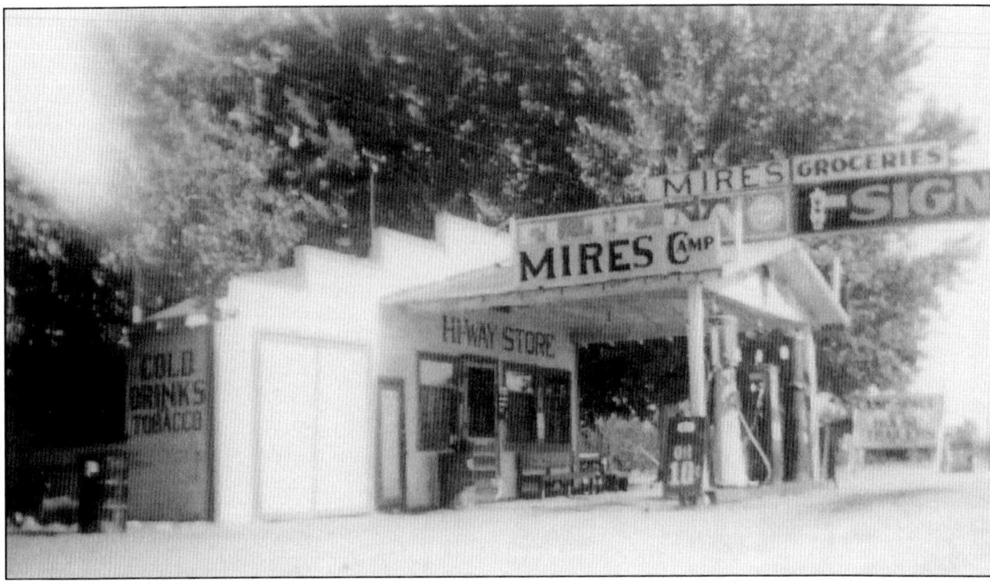

Isaac and Nilla Mires bought this Signal gas station in 1938. Besides the station and store, they also had cabins and provided campsites. The building was erected in 1936 and was located on Highway 99 west of Atwater. This business was leased to another individual in 1960 but burned in 1984.

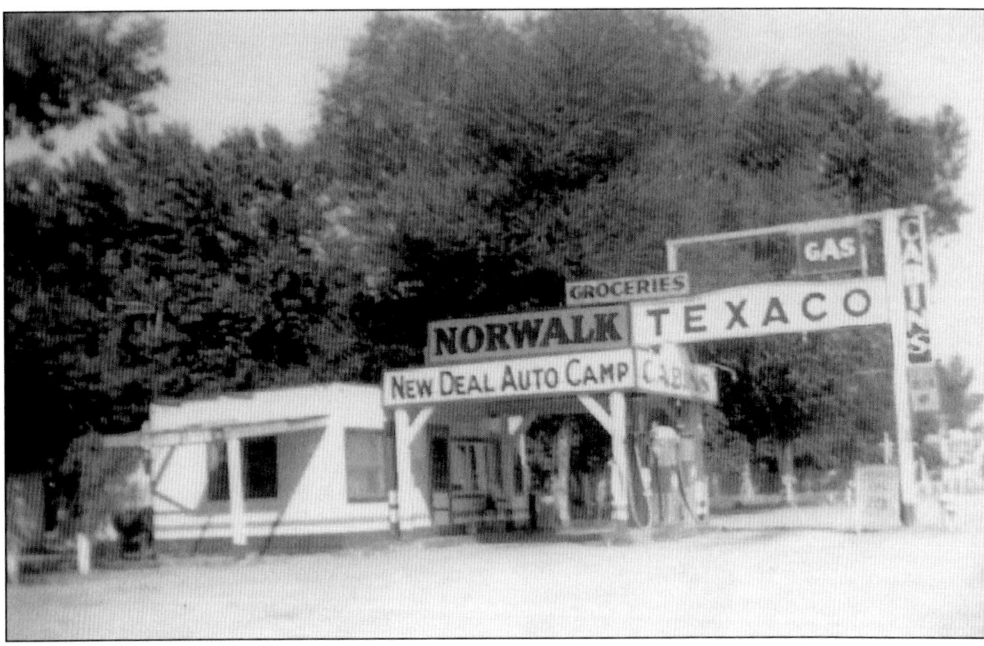

When the Meirs first came to Atwater, they leased part of this station that was located next to the Signal gas station that they bought two years later. The Norwalk Texaco was owned by the Whitmore family and also offered overnight cabins and groceries. This station burned in 1984 along with the Signal station. The site of both service stations is now a parking lot for the Atwater open-air market that takes place on Thursday and Sunday of each week.

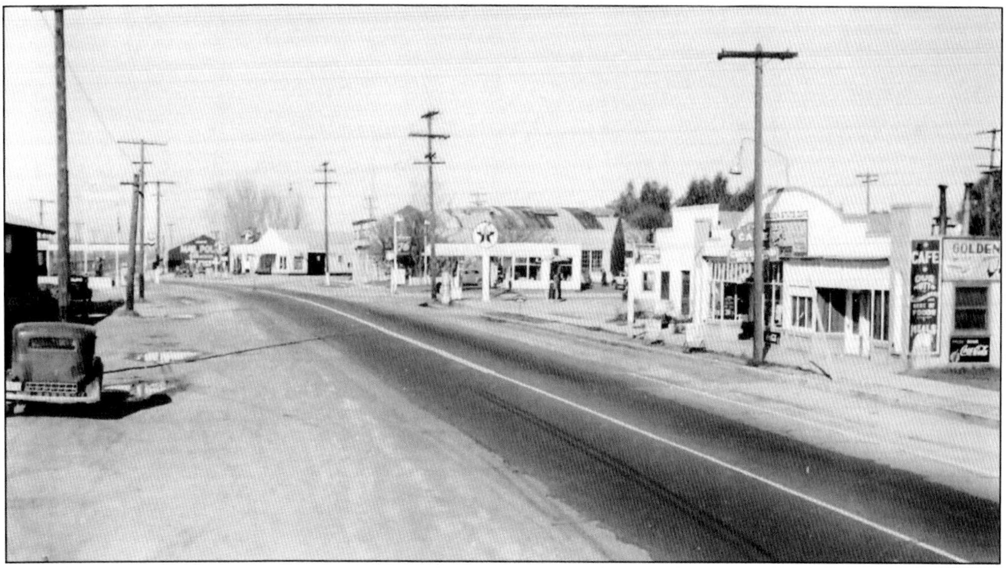

This 1940 photograph of Highway 99 (Atwater Boulevard) looks west. On the left-hand side are the edge of Joe Souza's packing shed and the Chevron station on the southeast corner of Winton Way. The old Golden State Café across the street was also a stop for Greyhound buses. The community also knew this building as the Travelers Café. The Texaco station site would become a modern Shell station in 1946 that was built by Bert Avellar and Francis "Macy" Maciel. The site would ultimately become a Kentucky Fried Chicken franchise. The Union 76 station building is still in the same location but now operates under a different name as an independent supplier. The domed building was Atwater Glass for many years. The white building on the northwest corner of Winton Way was originally Mike Delissio's garage, and in front is Silva's Signal service station. The large building in the distance with the Mail Pouch sign is where Waltamath's Machine Shop and Ed Wilhoite's first garage was located.

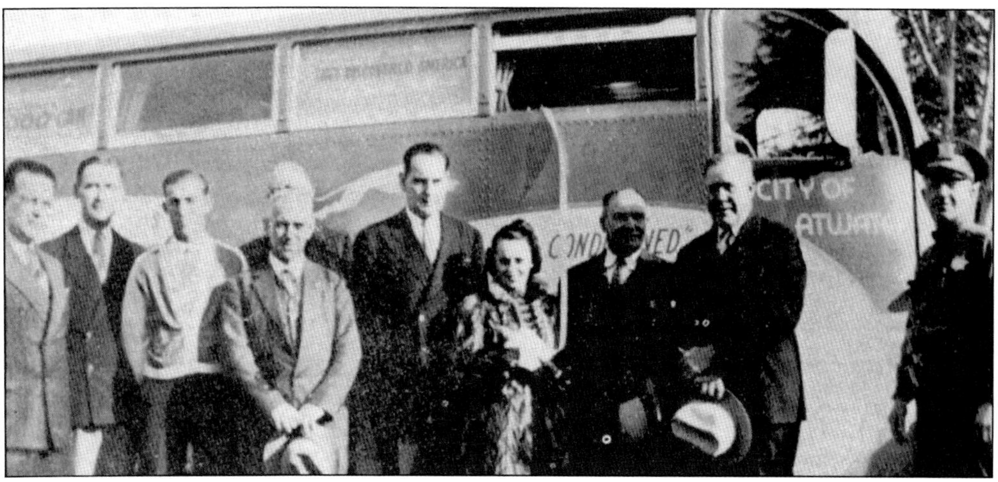

This photograph, taken in the late 1940s, shows the Greyhound bus named *The City of Atwater.* In 1929, The Pacific Greyhound Lines was granted a franchise to operate in the San Joaquin Valley. The larger and more dependable bus schedule allowed the citizens of small towns to travel for pleasure as well as business.

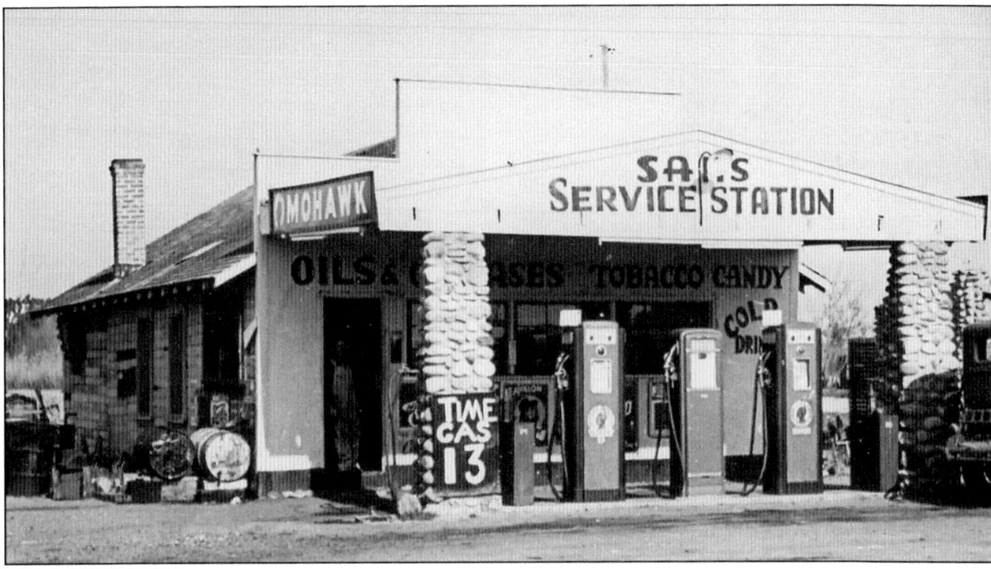

Sam's Mohawk service station was located on Highway 99 west of Atwater, where the present-day freeway on-ramp is located. Sam built this station and moved into it in 1941 after farming sweet potatoes and wine grapes for several years. This photograph was taken when the station was new.

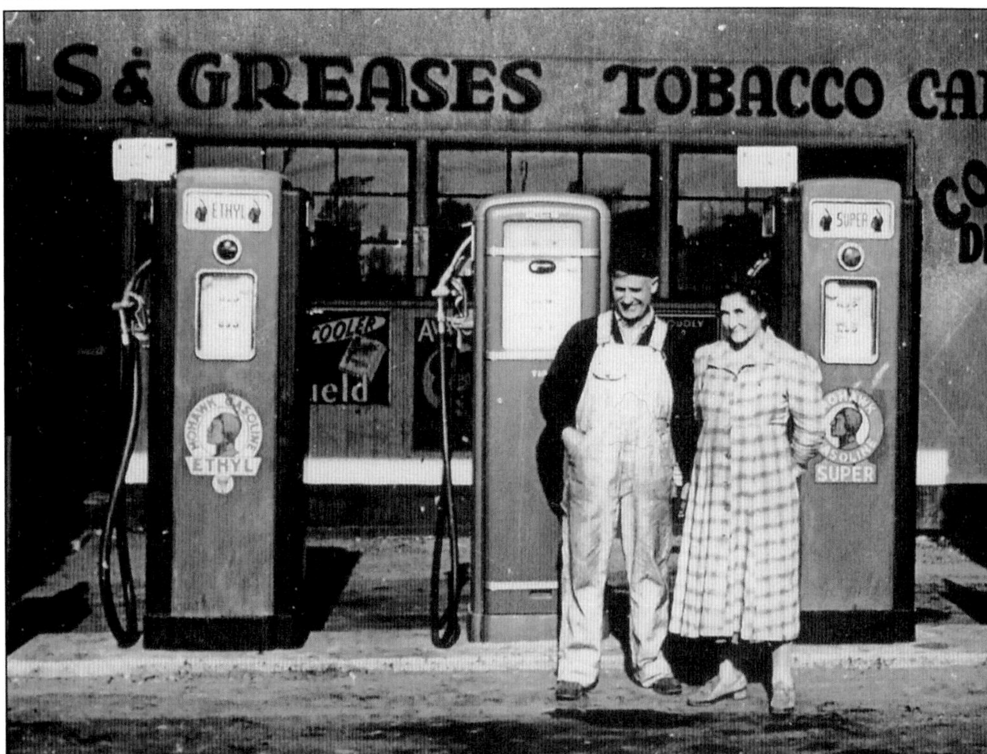

Sam and Helen Beutecal pose in front of their service station in 1941. Sam came to California in 1919, following his brother. He served in the United States Army Cavalry in 1908. Their son Sam Jr. was a tail gunner on a B-24 and was killed when his plane crashed during World War II.

Dave Silva operated the Signal service station on the corner of Winton Way and Highway 99 (Atwater Boulevard). The Silvas operated the station from 1941, when this picture was taken, until around 1961. Mrs. Silva still resides in their home on the corner of Grove Avenue and Winton Way.

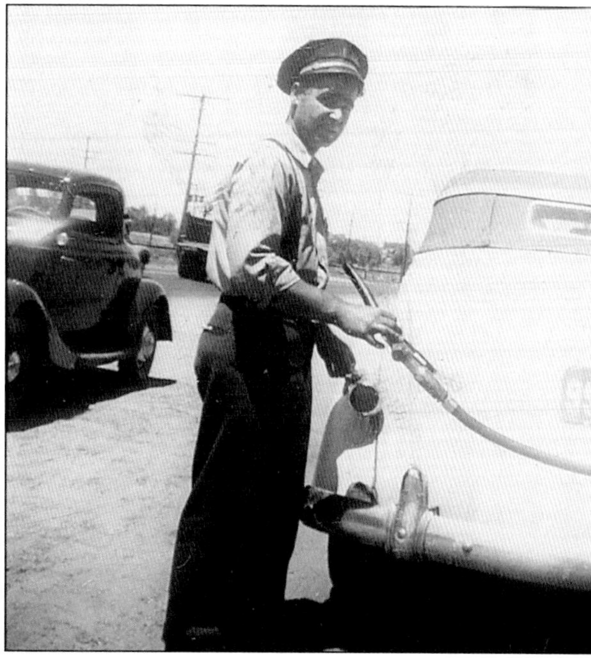

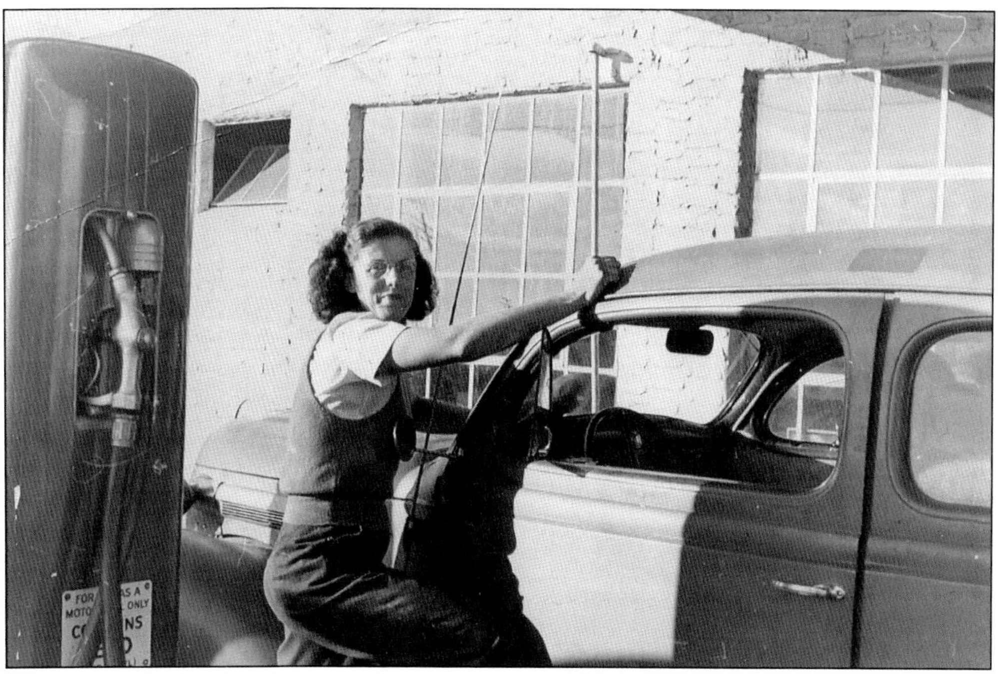

Assisting her husband at their Signal service station is Elvira Silva. Full service for the customer was the order of the day, and washing the windshield was part of that service.

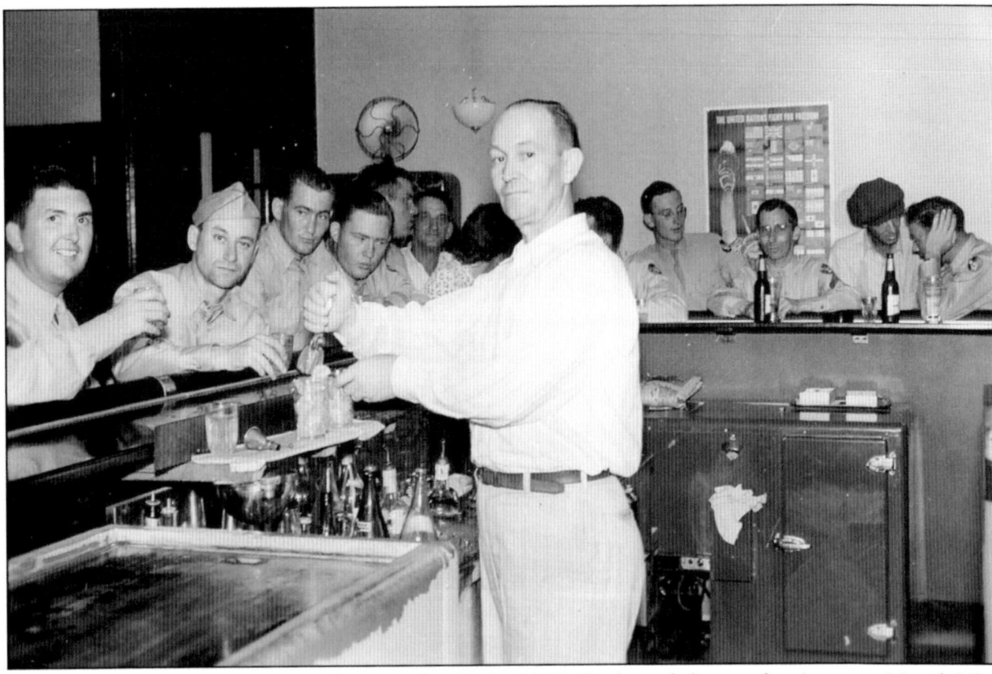

This photograph was taken on the Fourth of July, 1943. Carl tends bar at the Atwater Hotel. The patrons are gentlemen from the Merced Army Flying Field.

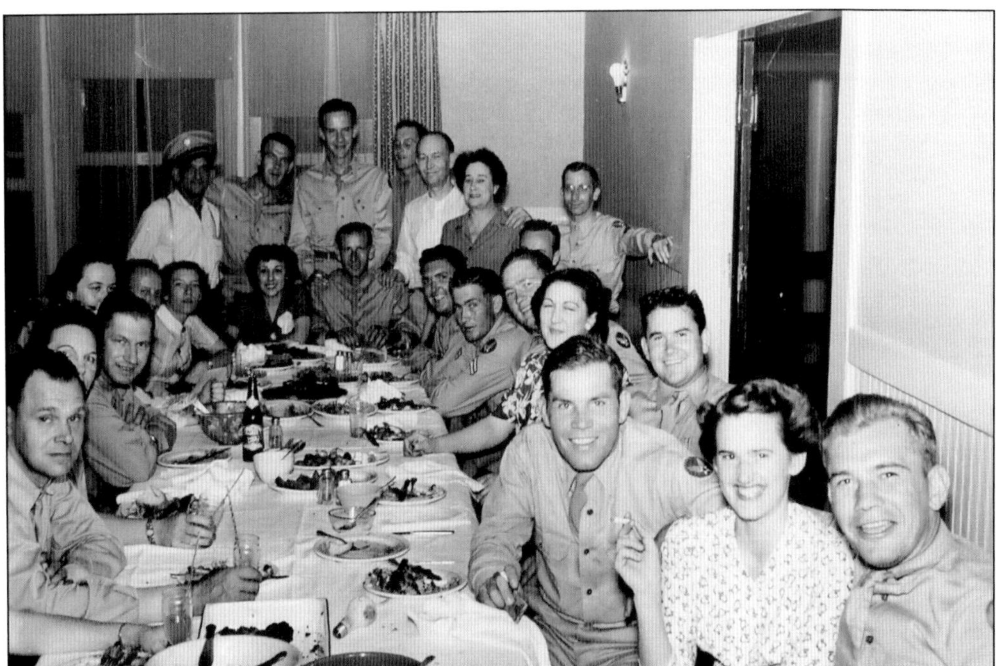

The boys from the base enjoy a family-style meal, also on the Fourth of July, 1943. The community made every effort to make the men stationed at the Army base during World War II feel at home. Carl and his wife, Alma, who managed the hotel and bar, are in the background.

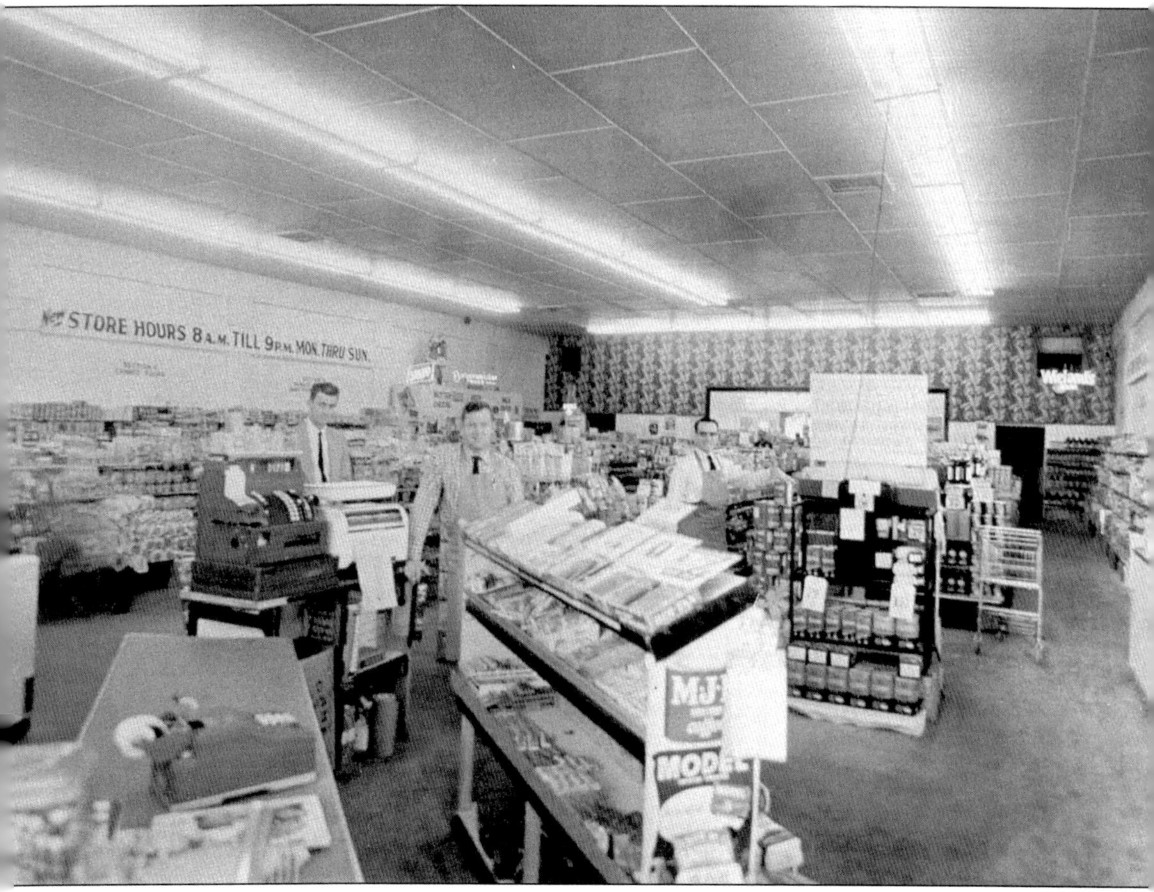

In 1946, Louis Passadori erected a large store on the northwest corner of Broadway and Third Street, on the site of the old Smith home that was moved to Sierra Vista Street and Olive Avenue. Salter's Pacific Food Market moved into this building. The photograph shows the new store, well stocked and ready for business.

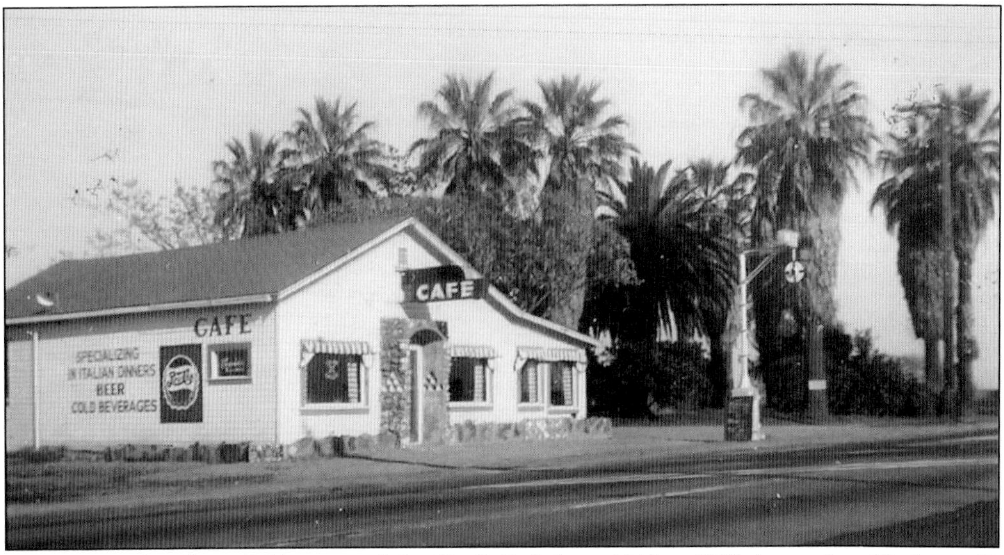

Elizabeth and William Fabbri owned the Shell Café from 1948 to 1955, located on Highway 99 going south toward Merced. Kenney's Cabinet Shop now occupies this site. The front entrance and the back bar area were lined with sea shells.

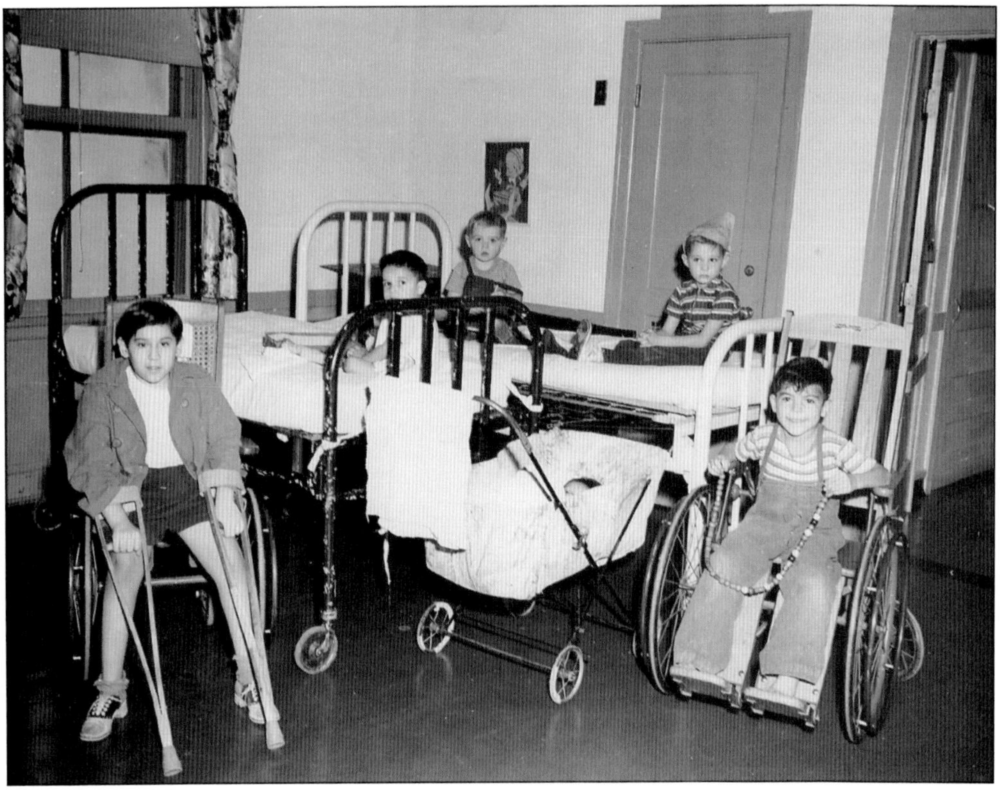

In 1937, Mrs. Sybil Crookham set up the "Sunshine School" for pediatric patients at the Bloss Hospital. Mrs. Crookham taught as many as 35 children. The school closed in 1942 but reopened in 1946 for patients with rheumatic fever, polio, and cerebral palsy. It remained open until 1957. This photograph, taken in 1948, shows some of the children who were hospitalized.

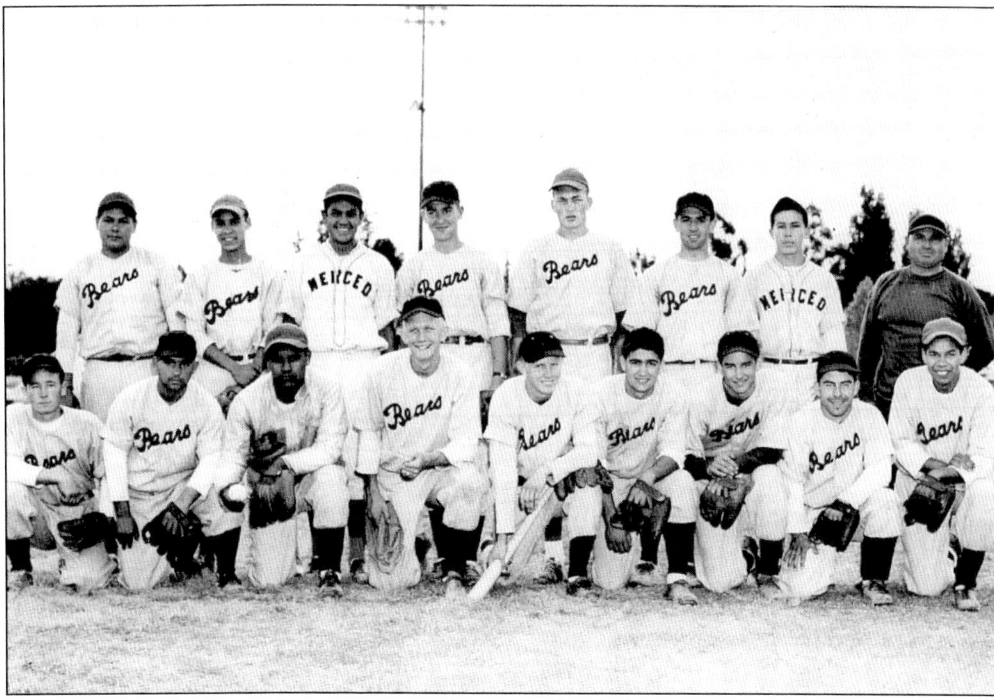

This photograph shows the 1948 Merced High School championship baseball team. Some of the members were boys from Atwater who attended Merced High School. The coach was Bill Joerg.

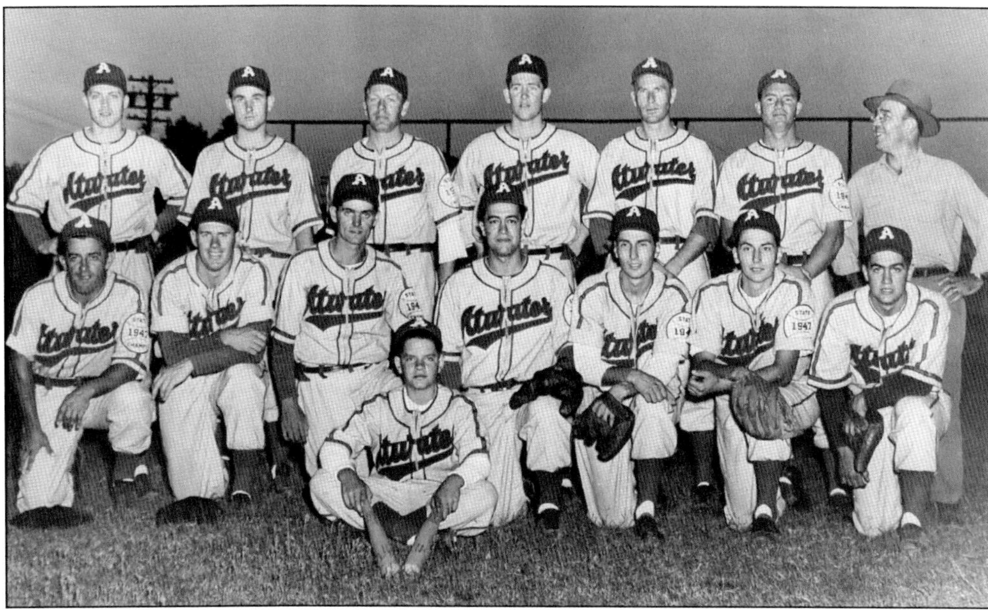

The Atwater Packers helped place Atwater on the map during the 1940s and 1950s. Team members of the 1948 season, from left to right, are (first row) Darrell Harworth, batboy; (second row) George Mandish, Vernon "Pinky" Bebernes, Don Garman, Ted Dallas, Harvey Toso, Harold Toso, and Bob Dallas; (second row) Johnny Cavalli, Harold Britton, Bing Miller, unidentified, Ray Nordell, Jack Hachett, and manager Johnny Pimentel.

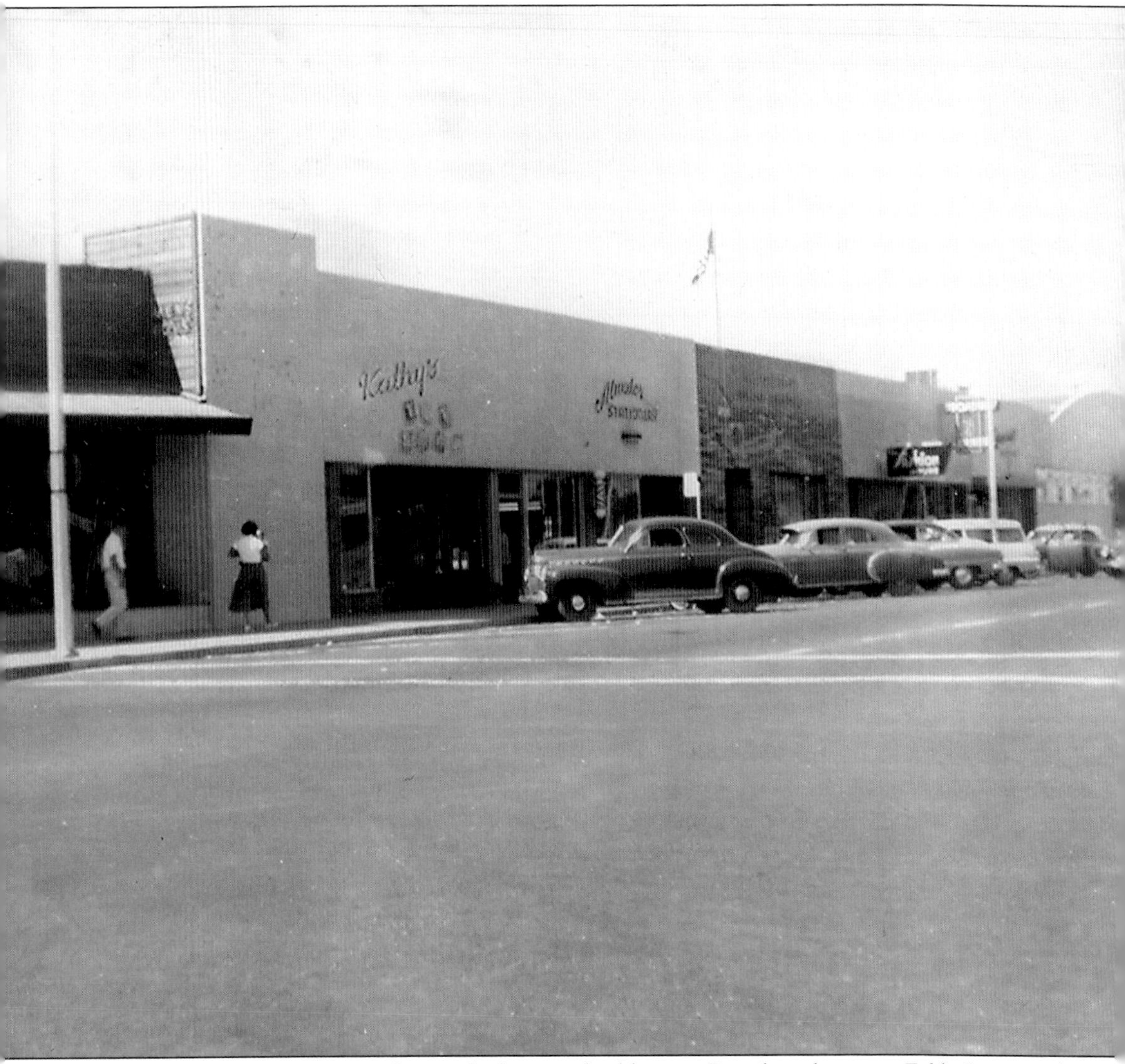

In 1952, Atwater was extremely proud of its new building on Broadway between Fifth Street and Winton Way. Manuel Smith erected this building and maintained ownership. The first occupants of the new block were Hunter's Men and Boys Shop (Clark Hunter, owner), Kathy's Tot Shop (Joe and Laura Saca, owners), Bud's Barber Shop (Bud and Pat Stanton, owners), Atwater Stationery (Harold and Katherine Holman, owners), United States Post Office (Joe Freitas, postmaster), The Fashion House (Adeline Wood, owner), Broadway Cleaners (Julian Aja, owner), The Corset Shop (Amelia Victorino, owner), Save Mart Supermarket (number two store), and Bernie's Liquor (the corner store). On the Fifth Street–side was Lloyd Cottrell's Shoe Repair. The Greyhound Bus ticket office was in Cottrell's shop. The only shop that remains as it was in 1952 is the barbershop. Vernon Mattos started working for Bud Stanton in 1956, and he purchased the business in 1967 with his wife, Norma. Interestingly, Norma's grandmother Ora was an Osborn, so this family has continued in the Atwater area.

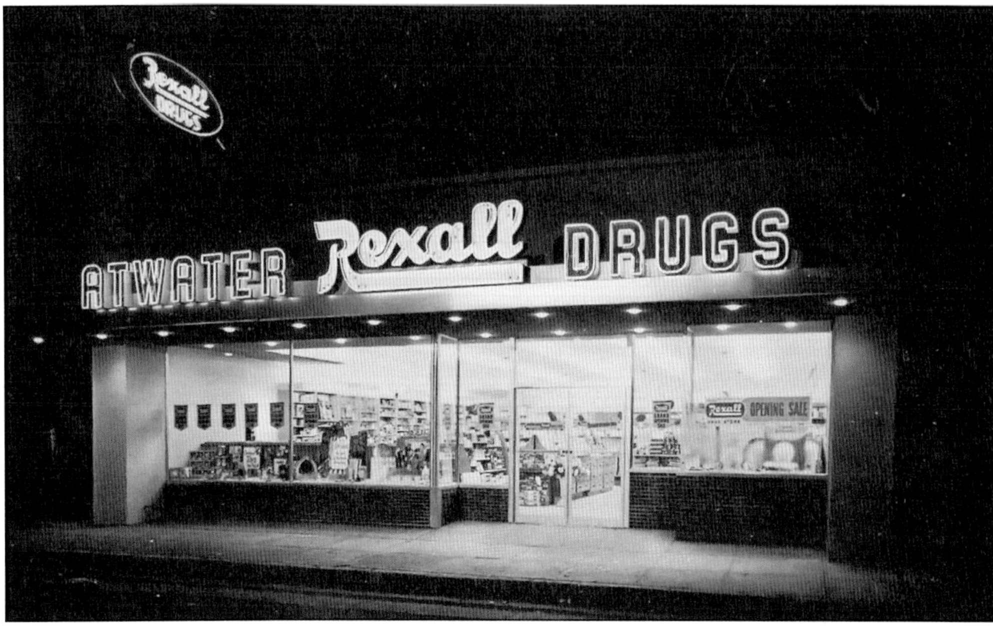

This night photograph shows the new building for the Atwater Rexall Drugs during its opening.

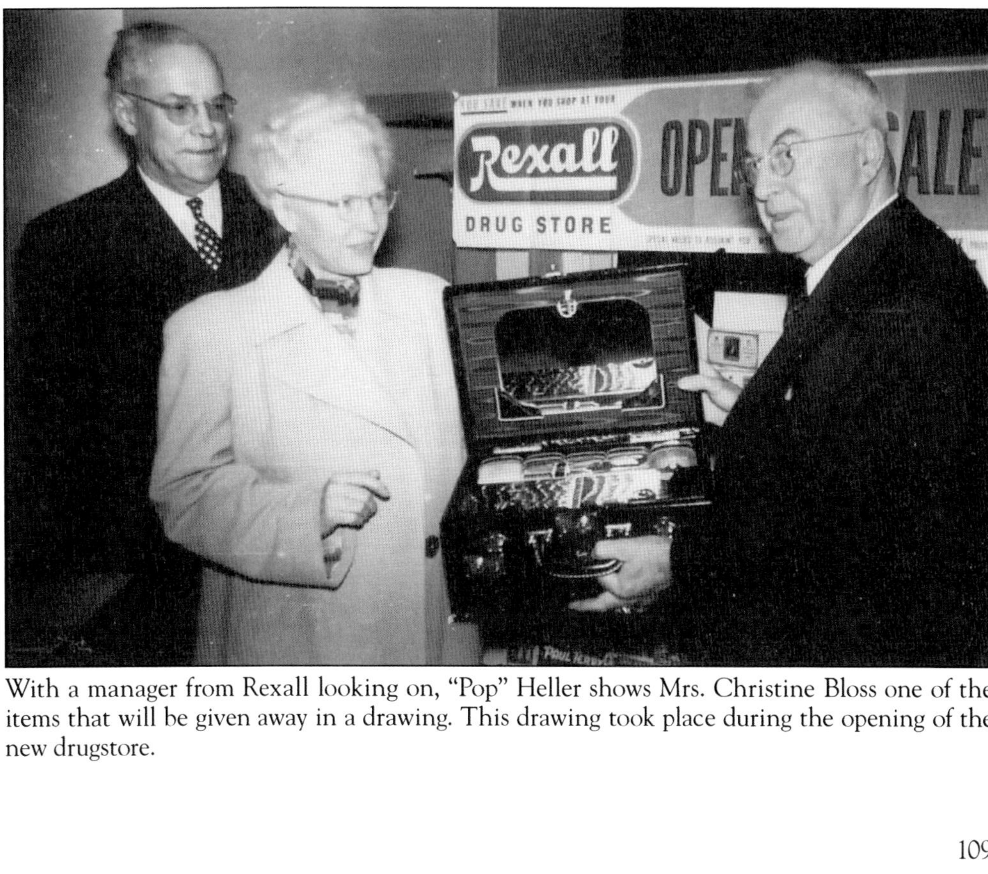

With a manager from Rexall looking on, "Pop" Heller shows Mrs. Christine Bloss one of the items that will be given away in a drawing. This drawing took place during the opening of the new drugstore.

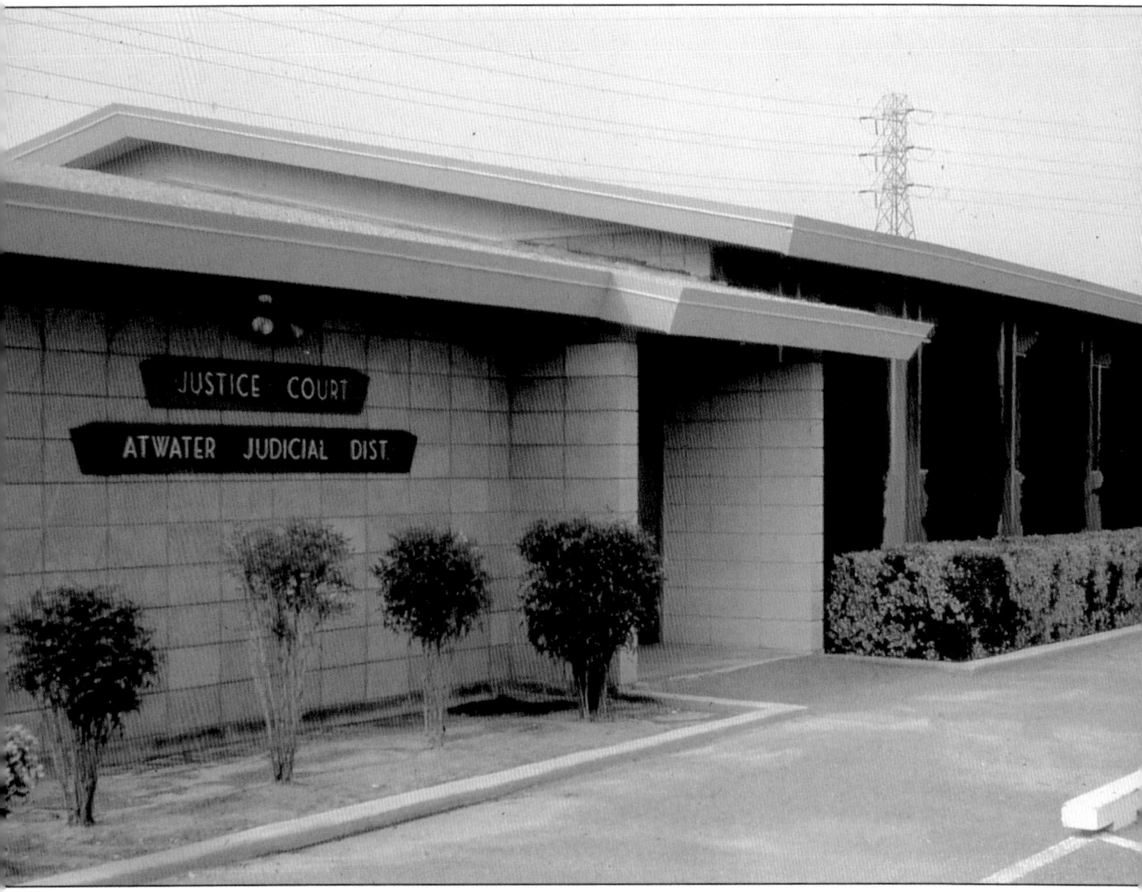

The Justice Court on Third Street finally outgrew its space and had to be replaced with a larger, more modern facility on the corner of Bellevue Road and Winton Way. It served the community for many years but was demolished in the 1980s.

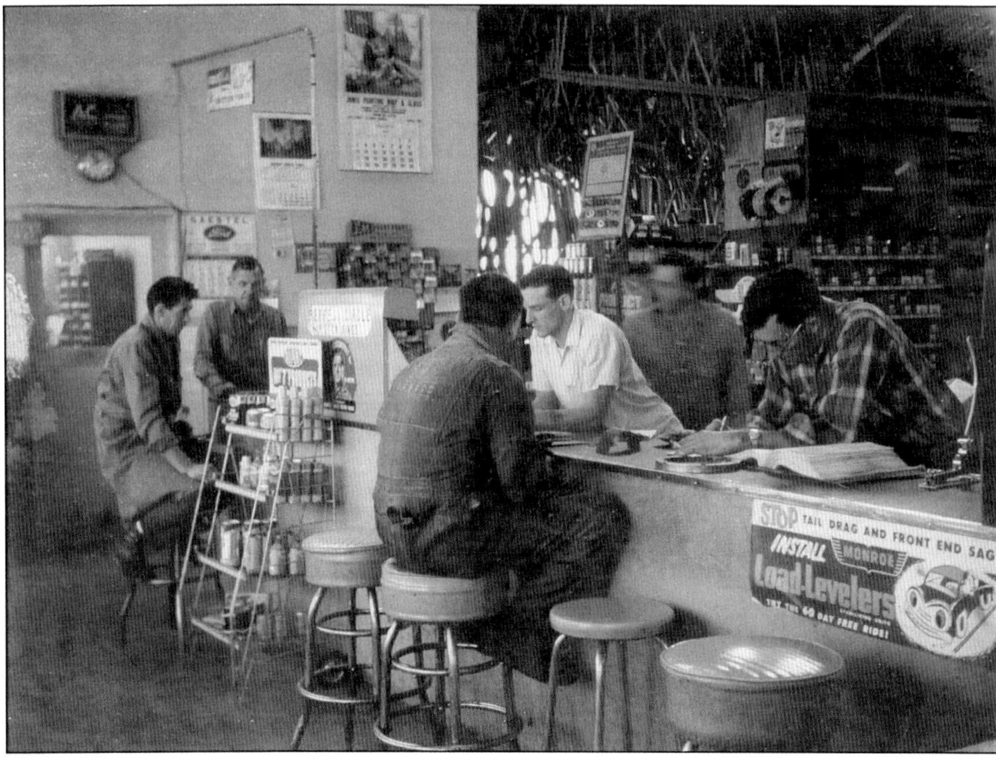

Located at 748 Broadway, the Atwater Auto Parts always did brisk business. The clerks pictured here are Ken Baldwin and Manuel Barcellos, and the customers are Elmer Bushee and Jerry Holzer. Today the business is known as Latta's Auto Supply.

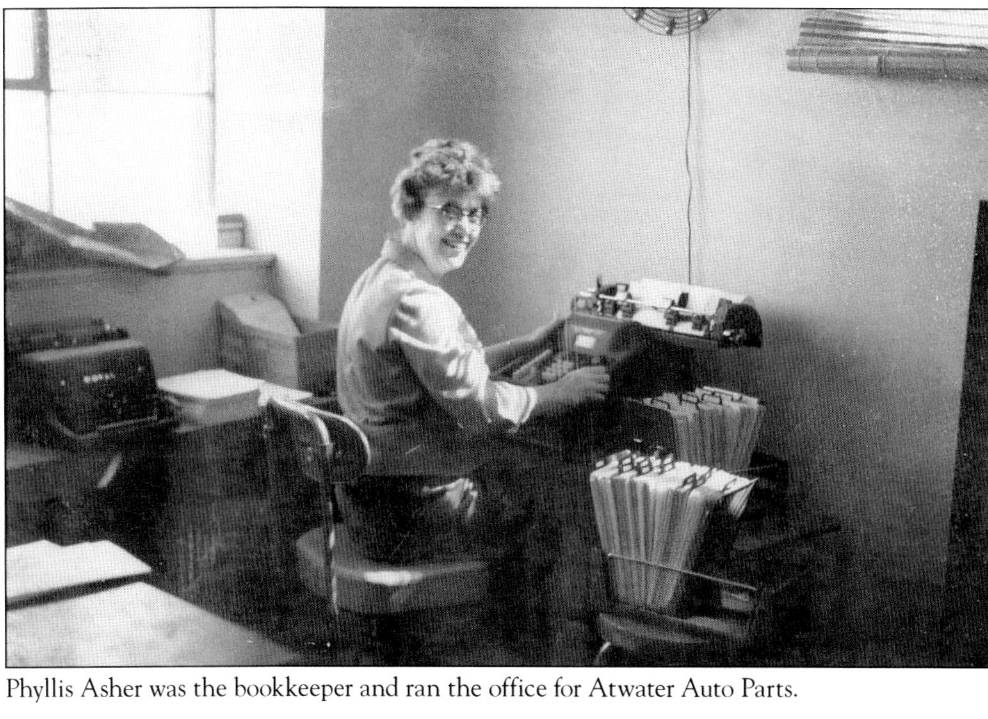

Phyllis Asher was the bookkeeper and ran the office for Atwater Auto Parts.

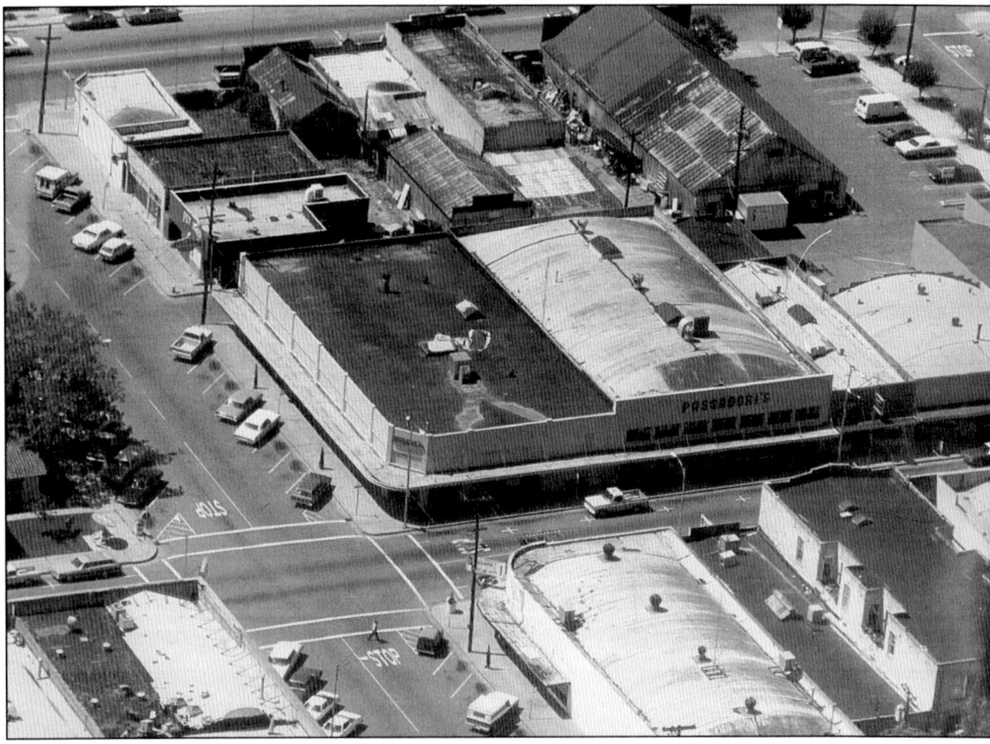

This is an aerial shot of downtown Atwater, at Third Street and Broadway, in the 1950s. Seen are Passadori's large furniture and hardware store. The Western auto store is now across the street where Salter's Pacific Market had been. The dome has been removed from the old bank building, and in the upper right hand corner the buildings on Atwater Boulevard have been removed and the space made into a parking lot.

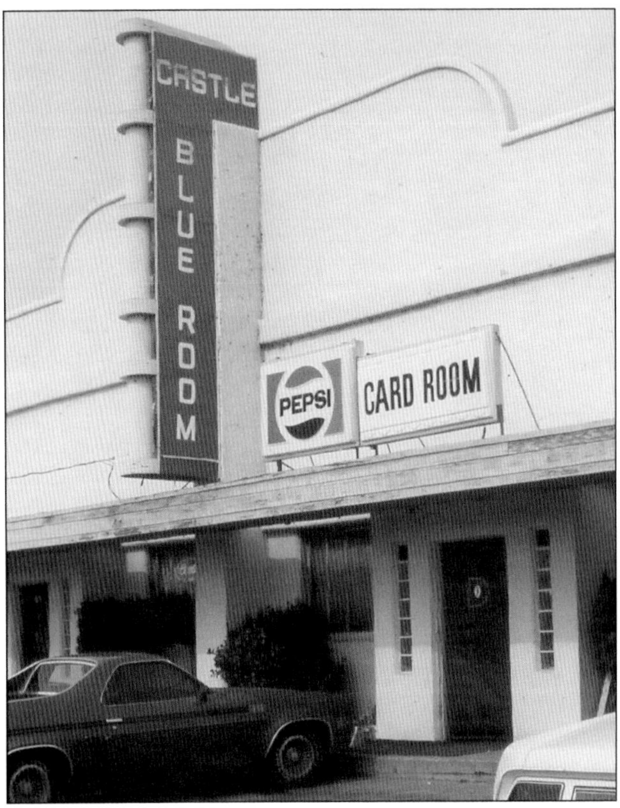

Located on Highway 99 (Atwater Boulevard) between First Street and High, this business was known as Dan's Castle Inn when it opened in 1946. In the late 1950s, it was sold to Dick Ashment and renamed Castle Blue Room. Built in the art deco style, it served as a lounge and card room and was the last home of the *Atwater Signal* while it was published in Atwater.

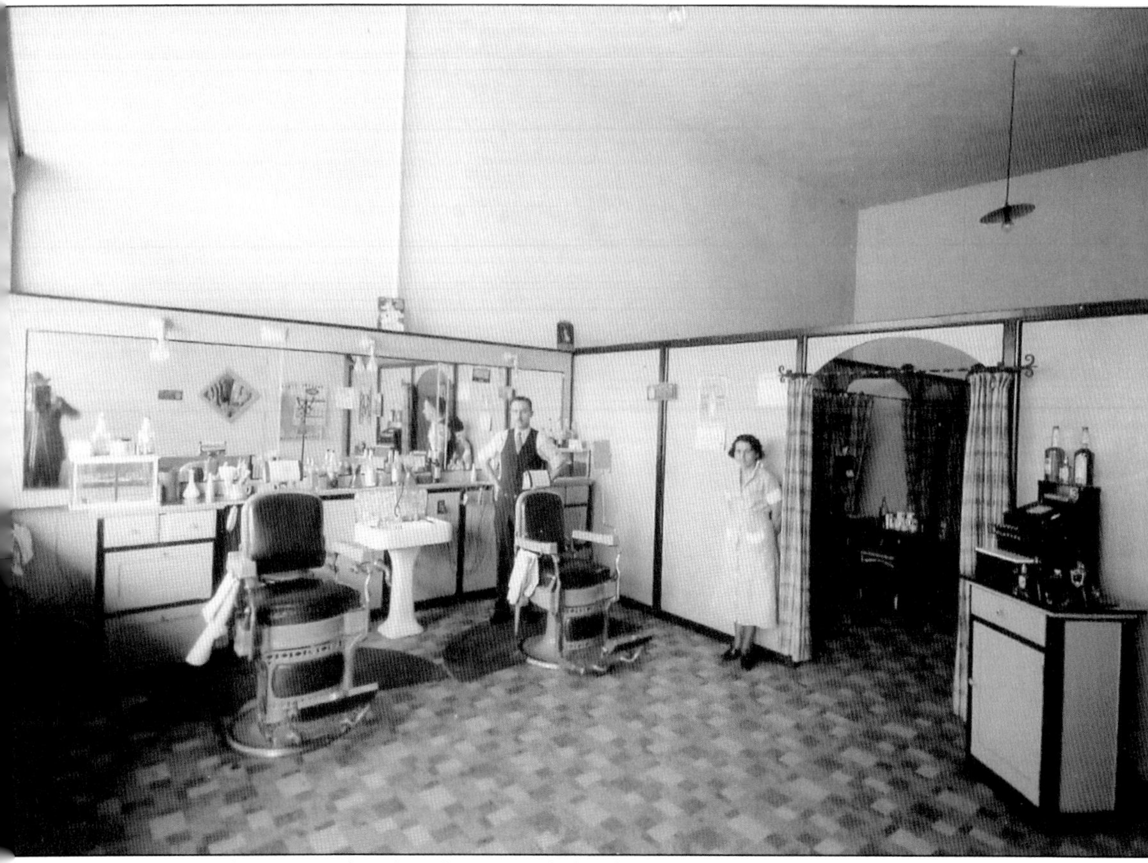

From 1935 until 1950, Nick Lubisich operated this barbershop in the Bloss building on Third Street. Mr. Lubisich closed it and, with his wife, spent a year or two in Europe, where they had family. In 1952, they returned and he opened the N&O Barber Shop on Broadway in the remodeled bank building.

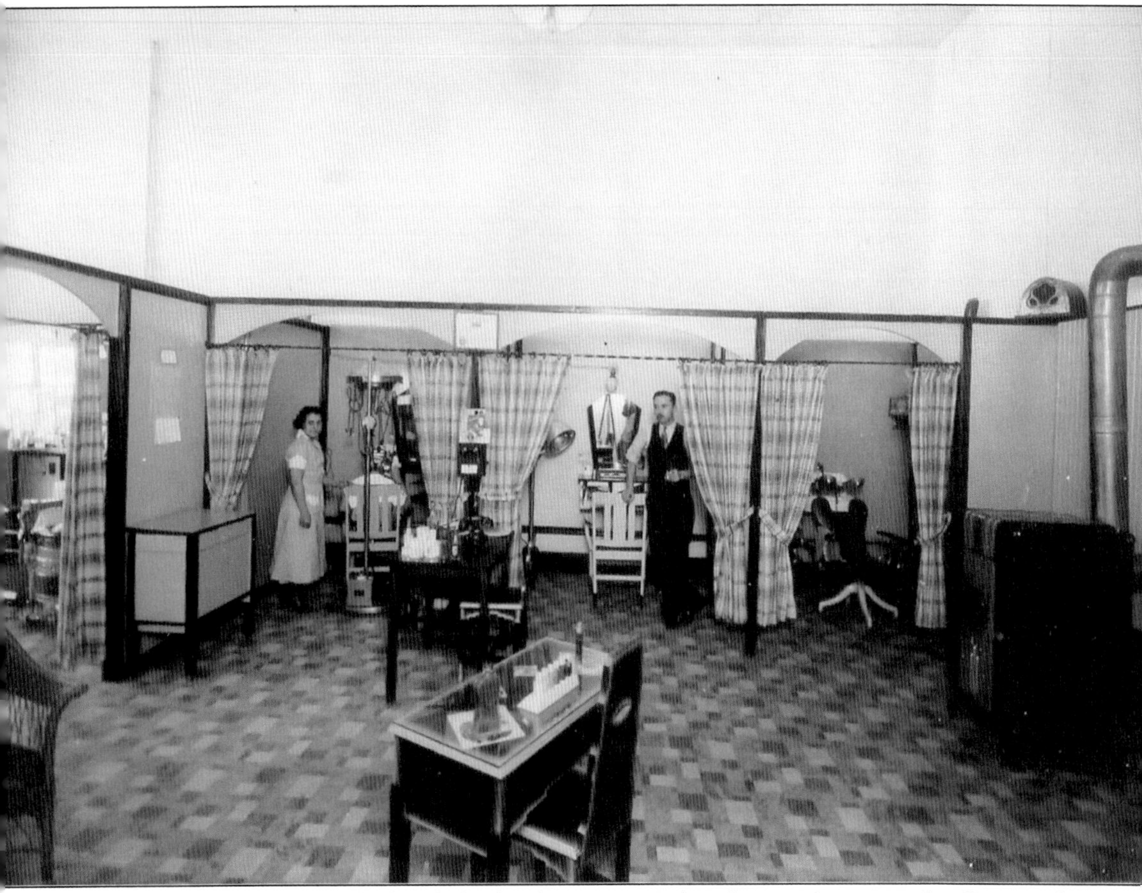

In conjunction with her husband's barbershop, Mary Lubisich ran a beauty parlor. During this time, she and her husband also raised their niece Nada Lubisich (Pazin), who lost her parents when she was in third grade.

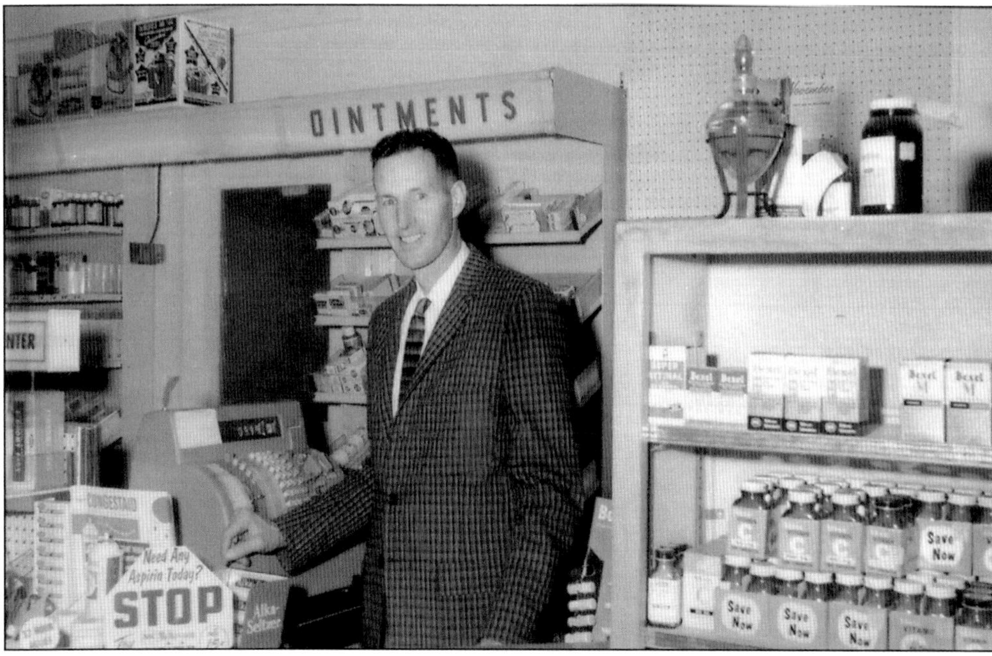

In November 1951, Joseph MacDonald opened his drugstore in the old bank building that had been remodeled by Louis Passadori. This was the second pharmacy in Atwater. Mr. MacDonald and his wife, Edith, became very active in the civic affairs of Atwater. In April 1954, Joseph was elected to the city council, and in April 1956 he was elected mayor. MacDonald's progressed steadily, and by the 1970s the business was moved to a larger facility on Broadway near Winton Way. On February 7, 1980, the Bertelli family bought the business, now known as Bertelli's Drugs.

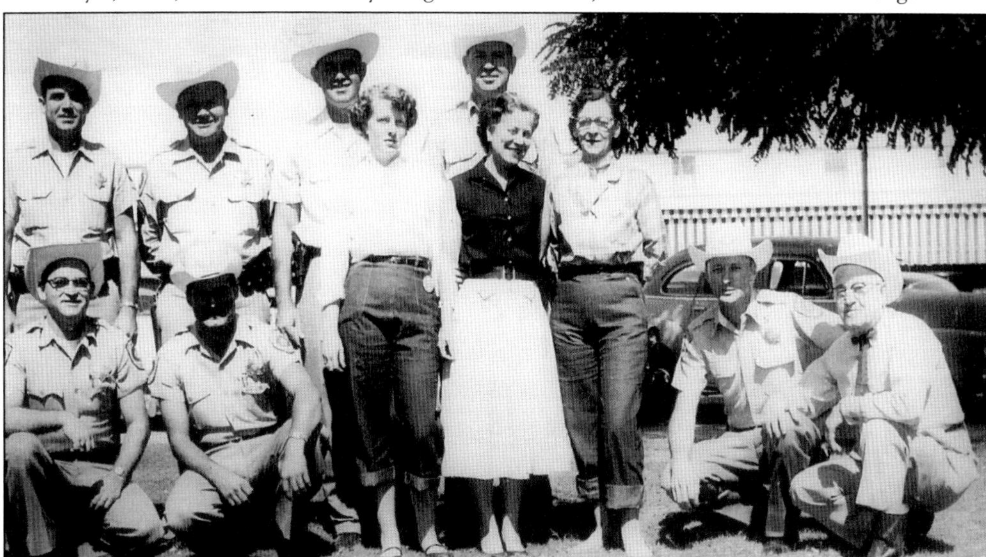

Some Atwater residents were involved in providing security for the Merced County Fair in 1955. Pictured here, from left to right, are (kneeling) Jess "Pooch" Bowling, Eldon George, Quinn Young, and E. L. Walter; (standing, first row) Wanda Austin (justice court secretary), Leona Demout (police department secretary), and Ann Addams (justice court secretary); and (standing, back row) Ervin "Dude" Milton, Dick Staggs, Larry Cardoza, and Jerry Cole.

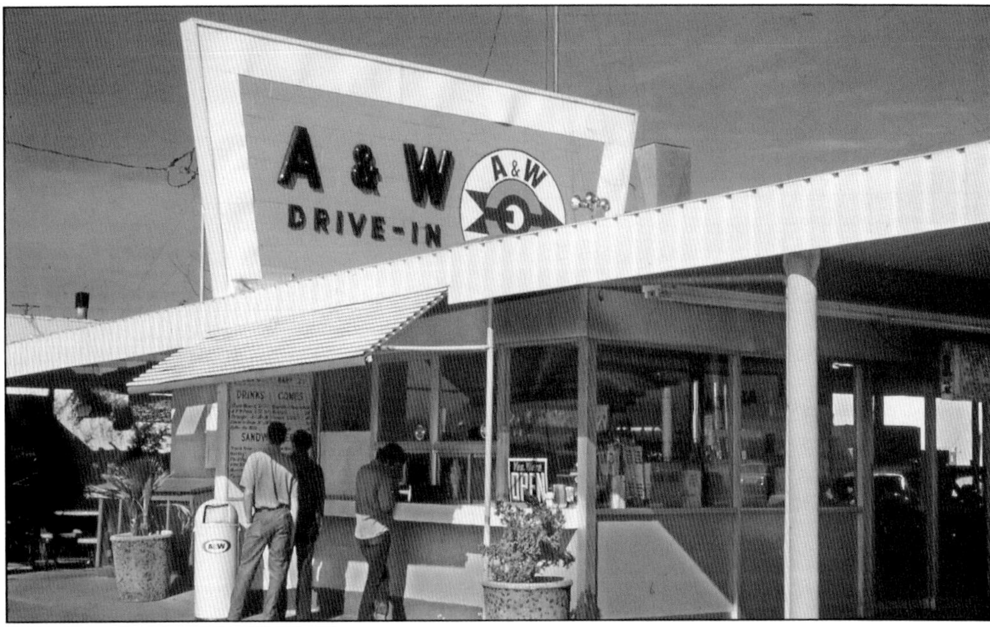

The Atwater Hotel, a former city landmark, was dismantled in 1955. It had been in use for 45 years and was in need of repairs that were ultimately deemed too costly. The new A&W Root Beer Drive-In was erected on the corner. The drive-in building is still on the corner of Fourth and Atwater Boulevard but it is now a Mexican restaurant.

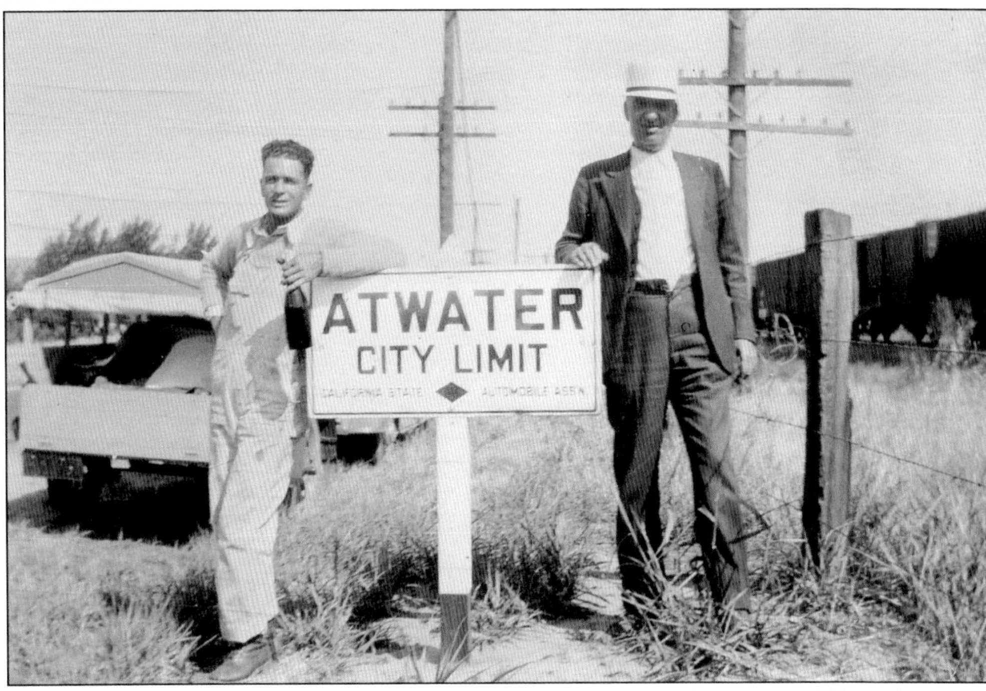

If you were traveling south on Highway 99 in the 1930s and 1940s, this sign would have been your first encounter with Atwater. Charles Vierra, on the left, and an unidentified gentleman pose with the sign when it was first erected. The California State Automobile Association apparently gave away these city signs.

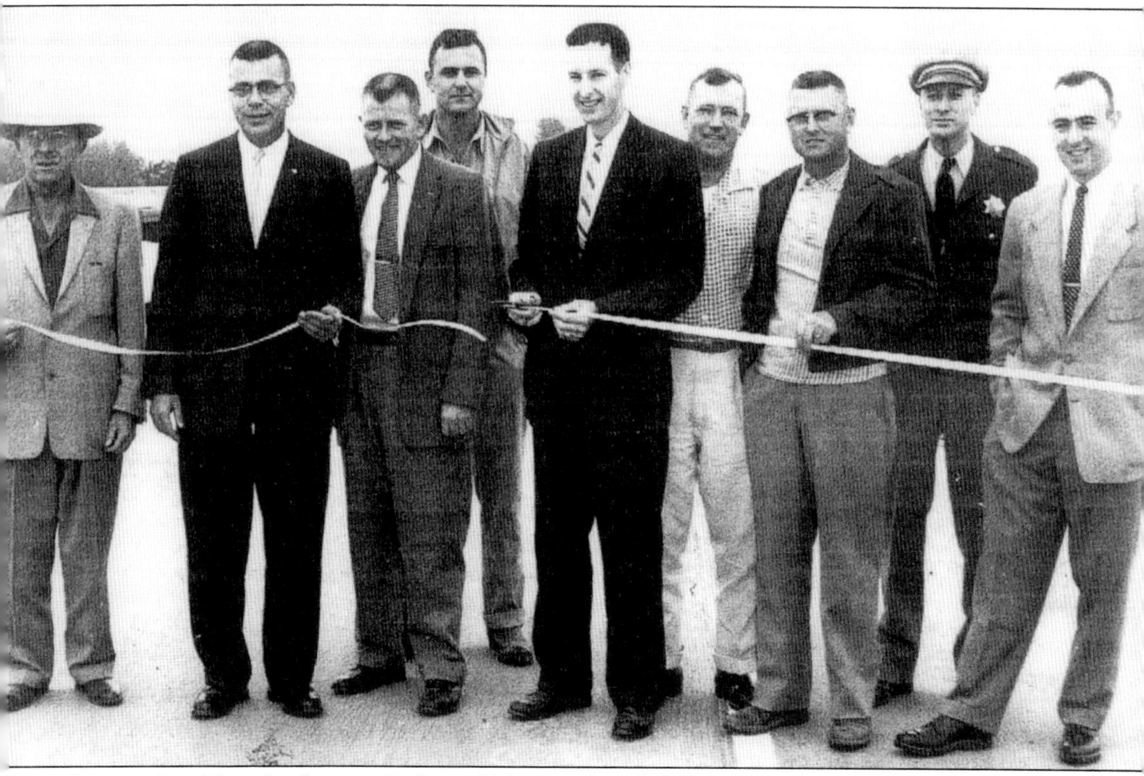

Cutting the ribbon for the new Highway 99 bypass, from left to right, are William L. Hurd, district construction manager of the California State Highway Department; Bill Spafford, Atwater city administrator; Stanley Court, councilman; B. W. Gillispie, highway engineer; Joseph D. MacDonald, mayor; Woodie Salter, councilman; Ernie Buller, councilman; Quinn Young, chief of police; and Gerald Passadori, chamber of commerce president. This photograph was taken in 1957.

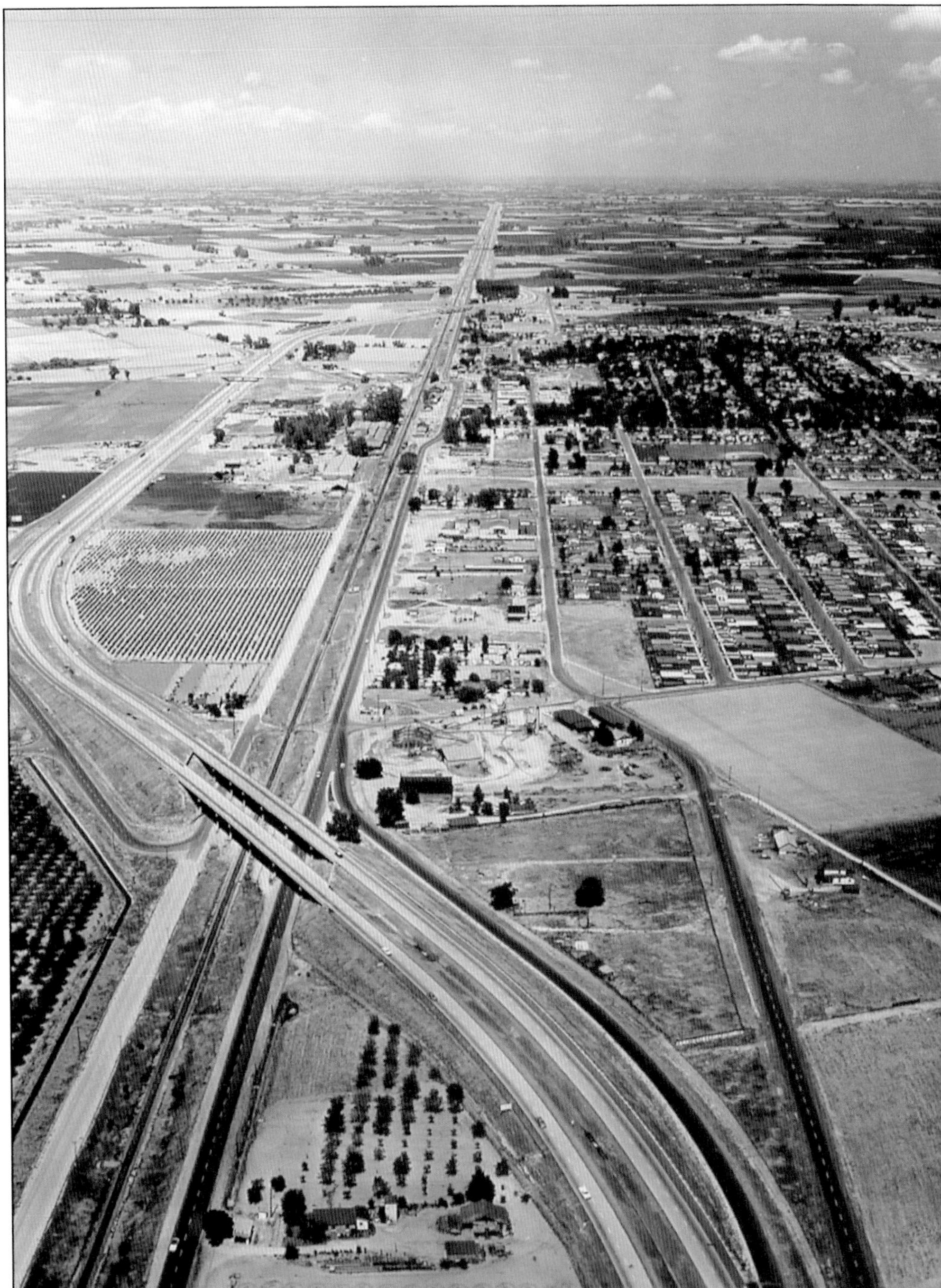

This aerial view shows the new Highway 99 bypass completed around Atwater. When this was finished in 1957, the old highway was renamed Atwater Boulevard. Though this bypass was a boon to travelers on the freeway, it tolled the death knell to many of the small businesses located on the old road. Atwater survived, however, and continued to grow in population.

Six

Merced Army Air Field and Castle Air Force Base

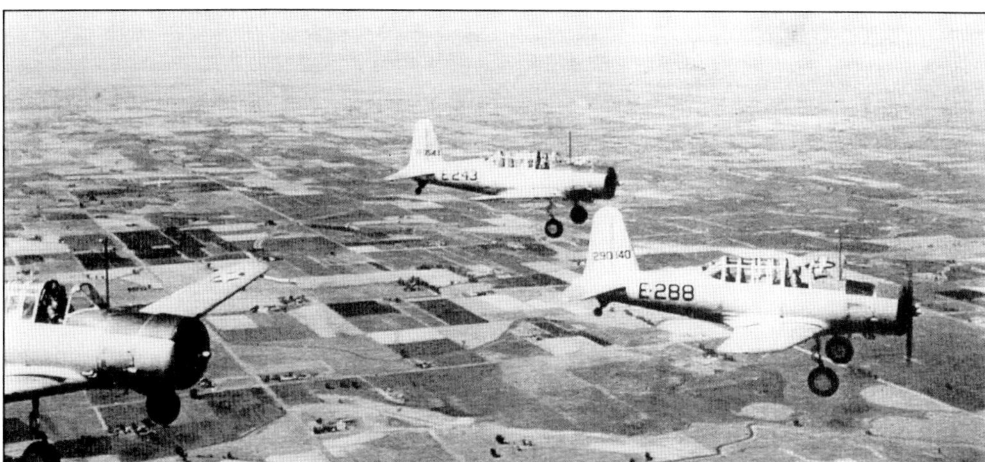

Three training aircraft from Merced Army Air Field fly over the San Joaquin Valley.

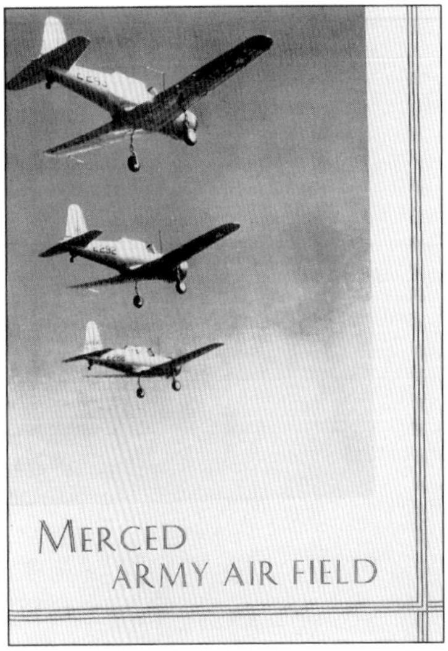

The base was officially established on September 20, 1941. No personnel were sent to the base until October 8 of that year, when a small cadre of enlisted men arrived from Moffett Field. These men and the first officers to arrive were quartered in hotels in Merced. A makeshift headquarters was set up at the clerk's desk in the Tioga Hotel. These offices were used until December 1, 1941, when construction at the base had advanced to the point where the office buildings could be used. The building of two hangers and a control tower were started on September 22, 1941. The first aircraft assigned to the base were three BT-13As that were kept at the Merced Municipal Airport until the runway at the field was completed. By December 7, 1941, there were at least 34 of these trainers at the airport that were transferred that night to the airfield. After the surrender of Germany and Japan in 1945, the field was deactivated for a few months. On April 6, 1946, Gen. Henry H. "Hap" Arnold reactivated the base, and it was named for Gen. Fredrick Castle, a Medal of Honor winner who was killed on a bombing raid over Germany on December 24, 1944. In September 1947, when the Army Air Corps became the United States Air Force, the group at Castle was reorganized as the 93rd Bombardment Wing, a unit of the 15th Air Force and Strategic Air Command. Castle Field became Castle Air Force Base and served as a training facility for the Air Force until 1995, when it was officially closed. The base and the community of Atwater had very close ties over the years and it was with regret that the relationship came to an end. The property is being redeveloped by the County of Merced under the name of Castle Airport Aviation and Development Center.

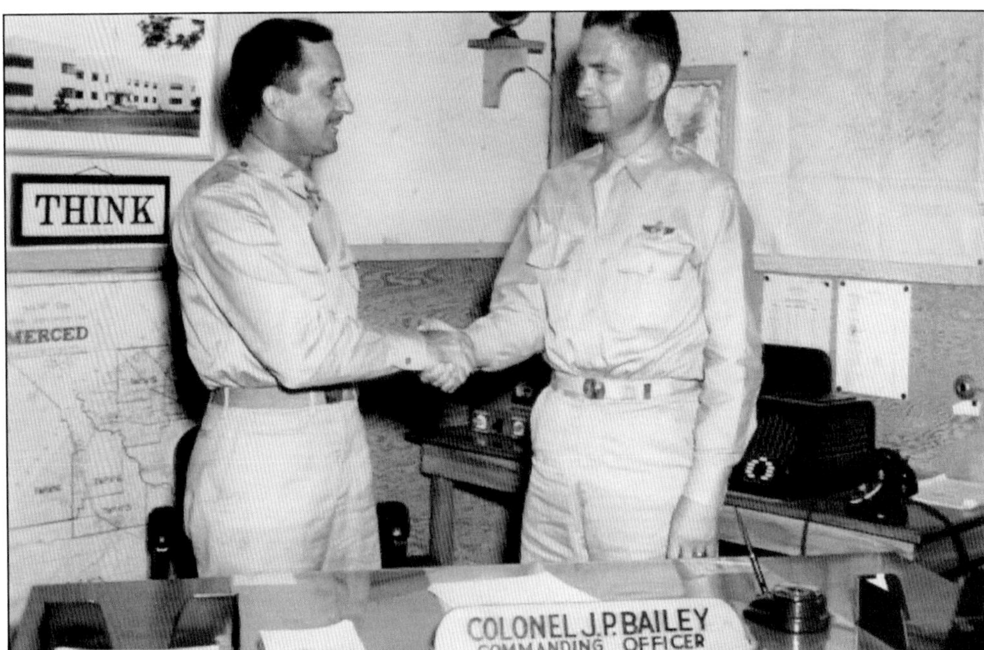

Lt. Col. Joseph P. Bailey (left) was the first base commander. Here he greets an unidentified visitor to his office.

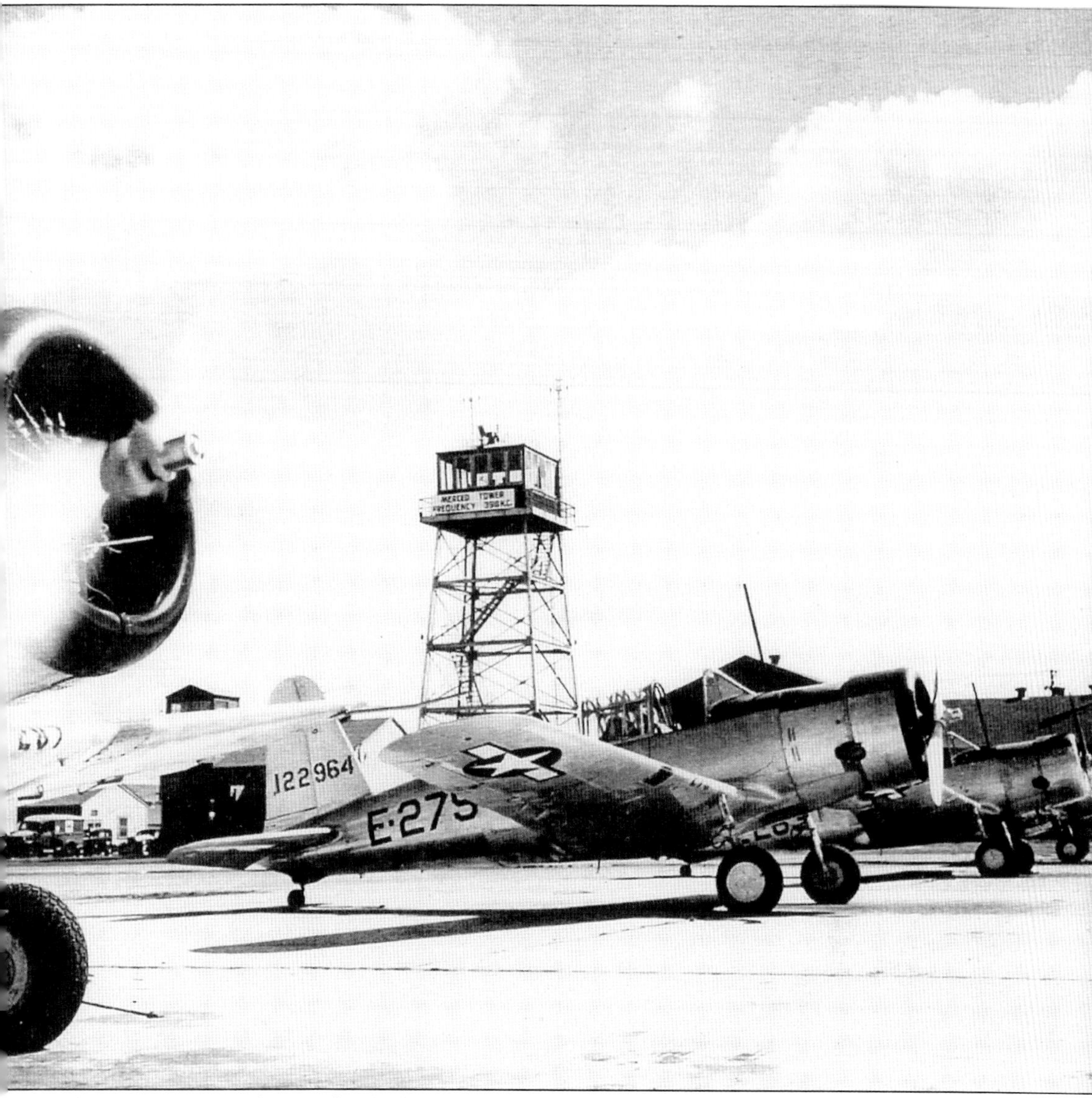

The original control tower for the base looks out over the aircraft on the tarmac.

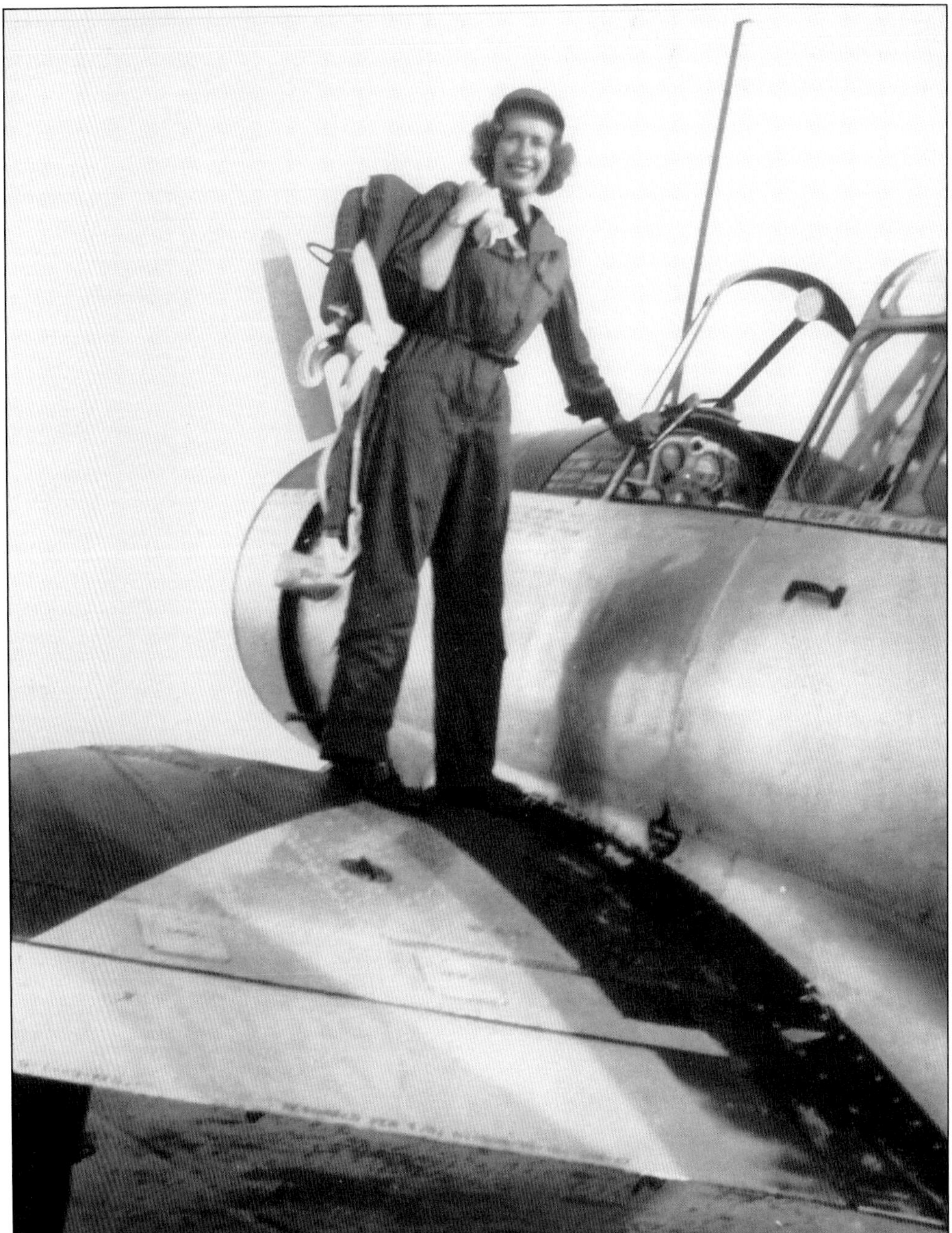

Women in the Air Corps were known as WASPs. Dorthy Meyn Ritscher went through the pilot program at Merced Army Air Field in 1944. These women were vital in ferrying aircraft to needed destinations to relieve the men for combat duty. Miss Ritscher's uniform is on display in the Castle Air Museum.

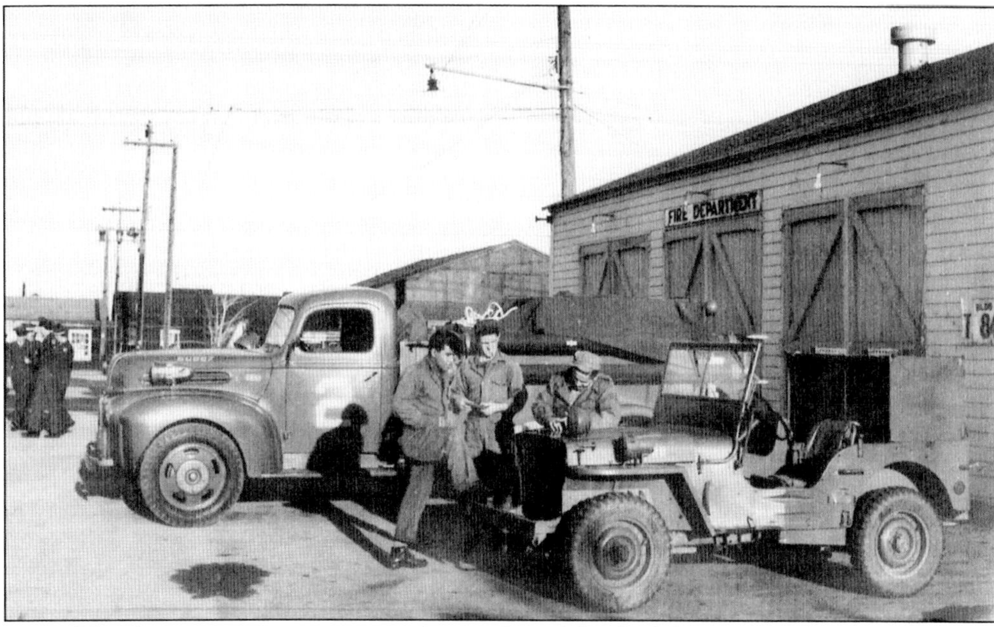

A good fire department was a necessity for any base. The shed shown to the left of the building contained a 12,000-pound, carbon-dioxide, low-pressure storage tank that was used to fill both Cardox trucks (also refrigerated, low-pressure units) and fire extinguishers. Also pictured is a pumper truck and the chief's red fire jeep. The large box on the rear of the jeep is the two-way radio. Pictured, from left to right, are J. Montes, Phillip Compton, and Paul Yanka.

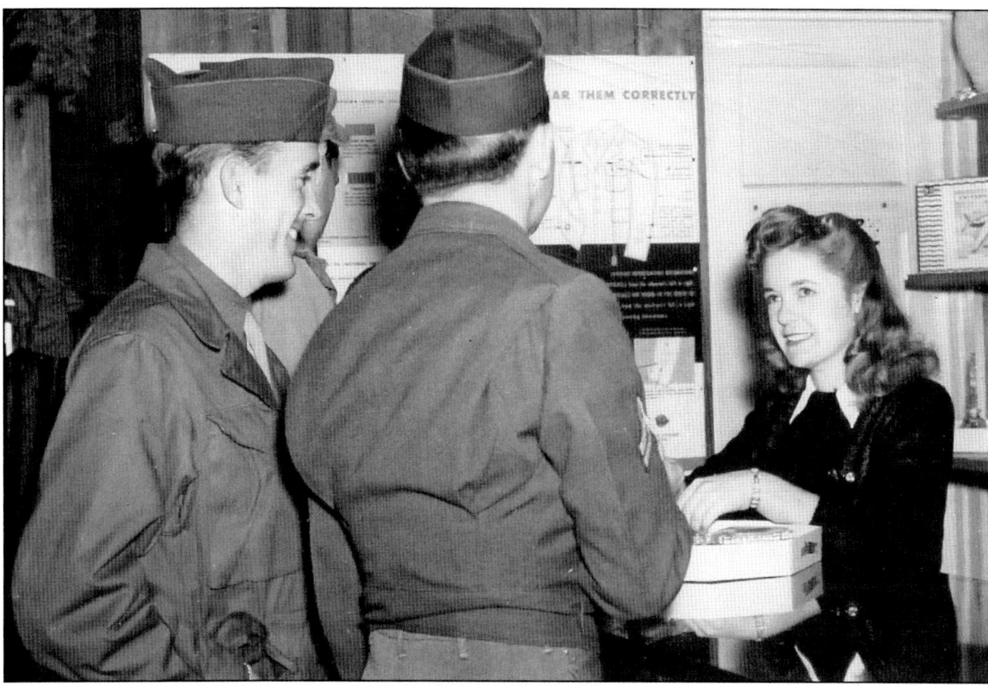

Purchasing some necessary items, these young men are shopping at the post exchange. Waiting on them is Helen Kangis (Rice) from Atwater. Miss Rice worked as a civilian in the exchange for several years.

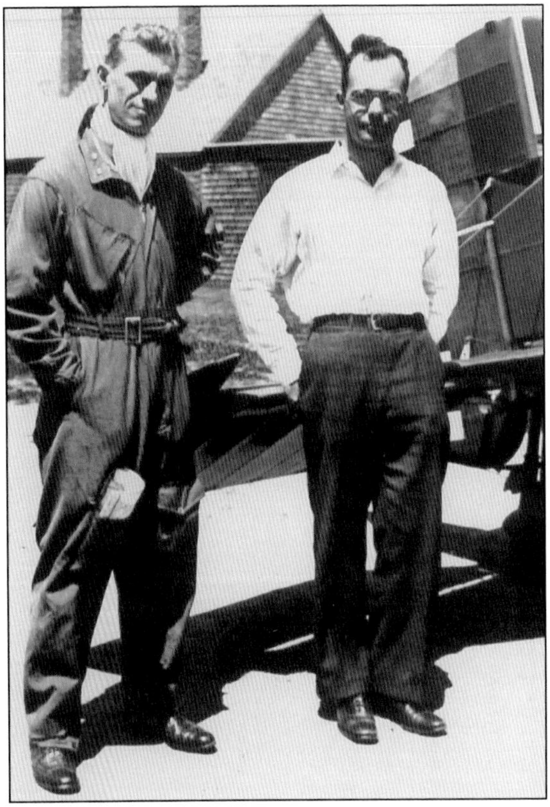

This photograph of the namesake of Castle Air Force Base, Gen. Fredrick Castle, was taken in 1935. The man on the right is unidentified.

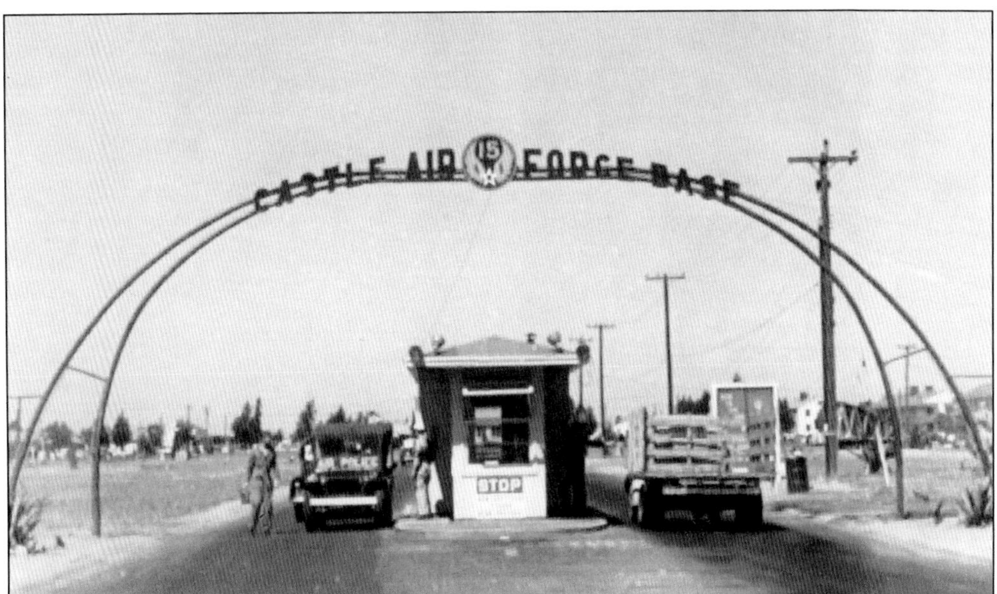

This post-1947 image shows the main gate after the facility became Castle Air Force Base.

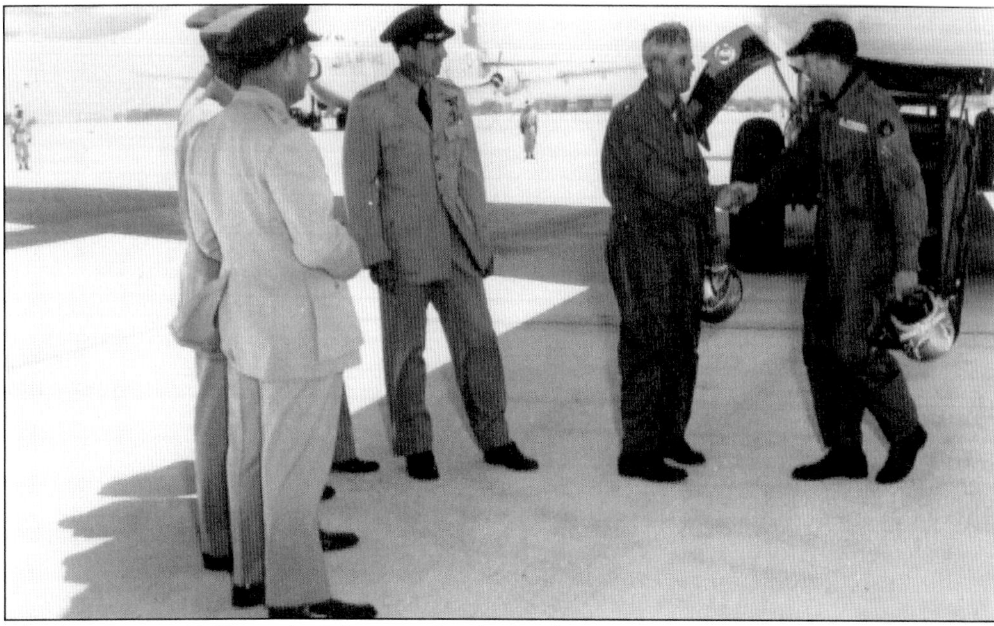

The first Boeing B-52 touched down at Castle Air force Base on June 20, 1955. Here General Eubank and Major Howard congratulate each another on the arrival. Shortly thereafter, the 93rd Bombardment Wing began training B-52 crews for SAC. In 1957, with the arrival of KC-135s (flying gas stations), the training program increased to include crews for the Stratotanker.

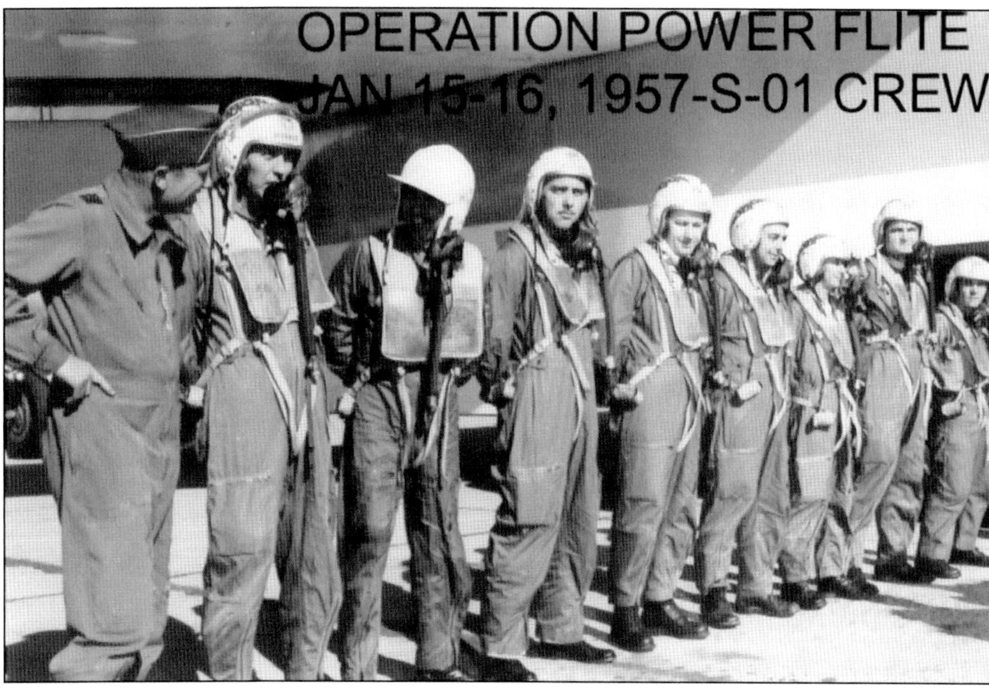

On January 16, 1957, three of the 93rd Bomb Wing B-52s completed a project called "Power Flight." This was a record-setting, nonstop flight around the world in 45 hours and 19 minutes. Pictured are members of select crew S-01, one of the three that accomplished this feat. Normally a B-52 carries a crew of six; however, for this job there were additional relief crewmembers.

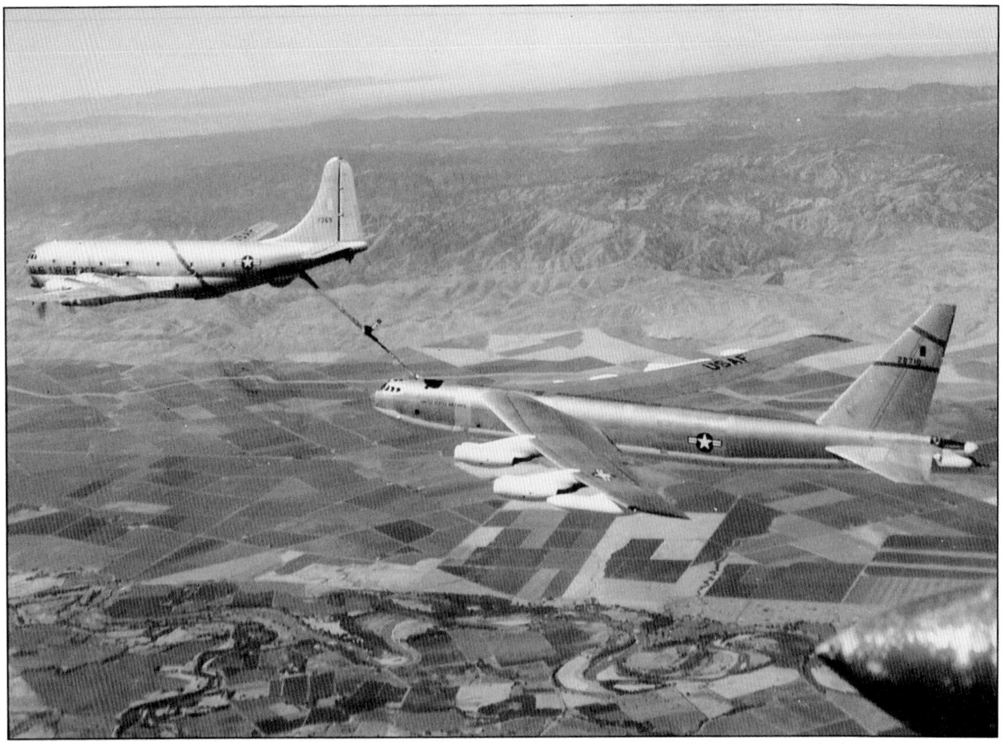

A forerunner of the KC-135 was the KC-97, a propeller-driven tanker. To refuel the jet-engine B-52, the tanker had to fly at full speed and the bomber at a very low speed. The two are shown here over the San Joaquin Valley.

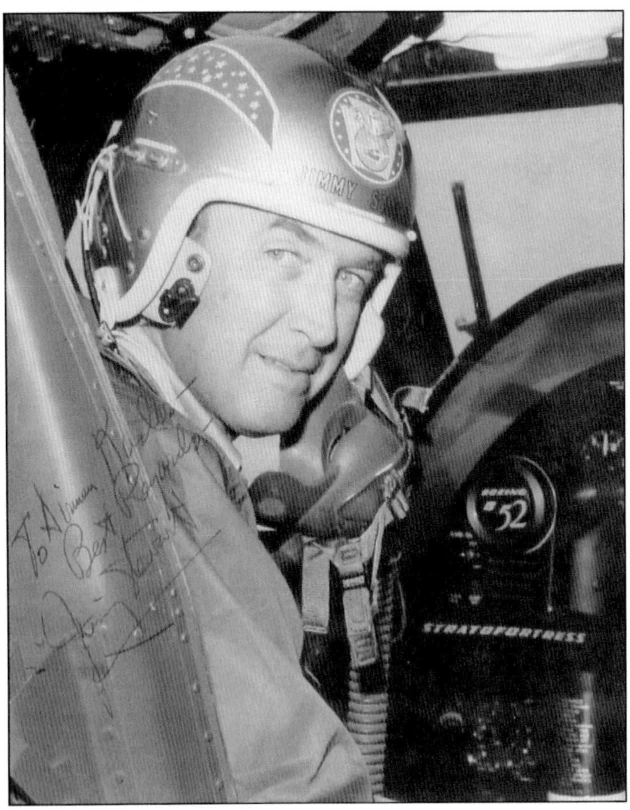

In 1955, *Strategic Air Command*, a movie starring James Stewart, was filmed at Castle Air Force Base. Mr. Stewart was certainly not unfamiliar with flying. He served as a pilot during World War II and continued in the Air Force Reserve, attaining the rank of general. More familiarly known as Jimmy, here he is in the cockpit of a B-52.

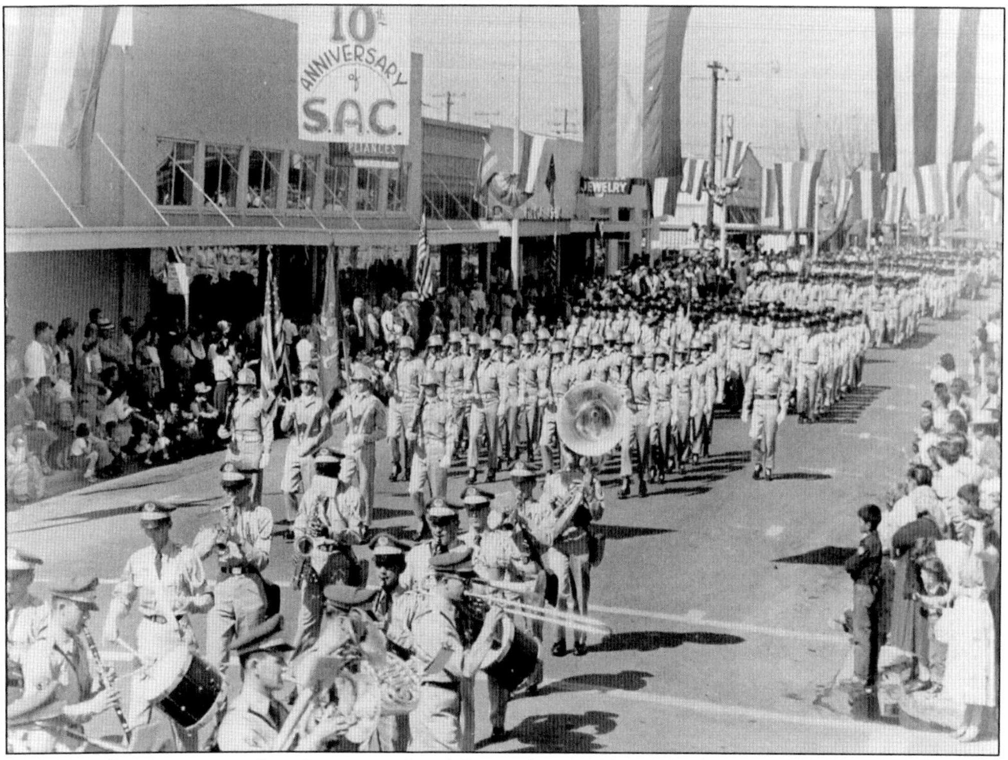

In 1957, the Strategic Air Command celebrated its 10th anniversary with a parade for the surrounding communities and an open house at the base.

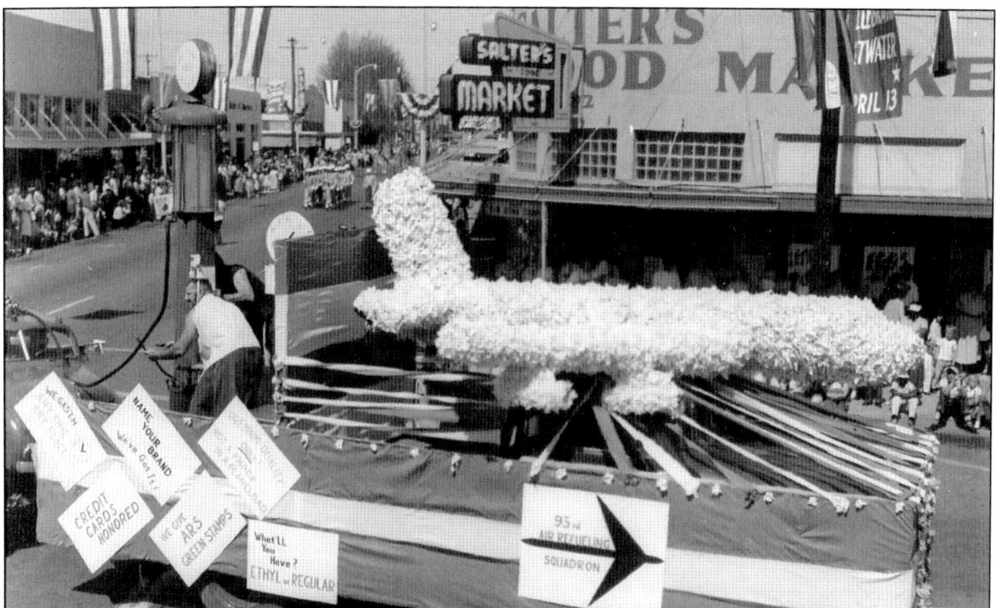

Always eager to participate in community activities, the men and women at Castle enjoyed a good parade. This float featured a crepe-paper model of a KC-135 that was entered in the Fourth of July Parade in Atwater. The photograph was taken at the corner of Third Street and Broadway.

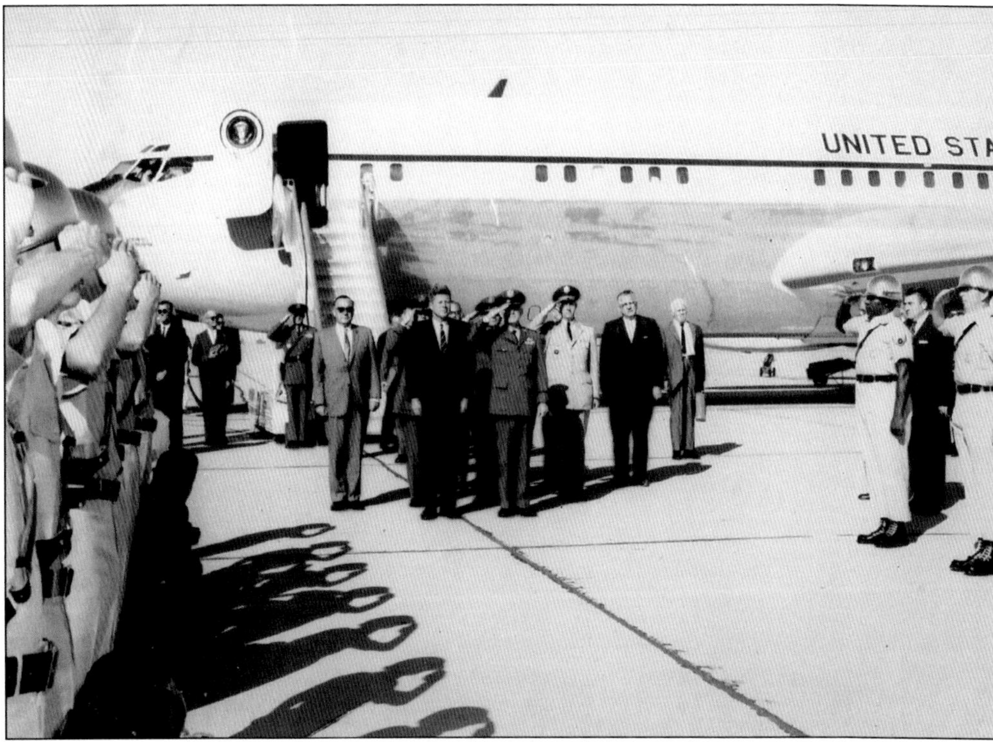

Pres. John F. Kennedy is greeted at Castle Air Force Base on August 17, 1962. The president, along with California governor Pat Brown, came to the San Joaquin Valley to commence the San Luis Dam Project west of Los Banos. He also spent one night in Yosemite National Park.

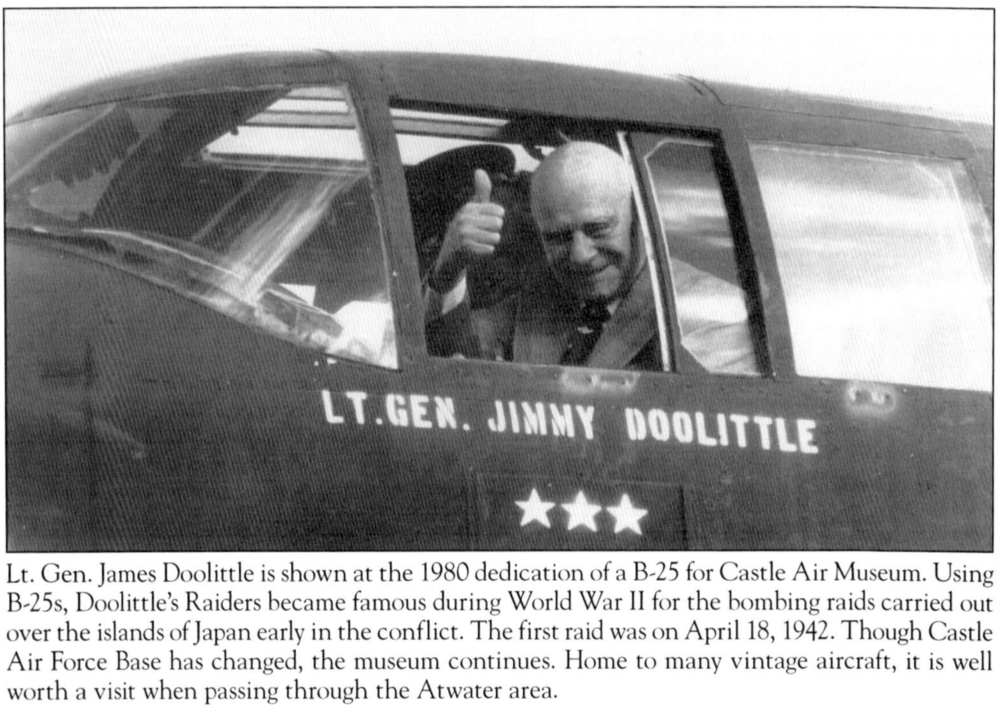

Lt. Gen. James Doolittle is shown at the 1980 dedication of a B-25 for Castle Air Museum. Using B-25s, Doolittle's Raiders became famous during World War II for the bombing raids carried out over the islands of Japan early in the conflict. The first raid was on April 18, 1942. Though Castle Air Force Base has changed, the museum continues. Home to many vintage aircraft, it is well worth a visit when passing through the Atwater area.